# A GRIEF
## OUT OF
### SEASON

# A GRIEF OUT OF SEASON

## *When Your Parents Divorce in Your Adult Years*

NOELLE FINTUSHEL (Oxenhandler)
and
NANCY HILLARD, Ph.D.

*Little, Brown and Company*

BOSTON   TORONTO   LONDON

OC 10 '03

306.89
Ox z g

FIRST EDITION

LIBRARY OF CONGRESS CATALOGING-IN-PUBLICATION DATA

Fintushel, Noelle, 1952–
    A grief out of season : when your parents divorce in your adult
years / Noelle Fintushel and Nancy Hillard. — 1st ed.
        p.  cm.
    Includes bibliographical references.
    ISBN 0-316-36351-0
    1. Divorce — United States.   2. Children of divorced parents —
United States.   3. Adult children — United States.   4. Aging
parents — United States.   I. Nancy Hillard.   II. Title.
HQ834.F56   1991
 306.89 — dc20                                              90-23179

10  9  8  7  6  5  4  3  2  1

MV-PA

Published simultaneously in Canada by Little, Brown & Company
(Canada) Limited

PRINTED IN THE UNITED STATES OF AMERICA

*For C.W.M.,*
*who saw me through the first round.*
*For Eliot,*
*past counting —*
*and for all the members of my family.*

*For Kathy, Terry, and Jeffrey,*
*who have taught me much through the years*
*about how divorce affects children.*
*And for Bob,*
*who has taught me to love, and to give,*
*and to create a new family.*

N.H.

What falls away, falls away; what belongs to us remains with us, for everything proceeds according to laws greater than our own insight. One must live in oneself and think of the whole of life, of all its millions of possibilities, expanses and futures, in the face of which there is nothing past or lost.

*Attributed to*
RAINER MARIA RILKE

# Contents

# About This Book

This book is divided in two parts. Part I, "A Map of the Terrain," lays the groundwork, seeking to understand the underlying sources of the adult child's pain. Part II, "The Journey," focuses on the more practical issues that confront the adult child at each stage of development.

All of the quotes in this book are based on actual case material obtained from personal interviews, written correspondence, and a printed questionnaire. Though the ages given are exact, all names and other identifying characteristics have been changed. In a few cases, we have created a composite example, in order to further protect the identity of certain interviewees.

# *Acknowledgments*

This book would not have been possible without the help of many people. I especially wish to thank:

*Nancy and Bob,* without whom nothing
*Rose,* for her boundless generosity
*My grandmother,* who keeps us all intertwined
*My mother,* who helped give me an attic to write in and a happy ending to write about
*Mollie,* for the WANG that changed my life
*Nikki Longaker,* who shared many insights
*Becky and her siblings*
*Barbara Foley Wilson* of the National Center for Health Statistics
*Peg Steffan* of Rochester Displaced Homemakers
*The Mediation Center of Rochester*
*Harriet and the Blue Mountain Center*
*Jennifer Josephy,* my editor
*Carol Mann,* my agent
*And all of those who shared their stories with us, especially my dear friend Sue*

— N.F.

# Introduction

The rate of divorce among couples married twenty years and more has risen dramatically in recent years and is expected to go on rising. In fact, although divorce rates overall have held steady, in this segment of the population they have continued to climb. Fortunately, a growing body of literature has begun to explore the special difficulties of the "gray divorce."

But what of the difficulties encountered by the children of these couples? There are at least two and one-half million adults who have lived through their parents' divorce in the last ten years. We have yet to encounter a single book that addresses their situation, as compared with the staggering number of books on other aspects of divorce.

True, in recent years there has been some recognition. In 1984, a research team at the University of Pennsylvania reported on the greater than expected impact of parental divorce on college students. In 1985, the movie *Twice in a Lifetime* explored the breakup of an older couple and its effect on their adult children. These gave rise to a brief flurry of interest in the press. Since then there have been a few short articles in scholarly journals, an episode on "thirtysomething," and an opening segment on a national talk show. On February 8, 1990, an article in the *New York Times Magazine* explored the effects of parental divorce on fifty college students.

These signs are encouraging, but they remain small blips surrounded by silence. The silence is symptomatic of one of the greatest difficulties faced by the adult whose parents divorce: the belief that it isn't supposed to be a problem.

Consider Mindy, whose parents divorced when she was twenty-two. Because she and her eighteen-year-old sister were distraught over their parents' divorce, it was recommended they see a counselor at the local divorce mediation center. Though Mindy had been feeling suicidal for several months, the counselor told her, "You're so lucky to be going through it at this stage of your life and not when you were little."

Callous as this may seem, it represents the prevailing attitude. "After all, you're grown-up. You had a family when you needed it. Now you're living on your own. Perhaps you're even married with children. What's the big deal?"

The premise of this book is that it *is* a big deal when parents divorce — no matter how old or independent their children. Divorce forces adult children back into intense reinvolvement with their parents. It thrusts upon them the immense responsibility of helping one or both — often severely depressed — parents adjust to radical changes in their lives. For adult children it brings about a painful and prolonged confrontation with the past, which is deeply unsettling to their own sense of self and threatening to other important relationships in their lives.

People have asked us: "Eventually adult children will have to face the death of their parents. Compared to this ultimate loss, isn't divorce a relatively minor matter?"

The answer is no. In the first place, divorce *is* a death. It involves the irrevocable loss of much that was cherished and familiar. The grief that people experience over the rupture of their family is in many ways indistinguishable from the grief of losing a loved one. *The added grief in divorce is the way it dis-*

*turbs and uproots the past.* Death often imparts a gentle glow to family memories; divorce unleashes intense negativity. It demands a painful and often disillusioning revision of "the way we were."

Finally, as so many people told us, divorce never ends, particularly when it dissolves a marriage of many years. Divorce is a long and complicated process, fraught with ambiguity, surrounded by few social supports, and often without a sense of closure. Husband and wife may go their separate ways, but children remain connected to both parents, often caught in a continuing cross fire of bitterness and resentment.

If there are already so many books for children of divorce, why a special book for grown-up children?

Because their situation is unique. The grief, rage, and guilt may be the same as for any child of divorce, but they are occurring in a very different context.

Young adults may find their parents divorcing just as they themselves are beginning to feel truly independent for the first time. The disruption of divorce may seriously shake such independence. It may be happening just as the question of commitment is becoming real and urgent as never before, and it can create doubts about cherished assumptions. It can happen when the whole movement of their being is forward. Just as they are becoming intensely involved in forging a career, in learning to live intimately with another person, their parents' divorce can be a powerful tide sweeping them backward into old emotions and entanglements they thought were left safely behind.

For those who are somewhat older, it is likely that they are already in the midst of major responsibilities with a career, a spouse, and perhaps children who need their time, energy, and understanding. These family members may not be able to understand the intense emotions that arise as a result of the divorce.

Besides these differences of context, there are often very stringent expectations as to how adult children *should* behave.

Most important, adult children often share these expectations. Generally, they do not feel entitled to the same freedom of expression, the acting out, or the withdrawal of a child or teenager. As adults, they feel they must simply absorb the new emotions and responsibilities while keeping up the same level of daily functioning.

Moreover, the distinct possibility exists that families who experience late divorce are unique in some important respects. Often, if a marriage has lasted long enough for the children to be grown-up, it's because some things were working. There was apparent stability. Many we interviewed insisted that theirs was a happy family before the divorce, a strong family, even a model family. When such a family dissolves, the shock, disbelief, and disorientation can be overwhelming.

All of this means that an adult's experience of parental divorce is different from that of a child or teenager. Not more or less difficult necessarily, but different — and different in a way that needs to be understood. Ironically, as recent studies reveal the long-term traumatic effects of divorce on younger children, it is possible that more and more couples will try to postpone divorcing until their children are grown and "won't be affected by it." This makes it all the more urgent to understand the grief out of season.

When Noelle first mentioned her project to me, I was struck immediately with its potential, with the need for creating recognition and understanding of these forgotten "children" of divorce. Professional colleagues agreed. As therapists, with pitifully little information available, we have had to rely on our own powers of empathy and on our ability to extrapolate from the young child's experience of divorce. How many of us, in ignorance, have echoed the counselor's remark to the deeply depressed Mindy, "You're so lucky to be going through it at this stage"?

Only a few of the millions of adult children of divorce reach out for structured therapy. Most struggle through alone or with the help of sympathetic friends, mates, siblings, parents. Many of them eventually find that the pain has been growth producing. But we can and we should remove some of the obstacles along the way.

This book addresses the two urgent needs of adult children facing parental divorce: to understand what's going on inside and to have strategies for dealing with it. Understanding the range and intensity of the adult child's reaction to divorce is, in itself, therapeutic. But it is not enough. Late divorce throws an entire family system into chaos, and a seemingly infinite number of practical questions arise: What can I do to help? How involved should I get? Should I take sides? What happens to my own marriage and family life?

To answer these questions, we turned to more than one hundred adult children of divorce, whose stories have provided the raw material for this book. Some of them were originally seen as clients; some were friends and acquaintances; others were reached more systematically through a printed questionnaire.[1]

Not only is this the first book on the topic, but to date it represents the largest study ever done and involves the most diverse group of subjects. Though virtually all are middle-class and well educated, they come from across the United States. They represent a range of family backgrounds: from close-knit, stable, and harmonious to severely chaotic and abusive. The youngest person was eighteen at the time of her parents' divorce; the oldest, forty-six.

The research clearly shows that late-divorce families are prone to very bitter disturbances. Rigid alliances form; the father-child relationship is especially vulnerable. Much of the harm is done in the acute, initial phase of divorce — largely because parents are unprepared for the intensity of their adult children's reaction. Assumptions are made; communication is handled in a very insensitive manner. One of our chief concerns is to provide information — for parents *and* children — that will lessen the damage done at this critical time.

However, it has become equally clear that late-stage divorce is *not* a fleeting crisis, a neatly time-limited phenomenon. One of our biggest surprises was the number and intensity of responses from adults whose parents had been divorced ten or more years. And in follow-up interviews over a span of ten years, we have been able to observe the ongoing adjustment of those we originally interviewed. We found that late-stage divorce produces profound and painful reverberations for many years, and we have designed the book to be relevant to adult children in the long aftermath of divorce.

The response of Liza, now thirty-four, was typical of many we received:

> My parents' divorce thirteen years ago affected me much more than I even realize today. I think it shattered every illusion I ever had about what a 'good marriage' is or could be. More than I want to admit — I think it still has an effect on me and my 'single' status at this point in my life. . . . It's interesting, even though I've gone through counseling at different times in my life for other personal issues — I never really discussed my parents' divorce. It's always been something I wanted to hide. Even though writing this makes me cry — I know it's good for me to acknowledge all those feelings that are really still there.

It has been said that good therapists provide an atmosphere in which their clients can reveal where and how they hurt. This nonjudgmental atmosphere diminishes the shame, guilt, and fear that make all of us want to hide from our deepest feelings. Once expressed, as slowly and gently as need be, feelings can be ventilated, discussed, and reinterpreted until the client is able to reintegrate them in a less painful, more mature way.

Gradually, the client is able to acknowledge: "This is where it hurts. This is why. This will make it better." The wound has been opened. The infection has drained. Healing begins.

Self-help groups are successful because they provide a comparable kind of atmosphere. Those who have experienced a particular problem, physical or emotional, move past shame and embarrassment, past anger and accusation. They reject denial and avoidance in favor of openness. They know that exposing pain will eventually lead to healing. They say to the others: "We have experienced that. We know how it feels. We know the pitfalls along the way. These things have helped us. You may want to try them."

Noelle and the other participants in this study constitute the first self-help group for adult children of late divorce. As such, they make a significant contribution to others in their situation and to the professional community, which has for so long ignored their plight. And they will help parents, too, who want to understand the welter of emotional reactions that beset their children.

As a therapist, I have felt privileged to join them in their struggle to make a clearing, to explore and to describe a hitherto uncharted territory. I have seen my job as helping to create that clearing — defining the boundaries, anticipating obstacles, providing a certain kind of perspective.

But this book is above all *their* book, and it is their way of reaching out to the millions of adult children of divorce, as well as to their parents, husbands, wives, friends, and counselors.

Listen to them . . . and learn.

— Nancy Hillard, Ph.D.

# I

*A Map of the Terrain*

# 1

## Noelle's Story: Breaking the Silence

**M**y mother's hand, frantically arranging a collection of my little sister's artwork on my father's dresser. In a few moments we will go to the airport to meet him: he is flying back from ten weeks of teaching in France. He is coming back to have Christmas with us but will move out shortly after to live on his own.

My mother has recently received a letter bearing this news — but her hand is not convinced. More even than her first telling me over the phone, or my six-year-old sister's jumping up and down singing "Daddy's coming," it's this that makes me want to cave in and die. The sight of her hand arranging those little clay animals as if they had the power to lure him back.

Four years after my own parents' divorce, I sat in a poetry-writing class and read a young woman's poem as she wrote it in chalk on the board:

> *My mother's wedding band*
> There is a wistfulness even now
> as she twists the joint where it used to rest,
> a thirty year habit in platinum.

> Nothing remains,
> save this thin bare place
> on her left hand.

*Someone else who knew this disbelief of hands! Something unlocked in me, a pain I'd buried deep, thinking it so private in its particularness that no one could ever really understand.*

*She did. I introduced myself, and soon after Sue and I sat late at her kitchen table, pouring out our stories. It is from our relief at having found each other — from many nights over the kitchen table and walks in the woods — that the idea for this book first came to be. . . .*

When a family dissolves, it does so in what feels like a deeply private and singular way that no one else could possibly understand. One of the most healing aspects of working on this book has been the chance to meet with a whole spectrum of people, for us to hear one another's stories, and to realize that — despite the many differences among our personalities and our situations — in the very private nature of our pain there was a deep bond of common understanding. Sue's and others' stories are — in briefer form — interwoven throughout this book. For now I'll tell my own, without apologies for its quirkiness.

## Noelle's Story: Part I

*When I was three years old, my father left my mother, and she and I lived alone in Greenwich Village for a year, where she went to art school and I went to nursery school. Although my mother tells me that "we had a good year, considering," I have very few memories of this time, and they are all tinged with sadness.*

*I remember the narrow steps leading up to our apartment, the dark blue bedspread my mother hung on the wall. I remember the funny feeling I got when she gave me a gift "for being such a good girl" — something she'd never felt the need to do before. That was the moment I consciously perceived that I had been suffering from something and that I knew what it was: Daddy's gone.*

*My parents got back together at the end of this year and were together until their divorce nineteen years later, but something irrevocable had happened. No matter how harmonious things might have seemed, I had experienced a deep precariousness in the heart of my family. My greatest fear was that my father would leave us again.*

*I adored him utterly. His dark hair, his blue eyes. The smell of his pipe, the sound of his typewriter through the study door. At night he stroked my hair and sang to me until I fell asleep. When I grew older, he told me funny stories and read to me.*

*As a teenager, I cherished his books; the house was full of them, books of philosophy, literature, religion. Wherever I went about the house, my eyes danced over the titles and I ran my fingers along their backs. It became a ritual: choosing which of his books to hoard in my room. It was a painful moment when I first visited my mother after the divorce and saw her ransacked bookshelves, the odd jumble of books that were left to her and my sister. I remember thinking, "But how can my sister grow up in a house without his books?"*

*I was proud of the world we belonged to through my father. Proud that he was a professor, proud when I visited him in his office at the university or heard students call him "Doctor." Wherever we traveled, he had a web of connections to scholars, poets, painters. On his sabbaticals we lived in France, and I learned to speak French and to love France just as he did. In fact, I took up and embraced all his favorite things.*

*I loved my mother, too. She was vibrant and playful, full of good ideas for how to spend the day. We would sit on the floor for hours doing art projects together — paper circuses inside a cardboard box, collages from her magic pile of scraps. When we traveled, she was the explorer who found the perfect picnic spot in the bend of the river, the colossal sand dune to climb. . . .*

*But my mother was like the soil in which I grew, simply there, day and night, while my father was like the sun. Where he was, I felt a glow; I felt bathed in a kind of love-light. But, like the sun, he could disappear. When I thought of him going away, the feeling was "I will die. All the life will drain out of me, I will wither." One summer he was in Peru, working on a novel about the*

*Peace Corps, and I was terrified that something was going to happen to him. At night in my bunk at camp, I lay awake pleading with God that if he would send my father safely home to us, I would join the Peace Corps when I grew up. I would go to one of the earth's most desolate places, I would make water flow in a land of rock and dust, if only he would send my father back to me, and keep my heart from withering.*

*This became my central mission: to keep my father with us, to weave my family into a harmonious whole.*

*There was certainly an underlying terror at work. But it would be false to see it entirely in this light. For my family was at the same time a source of great delight to me, and I loved those activities and occasions that emphasized or celebrated our "family-ness."*

*I loved to set the table for dinner in the evening, a place for each of us, united around the circle of the table. Wherever we lived it was always beautiful to me, the walls painted my mother's unusual colors — ocher, mauve, slate gray — the yard full of the flowers and fruit trees she tended and pruned. I loved it when guests came and seemed to bask in the glow of our family. We always had a few special family-less friends who would spend holidays with us or drop in unexpectedly when they felt down and out, and I could feel the warmth of my family expanding outward to include them.*

*I was proud of my little brother, seven years younger than me. And when my sister was born in my seventeenth year, it seemed a miraculous gift. I was always proud to be with my family in public, and many of my friends were envious of me. So many of my friends' families were torn by strife during our teenage years, but in my family there were very few overt conflicts. On some level I was always aware of the ways in which my parents did not deeply connect with each other, were not true companions, soul mates. There were gaps, silences, flashes of irritation between them — but all on a fairly subtle level, obscured by the generally harmonious flow of family life. Not long ago an old friend of mine referred quite matter-of-factly to my ideal childhood.*

*Whatever it was, part myth, part reality, this "ideal family" was my* raison d'être, *my central emotional investment. When my parents split up, it was as though the very thing I had worked all my life to preserve just blew up in my face.*

*Now that I've heard others' stories, I'm aware that mine is much less dramatic than many. My parents' divorce was not a complete shock; there were no dizzying revelations; my father did not leave my mother for another woman. Rather, while escorting a group of students to France one autumn, he decided that when he returned he wanted to live on his own. He had always suffered from terrible migraines, and in the letter he wrote to my mother this was the reason he gave: since coming to France and living a quieter, more solitary existence, he found he was much freer of the agonizing headache attacks. It was an explanation that made sense and that didn't seem — at first, anyway — too terrible a rejection of my mother and the family.*

*But what was so difficult for me was precisely the way in which my father's decision confirmed deep, unspoken fears and flaws. It did not produce some radically new equation, it simply revealed what had always been there: that the bond between my parents was very fragile, that no matter how hard I tried, I couldn't keep my father with us. The fact that my relationship with my father would continue was not a relief to me — quite the opposite. I had always felt deeply uneasy that the bond between my father and me was stronger than that between him and my mother, and the divorce just brought this out in vivid color.*

*I felt trapped in a deeply contradictory situation. Having always been afraid that my father would leave us, I completely identified with my mother's desolation, fear, and sense of abandonment. Yet because I had always been temperamentally closer to my father, I could understand his need to leave, and this made me feel terribly guilty, like an accomplice.*

*As the oldest — the grown-up child — I felt it was my responsibility to care for everyone, to keep the lines of communication flowing, to be what one friend described as a shuttle diplomat. I felt unable to communicate with my brother, sixteen at the time, whose general response to the situation was to grow very aloof and withdrawn. And I felt the most extreme anguish for my six-year-old sister.*

*Gradually, we all began to adjust in our different ways. My mother and little sister resettled in another state; my mother found a job that brought her new interests and a new circle of friends;*

*my brother and sister and I learned the delicate art of relating to
our parents separately.*

*As of this writing, it's been sixteen years since my parents'
divorce. My parents have made new lives for themselves. In ways
I never thought possible, a new sense of family has evolved.*

For me, and for most of those we interviewed, the healing has
been a very gradual process. Often, it has been more lonely and
difficult than it needed to be. I believe that the silence surrounding the situation of the adult whose parents divorce must
come to an end. There is too much suffering involved, and too
much of the suffering comes from the silence itself, from the
denial that is at the root of it.

Furthermore, there is much to be gained from facing the
difficulty. Again and again this note has been sounded — in my
own life, and in the lives of the people I've spoken with. This is
not a book of easy solutions. That would be a betrayal of the
worst kind. The insights have come hard, and many of us would
trade them in to have our families back again as they used to
be. But for all of us in different ways there has come in time the
sense of something understood, something never before appreciated, something in fact very precious that our parents' divorce has given us.

# 2

## *Late Divorce*

Powerful currents of feeling and strong habits of identification link parent and child throughout life. In the wake of divorce, most of our respondents experienced heightened involvement with one or both parents; many of them assumed a significant degree of responsibility for their parents' emotional and practical well-being. Thus, it is not possible to understand the adult child's experience of divorce without some understanding of the parents'.

There is another reason, too, for providing this basic overview of late divorce. For adult children, intellectual understanding, getting a fix on the facts, is a primary coping mechanism. They want to get at the *why* of their parents' divorce and to place their own pain in a broader perspective.

Those who are in the very midst of the crisis may find this chapter too dry for their liking. We suggest that they skip it for now and turn to the remaining chapters, which deal, in a more immediate way, with both emotional and practical issues.

Before we examine the unique topography of late divorce, we need to have a basic understanding of divorce, pure and simple.

Divorce: The General Landscape

Of course, divorce is rarely pure and simple. The decision to divorce is generally a long and hard time coming, and divorce itself is best understood not as a single, discrete event but as a complex and long-term process. Judith Wallerstein, author of two authoritative books on the subject, wrote, "Divorce is deceptive. Legally it is a single event, but psychologically it is a chain — sometimes a never-ending chain — of events, relocations, and radically shifting relationships strung through time, a process that forever changes the lives of the people involved."[1]

Though both partners may have experienced longtime dissatisfactions with the marriage, divorce is not usually a mutual affair. It has been estimated that in 75 to 90 percent of all divorces, one spouse wants the marriage to end more than does the other.[2] The question of who divorces whom is an important one, for generally the partner who initiates the divorce fares better, both in the short and the long run. Of course, an important distinction must be made between who files for divorce and who actually sought the end of the relationship. Frequently it is the "injured party" who, whether as an expression of anger or a means of rescuing wounded pride, actually files for divorce. It is the question of who sought to end the relationship that carries the most weight emotionally.

The partner who initiates the divorce has a greater sense of choice and personal control over events. Perhaps even more important, the initiator has generally had more time to prepare for the upheaval. Long before communicating the actual decision to leave, he or she has already withdrawn emotionally to a significant extent and laid the groundwork for a new life.[3] Thus, while divorce is a painful and disrupting experience for both partners, generally one is at a decided disadvantage. For their part, children often perceive this imbalance, and this can have a profound impact on *their* experience of the divorce.

*Ambivalence*

Highly ambivalent feelings are typical of divorcing partners, who may express extreme negativity about each other and yet remain strongly attached and fearful of separation. There is often ambivalence about whether or not to divorce, about when and how to carry out the process, and about how to relate in the aftermath of divorce. Ambivalence is often more extreme in one partner than in the other, but even the one who clearly initiated the divorce may at times be paralyzed by confused and contradictory feelings.

## The Process

For both partners, the process of disengagement is very complex and unfolds on many levels. Those few researchers who have written about late divorce emphasized that the longer the marriage, the more numerous and involved the ties that must be loosened.[4]

First, the partners must withdraw the emotional energy that they have invested in each other; in psychoanalytic terms, they must "decathect." They must learn to live in such a way that the other person is no longer central to the meaning of their life, to their image of themselves, to their plans for the future.

Second, the partners must detach from the role of husband or wife that they have played in relation to each other. This not only affects their own sense of who they are and of the meaning and purpose of their life, but it also affects their social status and often brings about changed relationships to members of the extended family and to family friends.

Third, the partners must go through a major upheaval in the practical sphere of their life. Each must evolve a new measure of autonomy from the complex web of interdependencies that characterize most marriages. From finances to place of residence, vacation plans, habits of eating and sleeping — there is scarcely an aspect of daily life that is not affected by divorce.

Fourth, at the same time, divorce often triggers memories of earlier losses. In the pain of losing a partner, some people reexperience a childhood trauma. Whether or not they are fully conscious of the past, a primal experience of grief or abandonment may resurface, greatly intensifying the pain of the present.

## The Cultural Vacuum

Many of these changes and losses are akin to those experienced upon the death of a spouse, and the divorce transition is, in many ways, a process of mourning. There are some very important differences between death and divorce, however. Divorce is, culturally, a much less defined event. Despite the extraordinary prevalence of divorce in our society, few cultural guidelines exist. Although it represents a major transition in the life of an individual and a family, no ritual marks it; no clearly defined patterns of behavior support those going through it or those who might help them. If you go to a card store, you will find sections for New Baby, Wedding, Graduation, New House, New Job, Get Well, and Sympathy. You may find one or two cards for divorce in the Humor section, and that says it all. Divorce is an awkward subject, the brunt of lame jokes. When someone says, "I got my divorce," do we say, "Congratulations!" or "I'm so sorry"? For most people, divorce remains a lonely and confusing event. Not only does it confer an uncertain social status in the present, but — and in this respect it is most unlike a death in the family — it casts a shadow over the past. In our culture, divorce represents the very epitome of what sociologists call the painful state of anomie, or normlessness.

## Styles of Divorce

Researchers have observed distinctly different styles of divorce among couples, from highly communicative and cooperative to extremely hostile or disengaged. Though it is important to resist the temptation to oversimplify and pigeonhole their parents' predicament, a basic sense of the different styles of divorce can be helpful to adult children. It can give them a framework for understanding their parents' behavior; it can help them anticipate obstacles and seek appropriate help.[5]

## A "Good Divorce"?

Given the absence of clear cultural standards, is it possible to fashion a definition of a "good divorce"?

Some will say there is no such thing, if by *good* is meant "painless." Most of those whose profession it is to think about such things will agree that a minimum-damage divorce has the following characteristics:

1. Over time, a greater sense of mutuality evolves about the decision to divorce. Though one partner may have been very resistant initially and may continue to feel regret, gradually he or she comes to feel that there was something meaningful, appropriate, and positive about the parting of ways.
2. Ideally, both partners, along with other significant members of the family, come to feel that the divorce has, in fact, genuinely resolved certain serious problems.
3. Both partners arrive at an understanding of the relationship that, while reconciling them to the divorce, does not entirely negate the past.
4. Though they may not feel warm and friendly toward each other, the ex-spouses recognize the value of a cooperative attitude.
5. However, they do not entirely avoid conflict. When difficulties arise, they deal with each other constructively and face-to-face. On such occasions, they are able to keep to the issues at hand and remain relatively flexible as to possible solutions.
6. The ex-spouses do not demand that their children and other close friends and family members be divided in their loyalties.
7. The parents are able to maintain many of the original family's functions with minimal tension — coming together in times of need as well as for special family events and maintaining contact with in-laws and family friends.

## Late Divorce

As we turn to the special characteristics of late divorce, a word of caution is in order. The rather bleak picture we've painted thus far is about to get even bleaker. Especially for those whose parents are currently divorcing or have recently divorced, it is important to keep a sense of perspective. Many of those we interviewed had very positive stories to tell about the eventual outcome of their parents' divorce. They felt that their parents had changed in significant and positive ways, and details of their stories are woven throughout the chapters to come. Many of them involve the kind of changes that don't necessarily show up in statistics and broad generalizations. Diane's mother, for example, developed cancer within a year after her husband left her and never remarried. However, ten years later she has survived the cancer, she lives in a lovely condominium, earns a good salary as a teacher, has an active social life — and ice-skates three times a week! She will never forget the trauma of her divorce, but her life is rich in ways that aren't captured in the aerial view we present here.

### The Numbers

First, the numbers. ·

Researchers are emphatic and unambiguous: over the last few decades, there has been a substantial increase in the rate of late divorce. In recent years the phenomenon has been all the more striking, given that divorce rates for younger age groups have been holding relatively steady.

Barbara Foley Wilson, demographer with the National Center for Health Statistics in Hyattsville, Maryland, reported that between 1980 and 1987, divorce rates for men and women over fifty-five increased as much as 16 percent.[6]

Since our concern is with marriages that remain intact until the children are grown, the most relevant statistics are those that report the dissolution of marriages of long duration. Here, too, the numbers confirm the substantial increase. Between 1980 and 1987 the number of marriages that ended in divorce after lasting twenty years or more jumped by 8,000 — from 131,000 to 139,000, an increase of over 6 percent.[7]

In absolute numbers, how many adult children are affected by late divorce? Barbara Foley Wilson estimated that in 1987, a quarter of a million children over eighteen experienced their parents' divorce. When we consider that the emotional and practical disruption is not much different for those whose parents separate without legally divorcing, the numbers loom even larger.

With the end of the baby boom, the number of children involved per divorce has declined. However, this decline is partially offset by the increased rate of late divorce. The baby boomers have not produced as many children as their parents, but as they themselves become middle-aged and participate in the growing trend toward late divorce, we can anticipate that large numbers of adult children will continue to be affected each year by parental divorce.

All in all, we estimate that over the last ten years, some two and one-half million children of eighteen years and over have experienced their parents' divorce.

### What's Behind the Numbers?

Researchers agree that the dramatic increase in late divorce is expected to continue. Many factors have contributed to the trend, and none of them are likely to diminish in influence in the near future.

One very basic factor is the increased health and longevity of the aging population. Today most men and women can expect to have some twenty or more active years after their children have grown and left the household — a long time, indeed, for a spouse who feels trapped in an unsatisfactory marriage.

At the same time, new attitudes toward aging encourage older people to "go for it," extending the quest for fun, adventure, romance, and sexual fulfillment further into old age. This means that more than ever before, an unhappy spouse in a long-term marriage may be inclined to risk a rupture with the past in order to inaugurate a new phase of life.

Another factor enhancing the likelihood of taking this risk is the increased affluence of post–World War II Americans. Divorce, both the legal process itself and the setting up of two households, is expensive. Where there is greater affluence, there is greater likelihood that an unhappy spouse will assume the financial burden associated with divorce.

Changing attitudes toward divorce also play a key role. As the overall divorce rate has increased exponentially over the last twenty-five years, negative attitudes have eased. Fewer people perceive divorce as a permanent stigma, a failure and disgrace. As the laws have been liberalized and the no-fault option has become widely available, divorce need no longer entail official accusations of cruelty or adultery. All of this means that many people who might have felt morally or socially constrained from divorcing no longer feel so.

Another very complex influence on late divorce involves the changing roles of men and women. For the most part, couples married twenty-five years and longer, before the resurgence of feminism in the late 1960s and early 1970s, established their marriages according to fairly rigid notions of male and female roles. The man was the breadwinner, identifying himself primarily through his professional achievement and financial status. The woman was the homemaker, finding her sense of identity in her role as wife and mother. This, by the way, accounts for the sex-role stereotypes in so many of the examples throughout this book. It is not that we wish to promote fixed images of Dad-in-the-office and Mom-at-home. We are simply reflecting the actual situation of most of the couples whose children we interviewed.

Though the repercussions take many forms, it is clear that the radical changes in sex roles over the past twenty years have produced tremendous stress in many long-term marriages, and no doubt will continue to do so for some time.

Lastly, an interesting factor to consider is the increased psychological sophistication about certain chronic domestic problems. We heard a number of stories about parents who divorced because they were "no longer willing to be codependent" in relation to an alcoholic or abusive spouse.

## Divorce and Midlife Crisis

It is difficult to know the exact percentage of late divorce that is associated with what is commonly called the midlife crisis. Certainly, a number of those we interviewed told us that the divorce itself was preceded by significant changes in at least one parent's behavior. Usually this was the parent who initiated the divorce, and the changes often represented classic midlife-crisis symptoms. These parents had been unusually depressed and brooding or very emotionally volatile. If they articulated their feelings, it was to express an awareness of time passing and a longing for change, if not outright disappointment and regret about the course their life had taken. Sometimes this longing was accompanied by the stereotypical signs of midlife crisis: a heightened concern with appearance and a hunger for new, revitalizing experiences.

Whether or not these classic signs were present before the divorce, we found many children who observed them in the aftermath. They reported that one or both parents were casting about for a very different life-style, that they had changed the sort of company they kept, the values they espoused, the books they read, the way they dressed, and sometimes even the way they ate. Needless to say, when a child is adjusting not only to the separation of the parents and the breakup of the family but also to radically different behavior on the part of one or both parents, this quite drastically affects the experience of parental divorce.

### Two Milestones in Later Life

Those who work with divorcing couples note that late divorce tends to cluster around two milestone events. The first of these, and the one that most closely corresponds to the midlife crisis scenario, is when the first or last child goes off to college.[8] In our culture, this event represents one of the few clear rites of passage, a significant threshold dividing youth from young adulthood. For many parents, it signifies the end of active parenting. And for some parents this translates into "I've fulfilled my responsibility. The kids are launched. Now it's my time to be free." For those couples who were "just hanging on for the kids," there's a sense of emptiness, the need to find new meaning in their life, a meaning that the marriage itself is not able to provide.

The second milestone affecting late divorce is retirement. These couples have managed to live together for some twenty or more years in the empty nest but now face twenty-four-hour-a-day contact, a prospect that often strains a tenuous relationship. Clearly, a frequent rationale for such late divorces is "I've worked hard all my life. This is my last chance to do something for *me*." Other changes at this time of life may further tip the balance: a decline in the health of one partner, the stress of caring for an aged parent, or the reaction to the death of a parent. Where stress brings some couples closer together, it weakens the bonds for others.

## The Emotional Climate

When our respondents were asked to describe what their parents' marriage had been like, most of their stories fell into one of two broad categories.

The first group described their parents as not being very close and yet rarely, if ever, fighting. Some were aware that their parents had once had a more vital relationship, but then had a falling-out or had gradually drifted apart. In many cases, it was not until the divorce was announced that these children recognized that their parents did not have a close relationship.

The second described an atmosphere of nearly perpetual conflict between their parents. In some cases the tension was overt, even erupting as physical abuse; in other cases it was kept under control, but pervasive.[9]

As might be expected — and as we explore in our discussion of the family in Chapter 3 — the pervasive tone of marriage and family life has a very strong impact on the experience of divorce.

## Who Divorces Whom

In the stereotypical image of late divorce, a husband in the throes of midlife crisis abandons his faithful, graying wife and takes off in a hot rod with his new young love. Though we did indeed hear a number of stories that fit this scenario, the reality is more complex. In her article on divorce among the elderly, researcher Barbara Cain confirmed that for those over sixty it is overwhelmingly men who initiate divorce.[10] Among the middle-aged, research suggests that the disparity is not so great. Out of their sample of ninety-three subjects aged forty to fifty-nine, researchers Gunhild Hagestad and Michael Smyer found that 44 percent of the men and 47 percent of the women had felt "total control" over the process of divorce. They had taken the lead in the practical and legal aspects of dissolving the marriage, and the emotional initiative had been theirs as well.[11]

## The Impact of Late Divorce

There are some respects in which older divorced couples may be better off than their younger counterparts: they may be more financially stable, and they do not face the difficulties of caring for young children and competing for their custody. But divorce is a profoundly stressful event at any stage of life, and for the most part being older makes it more so.

As Hagestad and Smyer observed:

> For some middle-aged individuals, a decision to seek divorce is closely tied to issues of their life stage: a reordering of priorities; a new sense of freedom from social constraints; a realization of unfulfilled potentials. For others, divorce becomes a shattering of their whole life matrix at a time when they already feel vulnerable.[12]

There are many reasons for feeling vulnerable. Growing older is in itself a difficult process involving loss, relinquishment, uncertainty. Though increasing numbers of people over sixty are able to look forward to many rich and active years, at some point the inevitable sets in. Physical energy and attractiveness diminish; health problems increase; mental agility may decline. All of these problems are naturally associated with lowered self-esteem. Simultaneously, the support network shrinks as longtime friends and family members move away, grow infirm, or die.

In addition to these physical and emotional challenges, many retired people live on small fixed pensions and experience serious financial pressures.

For all of these reasons — physical, emotional, and financial — growing older makes daily life more difficult for many people. Divorce intensifies the already stressful process of aging, compounding feelings of loss and uncertainty. Most middle-aged divorced couples are years away from the actual experience of these problems but nonetheless feel them looming on the horizon. This imparts an urgent dimension to the experience of late divorce.

Divorce commonly brings up feelings of abandonment, and these feelings are intensified for partners who stand at or beyond the threshold of old age. For many long-term partners, having someone to grow old with was one of the chief virtues of marriage. They feel, with a sense of injustice and bitter irony, that they are being deprived of support just when they most need it. Because of the sheer number of years involved, the sense of loss and waste can be particularly painful for late-divorcing partners. An added bitterness arises for those cast-off partners who have been looking forward to the next phase of marriage with particular eagerness. An often-voiced sentiment is "We worked so hard all our lives, raising the children and earning money. These were going to be our golden years — and now they're shattered."

### Older Women and Divorce

Because of the high premium placed on a woman's youth and physical attractiveness, women whose husbands leave them late in life often experience a serious crisis of self-esteem. Also, the options available to older women are limited. Because women outlive men, and because men frequently form relationships with younger women, the pool of available partners is much smaller for women.

Women suffer financially, too. Despite recent changes in attitudes concerning women in the work force, the fact remains that women are at a decided financial disadvantage. Divorce, for women, almost always means a significant decrease in standard of living. For older women, the prospect of reentering the work force or establishing a new career can be quite daunting.

Judith Wallerstein has written that women who divorce while still in their twenties or early thirties have far more "second chances," both romantically and financially, than women who divorce in their late thirties or after forty.[13] Even when the drop in standard of living does not pose a serious practical threat, the psychological consequences can be profound.[14]

Many middle-aged women are part of what researchers call the sandwich generation. They have young adult children who are not yet fully launched, and at the same time, they are responsible for one or more aging relatives. Under the best of circumstances, their emotional and physical energies are stretched to the limit. The emotional and financial insecurity of divorce may push them beyond their powers of endurance.

On the deepest level, divorce has a major impact on the general sense of meaning and purpose in many older women's lives. Older women may not have the pressures and responsibilities of raising children, but without anyone to anchor them at home, many experience a profound sense of emptiness. When a woman's sense of identity has been wholly wrapped up in her role as wife and mother, she is threatened to the very core when these roles are thrown into question. It is obvious that divorce threatens a woman's identity as wife; what is less obvious is that she may feel equally threatened in her role as mother — even when her children are grown. One research team observed that for many women of an older generation, the roles of wife and mother are inextricably linked. They quoted one woman as saying, "I was so looking forward to becoming a grandmother."[15] In this woman's mind, a divorcée could not fully *be* a grandmother.

Many older women experience the collapse of their marriage as a terrible personal failure. Others, especially those in the oldest category, feel a sense of spiritual failure. For women with deeply traditional views, as one researcher has noted, marriage represents a sacred covenant.[16] Divorce means that they have not only lost a husband and a way of life, but that they are no longer right with God. They are deprived of what might have been their greatest consolation precisely when they need it most.

Another difficulty for the oldest women is the lack of social support. Despite the significant increase in late divorce, it is still relatively rare for those over sixty. Elderly women whose husbands leave them have few peers to share their plight: being a widow is very different from being a divorcée. We spoke with one man whose mother felt so disgraced by her divorce that she forbade him to tell anyone. Though she went on living in the same house and was clearly living alone, her son was forced to lie to the neighbors and friends who had known them for decades.

### Older Men and Divorce

For their part, men are not immune to the crises of self-confidence that accompany aging and intensify the trauma of divorce. Though they are generally more financially secure and more likely to find new partners, they are vulnerable in other ways.

Researchers consistently note that men do not develop social networks to the same degree that women do. A man who has been left by his wife and who does not find a new partner is particularly apt to experience loneliness and isolation.

Older single men are often not prepared to take good physical care of themselves. Nutrition is frequently poor among the elderly, and the issue is most critical where elderly men are concerned. Many older men have little experience in shopping for and preparing food and are generally not familiar with the demands of basic housekeeping.

Many of the problems that affect men and women respectively after late divorce have to do with the markedly different sex roles among older couples. In general, the older generation of men and women were raised to function symbiotically and are less equipped than their younger counterparts to live alone. Their adult children, raised at a time of more flexible expectations with regard to role and gender, must frequently step in to bridge the gaps: helping Mother to manage her finances or helping Dad take care of his physical needs. Often it is difficult for these children to fully understand how radical a readjustment their parents face.

Divorce, at whatever stage of family life it occurs, involves loss and disruption for all family members. It forces major adjustments in both the practical and emotional spheres of daily life. It challenges the past, reorders the patterns of daily existence, and makes the future more uncertain. The many difficulties of growing older further complicate the experience of late-divorcing couples. This, in turn, profoundly affects the experience of their adult children.

# 3

## *Toward a Deeper Understanding of the Family*

For many adult children, long after the initial crisis is over, a deep perplexity remains. In the words of one young woman:

> It's three years later, and I've seen my parents begin to build new lives. I'm not so desperately depressed anymore. I'm getting used to the separate holidays, the double sets of phone calls, the split-level sense of family I carry inside me: my family *then* and *now*. But what I still can't come to terms with is the intensity of what happened to me, how at age twenty-four, I was nearly unhinged by my parents' divorce.

This, we discovered, was the question of questions for adult children of divorce: *How is it that, long after leaving home and establishing a life for oneself, one can feel threatened — sometimes to the point of breakdown — over parental divorce?*

The answer lies in a deeper understanding of the family, and what follows is a very basic tool kit for this purpose. The concepts may seem somewhat abstract at this point, but they are vital to everything that follows and will become richer in meaning as each chapter unfolds. To understand the connection between the family and the self, and to understand what happens when a family comes apart, we need to understand how it is put together in the first place.

## The Family as a System

We tend to think very literally of the family as a sum of individuals with common genes and a shared past. Since, as adults, we're no longer living with this "sum" of people, we believe we should not be deeply affected by its reorganization. After all, no one has died, so what's the big deal? We may allow ourselves a certain sadness, but we perceive our sadness as nostalgia for the past and sympathy for our parents. That we ourselves feel shaken at the roots — this we cannot account for. It seems preposterous, even shameful.

Yet a family is much more than a mere sum of individuals, and a divorce is much more than a rearrangement of these individuals.

An important step in modern family therapy has been to recognize the family as a *system:* a dynamic network of relationships in which each part is influenced by every other part.[1]

From the very beginning of their relationship, a husband and wife tend to develop ways of relating to each other that are predictable. To take simple examples: The man and woman may adopt the traditional roles of breadwinner and housewife. They may reverse those roles. Or they may both work outside the home and share in household responsibilities. Whatever it might be, this initial choice simplifies daily life. By prescribing certain actions and proscribing others, it sets a pattern that allows the couple to get on with the business of living. Without having to engage in endless negotiations about who does what and when and how often, they both know what to expect and what is expected of them. A system is developing, and as long as it works practically and emotionally for each of them, it perpetuates itself and remains in balance.

Of course, in some family systems conflict works. A couple may fight often and appear to be in constant turmoil — yet they, too, have a system. It is conflictual, but it is one that, on some level, they have agreed to because it meets certain needs and has well-established patterns and rules. Every family system is unique, and no matter how anarchic it may appear to an outsider, it has its own elaborate network of rules.

As children arrive, they are drawn into this preexisting system, and in the process the system changes. For each of us, the pattern of relationships into which we are born is deeply formative of who we are.

## Kinds of Patterns

Patterns don't just govern the basic division of household roles. They evolve around every aspect of family life. How much do family members reveal about themselves? How do they handle anger, anxiety, sexual feelings? What is the family's connection to the outside world? Each decision, made either unconsciously or overtly or by some combination of the two, then leads to a multitude of guidelines or rules.

Many of these patterns have to do with limits: What can be expressed? How far can we go? How much change is permitted? As we'll see, one of the frightening things that happens in divorce is the stretching and breaking of limits.

## Boundaries

One very important cluster of patterns regulates boundaries among family members. How much do we reveal to one another about our feelings? What are the rules involving physical contact and privacy? What lines are drawn around adults and children in the family?

On the deepest level, boundaries have to do with identity and difference. To what degree can individuals see both others and themselves as separate, possessed of unique strengths and weaknesses, needs and desires? At one end of the scale, we see families whose members are highly enmeshed. Each individual's sense of self is fused with that of other family members; there is little sense of a distinct, autonomous "I." Individuals find it hard to express desires, make decisions, or take actions that do not conform with the values of the group.

At the other end of the scale are families whose members are highly disengaged. There is little intimacy; physical expression of closeness is limited, and communication is relatively superficial. Decisions are made and actions are taken separately, with little concern for their effect on the group.

Of course, we all start out highly fused. Infants really can't tell where they end and their mothers begin. Young children continue to see others, especially their parents, as extensions of themselves. The process of growing up naturally involves gaining a clearer sense of self in relation to others. However, even adults manifest striking differences in this capacity. Some otherwise quite competent grown-ups have difficulty with boundaries: they may be devastated by the slightest criticism, or project their own feelings onto others, or attempt to live vicariously through others. Ideally, the mature person is someone with a strong, autonomous sense of self who can nonetheless relate intimately and empathetically with others while respecting them as equally autonomous beings.

The concept of boundaries is one of the most important for understanding the impact of divorce on adult children. As we'll see in later chapters, one of the things that frequently happens in divorce is a disturbing shift in boundaries: a parent suddenly becomes a peer; a child becomes a confidant or a go-between.

Even more fundamentally, the concept is important because of the assumption that simply because people are adults, their boundaries are clear and firmly established; they know where their own life ends and their parents' begins. But this is not necessarily the case. It is possible to appear quite autonomous externally — to move out of the house, find a job and a circle of friends — while remaining emotionally tied to one's parents and family. Too often an adult child who is severely distressed by parental divorce is dismissed as immature. In fact, not everyone starts from the same base: some families are highly enmeshed, making separation extremely difficult. And ironically, at the very moment that parental divorce exposes the urgent need for separation, the stress and upheaval make separation more difficult.

## Triangles

Another important concept for understanding the structure — and rupture — of family systems is the triangle. If asked to imagine a perfect relationship, most of us think automatically in terms of a twosome: husband-and-wife, mother-and-child. Family theorists, however, find something inherently unstable in a relationship of two. Couples tend to "spill over," drawing a third party into the dynamic between them.

Anyone may be "triangled in" to the relationship between a husband and wife. A problematic parent-in-law may become the focus of the couple's concern, drawing attention away from difficulties in their own relationship. Or a close friend may be drawn in as confidant and tension defuser. In families, the third party is most often a child. What happens, then, when the couple dissolves?

Noelle's family provides a classic example of a mother-father-child triangle. Her role in the family was to shore up her parents' marriage, serving as her father's confidante and soul mate and as the family's chief connector. This role was one that Noelle had assumed very early in life; it structured her relation to her parents and was very much a part of her sense of self. When her parents divorced, she felt a profound and frightening sense of dislocation.

## Problematic Patterns

In our original example of breadwinner-husband and home-maker-wife, the patterns arose in a complementary way to promote the smooth, predictable flow of daily life. While this is a valid description of many family patterns, the reality is far more complex.

What originally began as a complementary flow of mutually enhancing qualities may become rigidly polarized. If Mom is "the emotional one" in the family, she does all the expressing, connecting, interpreting. If Dad is "the practical one," he handles the "real" world and earns the money. This may be fine until the day Mom collapses from lack of self-confidence or Dad wakes up and realizes he's a stranger to his children.

Yet even when they have become useless or harmful, family patterns exert a powerful momentum. They have been repeated so often than they acquire an aura of necessity. At the very least they assure a familiar, predictable world — no matter how limited or painful that world might be. Even when a member of the family is disapproved of, perceived as the black sheep, for example, this is often a role that the family — albeit unconsciously and even in spite of itself — reinforces.

Changing fundamental family patterns — no matter how useless or negative those patterns might be — stirs up tremendous anxiety and fear of the unknown. This basic fact is crucial to our understanding of what happens in divorce.

## The Healthy Family

Nearly every family theorist has a different way of defining the healthy family. Broadly speaking, however, we could say that in the healthy family habitual patterns promote smooth functioning and help insulate against anxiety, without being overly rigid. Family members have many complementary roles, without polarization of strengths and weaknesses. They can communicate openly about many subjects and express a wide range of emotions. What triangles exist in the family are not held together by excessive anxiety; they provide subsystems of support, without turning into rigid, exclusive alliances. Boundaries exist that are appropriate according to the age, sex, and relationship of family members. There is closeness without enmeshment, privacy and autonomy without isolation. When conflicts arise, family members are free to express differing opinions and to explore a range of possible solutions.

A key word for most family theorists is *flexibility.* It is the given of any system that it strives for continuity. In the family system, the risk is that continuity will be maintained at the price of great rigidity. This not only limits each individual's potential growth, but it makes the family vulnerable to any internal or external stresses. A certain pattern may work very well for a family at one time, but — as the children grow, or Dad gets fired, or Mom takes a new job — it may no longer be functional. Lack of flexibility is no doubt an important part of what leads to divorce in the first place. Certainly it is a crucial factor in how well family members survive divorce.

## Laura's Family

Now that we've assembled our basic tool kit for understanding the dynamics of family life, let's look more closely at an actual family.

Laura was twenty-seven when her parents divorced; her five siblings ranged in age from seventeen to thirty. Her parents had been married for thirty-four years when her father left her mother to marry his young secretary.

Laura's father was a successful state senator. From the beginning of their relationship, Laura's mother looked up to her husband with a certain awe, and as her children were born, they were drawn into this basic dynamic.

In Laura's words:

> We saw our father as a combination of saint and superman, a hero. He was extremely busy, and our family life was centered around his brief appearances. There was the feeling that as soon as he walked in the door, we had to immediately begin savoring the precious moments that we had with him. We were always "on" for him, performing. There were so many of us kids, and I was shy and somewhat awkward and always craving for more attention from him. That's probably the dominant feeling I associate with my childhood. Waiting hungrily for a look from him, a smile, an encouraging word. The ecstasy when I got it. The feeling of never getting enough.

For two years following her parents' divorce, Laura was severely depressed and at several points felt close to breakdown. She explained:

I had such pride in my parents, such pride in my big hearty family. In fact — as I now see it — the core of my own sense of self-worth was pride in my family, and especially in my father.

It was a shock when I realized that in fact my whole sense of the family, of the lineage, was associated with my father and his side of the family. Even though only my youngest sister was still living at home, when he left my mother I felt that he was leaving the family. I felt a terrible sense of rejection. I mean that I felt personally rejected and abandoned — because my identification with the family was so strong, because I had so little sense of self apart from the family. And though there was only one of him and seven of us, when he left I felt there was nothing left of the family, that we were totally devalued, worthless.

## The Internalized Family

What Laura's story reveals is the power of the family we carry within us. It is not something that an X ray would show or a surgeon's hands would discover, but it operates as a very real force in our lives. It's a certain way of construing the world, of patterning relationships, providing a set of values and beliefs about who we are in relation to others. Whether it's "I'm the quiet one," "I'm the bubbly one," or "I'm the troublemaker," at the core of our perception of ourselves is a sense of our place within the family. Long after we have left our parents' home and established a life of our own, this primal sense of place continues to operate out of the set of deeply ingrained images that *is* the internalized family. Whether we revere it or rebel against it, no matter what our level of awareness, in some way we live our lives in relation to the family we carry within us.

Of course, family systems vary tremendously as to how "open" or "closed" they are. In some families there is considerable freedom for members to become more autonomous. But that internal family is always there at the core. This is the radical contribution of family systems theory. It enables us to see the family as an emotional unit and the individual as a part of that unit, not simply as an autonomous psychological entity.

The trauma of divorce is an explosion of the inner family, the system of beliefs, and the patterns of relationships that form our primal sense of orientation. In a very real sense, the whole family gets divorced. And temporarily, at least, the grown-up child is also divorced from his or her concept of self.

## Rules, Myths — and Their Unraveling

One of the first things that happens in a divorcing family is the overturning of certain rules. These are not the "No snacks before dinner" variety, but those rarely stated rules that involve the complicated intermeshing of roles in a family and its sense of limits. What can be said? How much can be expressed? How angry are we allowed to get? And so forth.

One young woman described an evening that she remembered with particular horror:

> It was shortly after my mother had announced her plan to leave, but she hadn't moved out yet. We were all at the dinner table, and the tension level, needless to say, was running very high. My mother was speaking — as if very casually — about her dream the night before in which she had encountered a tall, withered rhododendron plant and had said to herself emphatically, "I'm tired of taking care of a dying plant." Because my father was so often ill, it was clear to me that this "plant" was my father. I left the table, ran upstairs to my room and fell on the floor sobbing. It felt so wretched that my lovely family had come to this Ingmar Bergman–like state where husband and wife casually said this sort of thing to one another over the table — but I've never been able to understand why that particular remark set me off that way. I mean I felt close to hysteria.

As she talked through this incident in therapy, it became clear that a basic family rule had been violated. As long as her parents were together, it was not possible for her mother to openly express disgust and exasperation with her husband's illness. Her remark make it clear how radically the family ways were changing.

Underlying the system of rules is the family mythology. It is made up of fundamental beliefs, shared by family members, about family roles and relationships. These myths need not be verbalized or even acknowledged by family members — indeed, they generally are *not*, and this is part of what makes them so powerful. They are usually not apparent to an outsider and, if stated, might seem blatantly untrue. Yet within the family system, the myths are shared.

If put into words, the family myth might sound like Laura's: "Daddy is a very important person. Our family always supports him. We wait for him to come home, and when he does we must make him realize how much we appreciate him." Though the basic underlying myth may be as simple as this, it gives rise to a complex system of beliefs and rules: "Since Daddy is the most important person in our family, any weakness of his must be overlooked, no — must not even be seen. Therefore . . ."

In this way the family myth determines a great deal of each member's beliefs and behaviors. Such myths are not necessarily pathological; indeed, they contribute to smooth functioning. Their negative force exists only when the myth is far from reality and rigidly fixed.

### The Myth Explodes

This was the case with Laura's family.

One of her brothers discovered that their father was having an affair with his young secretary — a woman that he frequently brought to family gatherings. In fact, as far back as any of them could remember, he had always brought young, unmarried women to their home. But it was only now that they recognized the tremendous ambivalence they had always felt toward these women. Until then, the family myth simply would not allow the recognition — let alone the expression — of such feelings. Laura remembered that once on her birthday, when she dared to protest that one of these women was going to be there, she was reprimanded by her mother, who told her: "How can you be so selfish? Our family has so much to share. This woman is very lonely, and your father is so generous to invite her."

In families that perceive themselves as happy, as Laura's did, the myths are especially difficult to challenge. Indeed, family theorists find that "happy" families are the most resistant to insight. There is little motivation for family members to see into the workings of the system when the system is running smoothly, with each person's sense of who they want to be meshing with the image of who they're supposed to be. Interestingly, one of Laura's brothers, Stan, was hospitalized for a mental breakdown not long *before* the revelations about his father actually came out. At a very deep level he sensed the contradiction between the myth and the reality, and being very closely identified with his idealized father, the pressure was more than he could bear. In fact, it is not uncommon for the family's contradictions to first erupt as physical or psychological symptoms in one member.

For Stan, as later for Laura in her acute depression, the process of healing meant evolving a sense of self that was not so dependent on the image of their father as a superman. And while this was their primary task as individuals, as a family they had to develop new ways of relating to one another. With the central organizing principle of their life gone (Which of us is most worthy of Dad's love? Who is most like him? Who gets the most attention?), Laura, her five siblings, and her mother were almost like strangers:

> At first when we would get together without him, we were so awkward with each other. Something felt so hollow, absent at the core. We didn't know how to relate to one another without Dad at the center as the be-all and end-all, the source of all authority and value in our family. Isn't it incredible? Having to get to know your own family.

There were months of tension before they learned new ways of relating without Dad at the center and felt free to form a *new* family system.

The disparity between myth and reality need not be spectacular in order to induce a profound feeling of shock. In Julie's family, a central myth was "Dad is absentminded." Julie told us, "One of our family jokes was to imagine Dad taking a walk in the forest. As he walks, he keeps bumping into trees. Each times he does, he says, 'Oh, it's a tree. It's a tree.' " When it turned out that her father had been having a secret affair for over a year, his endearing absentmindedness began to seem more like an abandonment of his family.

Whether it's a spectacular explosion or a subtle erosion, the disintegration of many of the family's central myths and rules *is* what happens in a divorce. It is one of the reasons that a divorce is frequently more traumatic than a death in the family. For while one may grieve for the deceased person, his or her place within the family generally remains intact, and the family's images of itself not only live on but are often glorified. In the case of divorce, however, the opposite is true: these images come under sharp attack.

## Family Patterns in the Wake of Divorce

As these myths, rules, and images that form the internalized family dissolve, so do many of the familiar patterns of behavior that they sustain.

Some patterns change simply because they are clearly seen for the first time. Particularly in the acute stress of the initial phase, habitual defense mechanisms heighten. Family members play their role to the hilt, and the images stand out in high relief: this person is the hysterical one, this one is the rational, controlled one. Sometimes this tendency reaches nearly comic proportions. Laura's father had always insisted on being rational, but needless to say, in the wake of the revelations about his many years of infidelity, no one was feeling very rational. Nonetheless, at one of the first family powwows after the news broke, her father actually tried to implement parliamentary procedure!

Sometimes what is exposed is a basic triangle. One woman told us:

> My father was away on a trip and sent a letter to my mother telling her that he wanted to separate upon his return. I came home from college to be with my mother and together we went to pick up my father at the airport. Shortly after we got home, my mother said, "You go out for a walk with your father." I remember thinking, "This doesn't seem right. The first order of business should be that *they* sit down and talk." But my mother clearly wanted me to go with him, and so I did. Several days later, after I'd already gone back to school, my mother said to me bitterly over the phone, "I'm always the last to know what's going on around here."

Though she didn't label it "family triangle," this young woman was able to see for the first time how she had served as a go-between for her parents. In seeing it, she took the first step in detaching from it. Some family patterns are like those fairy-tale creatures whose power is predicated on darkness. The moment they're seen in the light of day, their power begins to dissipate.

Other patterns, once recognized, are actively destroyed. This was the case in Laura's family after their years of silent complicity had been acknowledged. They began to challenge one another, to struggle for levels of communication that earlier would have been taboo.

Still another way in which the patterns come apart is through a kind of general anarchy. Because "the worst" has happened, there is little left to protect. The deep sense of limits, the elaborate network of rules, spoken and unspoken, concerning what is permitted, is now meaningless. Forbidden things come out. Sometimes this is liberating, as when Laura's sister, in the ultimate defiance of her father's authority, yelled, "How are you going to get it *up* for this young chick?" or when Laura, defying the family dictum to be rational, allowed herself to weep in front of everyone. But more often it's very disturbing — as when the daughter heard the dream of the dying plant, or when a parent begins revealing sexual secrets, or when Scott's mother told him, "There's something I have never told you and never can tell you. But you should know that your father did an unspeakably terrible thing many years ago, when you were small."

Whether based on conscious recognition or not, whenever one person changes his or her role in a basic pattern, this alters the family dynamic for everyone else as well. When Laura's father left, she and her siblings had to learn to relate to one another in what felt like the vacuum of his absence. When Rebecca was told that her mother was leaving her father, she had to acknowledge his chronic mental illness for the first time. Her mother would no longer cover up for him, and Rebecca had to learn entirely new ways of coping with him. This, in turn, affected her relationship with other members of the family.

## Happy and Unhappy Families

Though some people indicated to us that their family life had been happier at one point, later growing more troubled or distant, most people had no trouble characterizing their family life as clearly falling on one side or the other of the happy/ unhappy line.[2] Needless to say, this distinction quite drastically shapes the experience of parental divorce.

### Two Families

Anna's experience of her family as "happy" did not mean that she perceived it as absolutely blissful and problem free. There were tensions, spoken and unspoken, that had occasionally erupted into outright conflict. But family life was basically stable and harmonious. Her parents were both artists and shared many of the same values and friendships. Anna was proud of her family and closely identified with it.

Anna's acute sense of shock upon learning of her parents' breakup was typical of children from "happy" families. As with many families of this type, the parents' relationship had receded to the background, with the greatest focus, energy, and identification directed at family life. Some adult children we questioned expressed a mixed feeling: "Somehow I knew it was coming, but I just couldn't believe it" or "I wasn't really surprised, but I just never thought it would really happen."

For many in this category, the shock is intensified by a sense of shame or embarrassment. They have grown up feeling that others admire or even envy their happy family — now they, too, are joining the ranks of children from "broken homes."

The extreme sense of disorientation that Anna suffered in the months following her parents' breakup is typical. She had a strong sense of identification with her family; her own values and way of life were closely modeled on her family's. Like her parents, Anna and her husband are both artists. The sudden realization that her family life had not been all that it seemed induced a crisis of doubt in her own life.

Ericka was one of those who unhesitatingly described her family background as unhappy. Her father was an alcoholic and family life was overshadowed by her parents' frequent and bitter arguments. Toward the end of our interview with her, we asked, "What do you miss most about your family as it used to be?" Tears came into her eyes as she realized, "Nothing."

Many of our respondents who had long perceived their families as troubled felt that the divorce itself was a rather anticlimactic event. Those from "happy" families remembered the moment of being told with vivid clarity and could usually reconstruct the time frame of the divorce without much difficulty. Those in the "unhappy" category were often rather hazy. There had been so many crises and climaxes leading up to it, that the divorce itself did not stand out in such sharp detail.

Another difference was that in the unhappy families, news of the parents' breakup did not usually generate the same degree of shock, disorientation, and self-doubt as in the happy families. Because family life had been unhappy for so long, these children had often been through an intense period of disillusionment and questioning at earlier times. However, most of them did not feel emotionally prepared for the actual reality of divorce.

The common assumption is that people in this category experience relief when their parents divorce. Some, of course, do. Bill's father was an alcoholic who was physically and emotionally abusive to his wife and children. From an early age Bill had been the responsible man in the family, and for many years he had wanted his mother to leave the marriage. When she finally did, Bill and his siblings came and helped their parents divide possessions and move out of the house. For many adult children, this day of final reckoning stands out as one of the most painful events of their life. But as Bill described it, there was a slight smile on his face. Having been through so many years of grief and chaos, he felt a certain pleasure in the speed and efficiency with which he and his siblings sent their parents on their separate ways.

Except for a handful of very extreme cases, the relief expressed to us by children from unhappy families was rarely pure and unadulterated. For these children, too, there was grief — even if, like Ericka's, it was a grief for something that had never been.

## Remarriage

When one parent remarries, new shock waves ripple through the already disrupted network of family patterns.

Of course, some patterns stay intact, unaffected by — or actually duplicated in — the new marriage. Amanda's mother had dominated her husband for many years with her powerful mood swings and very serious depressions. He finally managed to leave her, and for a short while after the separation Amanda felt closer to him than ever before. When he remarried, however, he chose a woman who, according to Amanda, was — in a different way — just as controlling as Amanda's mother had been. "He's just someone who needs to be completely sub-sumed in his marriage," Amanda said. The result was that she felt even more cut off from him than ever.

Other patterns simply fall away or atrophy, unable to find an energy source in the new relationship. Still others are actively rejected or destroyed.

### The Risk and the Possibility

Now we are in a position to understand the powerful impact of divorce.

In its mildest form, it gives rise to a frightening sense of exposure as the family's inner workings are revealed as never before. With the collapse of familiar patterns, family members often feel awkwardly exposed in front of one another, without the comforting insulation of their habitual roles.

Frequently, the sense of exposure is accompanied by a general feeling of disorientation, a kind of dizziness that comes from the familiar rules being out of play. One man told us, "It's like living in a country where overnight the currency is devalued."

Eventually, of course, it can be very liberating to be freed from the pattern of old beliefs. But initially it's as though the core, the foundation, that gave one's life meaning has dissolved. As one woman said, "My parents — for all their conflicts — had always been united in one thing: their criticism of me. When they divorced, it was as though the altar on which I'd offered myself up all my life no longer existed." The disrupted pattern may have been a negative one, but it informed her basic sense of self.

This is the source of the greatest misconception: it's assumed that because the adult child is no longer in formation, has passed through the vulnerable, impressionable stages of earlier growth, he or she will not be severely affected by parental divorce. "After all, you had security and stability when you really needed it. Why are you so upset now?" *Yet it's precisely because the adult child's sense of self has crystallized around a certain perception of the family, a perception that remains at the core of self, that it is so devastating when that perception explodes.*

Of course, not all adult children are equally shaken by their parents' divorce. Some family constellations make particular family members more vulnerable. Certainly not all adult children are so closely identified with their parents as were Laura, Stan, and Noelle. Not all have reached adulthood with so many of their most cherished assumptions intact. When families are highly enmeshed, when there has been a very intense identification with the family myth and a great disparity between that myth and reality, when rules have been rigid, communication restricted, roles highly polarized, triangles exclusive and tightly bound — we would expect divorce to have the most disruptive impact.

But whenever a couple with grown children splits up — no matter how mutual, how amicable a divorce it may be, and no matter how autonomous those children may appear — the very nature of families prevents a clean break. A divorce after many years of marriage is not like the pieces of a puzzle coming apart, with precisely defined, individualized parts remaining whole and intact. It is not a mere regrouping. Because of the mutually formative nature of family relationships, a divorce after twenty or so years of marriage profoundly alters the patterns of interconnection and thus shakes the roots of each member's self-perception.

# 4

## *What Any Child Feels When Parents Divorce*

Divorce is unique among family crises not so much in the intensity but in the range of emotions that it calls up. The sense of shock, loss, and disorientation may be as powerful and unsettling as in the wake of a death. But in the case of divorce, these feelings are frequently accompanied by others that are no less intense and often harder to acknowledge. Rage, bitterness, guilt, jealousy, shame — it is hard to imagine an experience that encompasses a wider spectrum of human emotions.

The presumption, all too often, is that adult children are not drawn into this powerful mix of emotions. Their role is to remain uncomfortably but sympathetically on the sidelines, carrying on with their own lives. Yet as we have seen, the very nature of families makes it unlikely that such powerful emotions will be neatly contained between the divorcing parents. In many cases, it is precisely because the children are grown that their parents, thinking them beyond any need of protection, pull them into the very center of the whirlwind.

What follows is a litany of the emotions most frequently and intensely experienced by sons and daughters, young and old, in the wake of their parents' divorce. While in the next chapter we

42

focus on the unique features of the adult child's situation, here we focus on the many profound — and sometimes startling — continuities between young and grown children.

## Shock

The dictionary defines *shock* as "a violent, sudden blow," and this is precisely how most children experience the news of divorce. Even if there has been conflict and talk of divorce before, they feel stunned that it is happening *now* and *in this particular way*.

A number of people told us, "I had often thought that my parents might get divorced. As a child, I even wished for it. But I never knew the reality would feel like this." As Sarah explained:

When my sister and I were growing up, our parents were always so busy. I used to fantasize that if they got divorced, they would each have more time for us. There would be long, uninterrupted tête-à-têtes. But the reality is that they are even more preoccupied with themselves than before. And of course, there are all the other aspects of divorce that hadn't figured into my fantasies — the anger, the money problems, all of that.

Adult children, one might think, would be more prepared for their parents' divorce. After all, as adults they have greater insight into the dynamics of intimate relationships. They are less dependent on their parents and hence capable of a more objective appraisal. Often, they have even served as sounding boards for their parents' marital grievances.

Yet fully 45 percent of our respondents said that their parents' divorce came as "a total surprise" — a figure that corresponds to the findings of other researchers.[1] How is it that so many adult children are caught off guard?

There are many reasons for not anticipating what later may seem obvious. One very significant factor is that it is possible for children to be very satisfied with the quality of family life without being very disturbed by, or even particularly aware of, unhappiness between the parents.

Of course, for some adult children there are simple logistic reasons for not being in the know. As one young man in his midtwenties explained, "I'd been on my own for four years, seeing my parents only on holidays, when everyone was on their best behavior and the emphasis was on the family celebration. I had absolutely no idea that their marriage was faltering."

Another woman told us:

> Until the moment my parents told me, I actually thought
> . they had been happily married for twenty-five years. So
> in that instant, I not only had to grasp the enormity of
> what was happening to them in the present, but suddenly
> I had twenty-five years of our shared past spinning around
> in my head, uprooted, unaccounted for.

She said she could not have been more surprised than if she had suddenly found out that her parents were not her real parents.

For very young adults at the tail end of adolescence, the turmoil in their own lives may obscure the parents' plight. For older adults, there are the consuming demands of their own commitments.

And on a very deep level there's fear — fear of opening up the dark welter of emotions that really does emerge when a family comes apart.


## Grief

Of all the feelings surrounding divorce, grief is the most complex and all-encompassing. And while for most people its acute phase subsides after the first year or so, the sense of loss is the one feeling that never disappears completely. Instead, it seems to submerge for periods of time and then to reemerge, revealing itself under a different aspect. For a young woman in her early twenties, it may be the loss of the family home that is hardest to bear. At thirty, it may be the lack of a loving pair of grandparents for her children.

## The Loss of the Family

Divorce, for all children, means the loss of the family as it has been. For the adult child, it means that never again will family members come together in the ways that are so deeply familiar after decades of shared existence.

If the family has been a relatively smoothly functioning one, then it is easy to see the loss involved. Now from the wealth of happy memories come stabs of pain: sitting around the dinner table, celebrating Christmas, bringing friends home, laughing over certain family jokes — none of this will ever be the same again.

Even when there are civilized attempts at reunions — at holidays or important events such as graduations and weddings — there will always be a feeling of strangeness or artificiality. No matter how successfully such occasions may come off, there will always be the feeling of something having "come off." For some, this is the most painful loss: the loss of spontaneity, of the simple taking-for-grantedness of one's family.

In part what is involved here is the loss of a particular vision of the family's future: things will not be as they have been; things will not be as one imagined them to be. For some, this loss is experienced in an all-pervasive and global way. As one young woman said, "I'd think of one thing that would never be the same again — like going as a family to my grandmother's house — and then I'd think of another and another — until I had this gigantic, overwhelming snowball." Others focus on a particular event, such as the wedding day they had always imagined, which now will be quite different from their dreams.

There is, then, a break in the sense of continuity between the family's past and its future. This break goes deeper still, however, for the past itself does not remain comfortably the same in memory. As we will see later, the revision of the past can be one of the most painful aspects of late divorce.

Even for families with a history of unhappiness, divorce brings a sense of loss. Many people told us that no matter how bad things were, they always cherished the hope that their family might one day be transformed into a happier one. When their parents divorced, that hope was extinguished once and for all.

## The Loss of the Family's World

No family exists in isolation, but rather, to a greater or lesser degree, incorporates others into it, defining itself in relation to them. Part of what it means to be a member of a family is to have certain patterns of relating to an extended group of people — aunts, uncles, cousins, neighbors, friends. All of this gets disrupted when parents divorce. Even under the best of circumstances, friends and relatives face the awkward business of relating separately to both halves of a once-united pair. Secrets, slips of the tongue, uncomfortable pauses, have a way of intruding upon conversations that once might have flowed with a natural ease. Worse, frequently people take sides, cutting off from one or the other branch of the family. At each "encampment" there is an atmosphere of bitterness and recrimination. In Diane's words:

> It's very hard when you have grown into an adult-type relationship with your parents' friends. You've come to really value them as friends, and now there is all this taking of sides. So that in addition to losing your family, sometimes you're losing other very close and long-term relationships as well.

All of this means the loss of the world that existed around and through one's family. This loss is compounded by a certain stigma that surrounds the experience of divorce. Research shows that families experiencing divorce do not receive the same degree of social support as in the case of death or illness.[2]

## The Loss of Parents as a Unit

No matter how difficult one's parents' relationship might have been, there is nonetheless a deeply rooted feeling that they belong together. Grown-up children have a tendency to ask, "Why am I grieving? After all, no one has died." But the breakup of a marriage *is* a loss, it *is* a death — the death of a relationship — a relationship that was one's first home, one's first world, the very air one breathed. Many find that their parents become different people when living apart. This means the loss of that part of each parent that, with the dissolution of the marriage and the family as it has been, will no longer exist.

There will be no more homecomings to Mom-and-Dad, no more phone calls with the two of them on the line; letters will have to be written in duplicate, holiday time carefully divided. Each will have to be visited in his or her own home, and at each place for a long time there will be an ache, a sense of "this is not right." One will never again be able to bring friends "home" in the same way as before. As one woman said:

> Though gradually you get used to it, initially it's strange
> when there is someone very important — a close friend, a
> lover, maybe even your fiancé — and they have never
> known your parents as a couple. They take it for granted
> that your parents are divorced, while you keep wanting to
> explain to them about your *real* family.

In fact, parents may outgrow this particular sense of loss sooner than their children. Each of them, after all, carries a memory of the twenty or so years of separate existence before they married, but their children have never known them apart from each other. What parents, in their need to break from the past and get on with their new lives, may come to think of as a long mistake remains — forever — the very ground of their children's being. "I guess I married him because everyone else was getting married," Marcy's mother told her daughter. Marcy could understand that intellectually, of course, but on the deepest level it was difficult to accept as so fluky and arbitrary the relationship that brought her into existence and was the world of her first years. It is not unlike the discovery that one was an "accidental baby." More than one person told us that their parents' divorce gave them a strange feeling of retroactive illegitimacy.

## The Loss of Parents as Parents

For some children, it is the divorce itself — the fact of a failed marriage, a broken commitment — that diminishes the status of their parents as parents, as figures worthy of respect and emulation. For others, the circumstances surrounding the divorce — the disturbing revelations or inconsiderate behavior — bring about this disillusionment.

And for many children — adults included — it is in the aftermath of the divorce that they first see their parents as truly vulnerable, and even out of control. "I had never seen my father cry before," was a frequent testimony. "My mother had always brought us up to be independent — now she was throwing herself at my feet," one young woman said.

Young children frequently experience their parents as less giving, less available as parents following their divorce. Adult children, too — though their daily physical well-being may not be at stake — may feel the loss of their parents' devotion to parenting. Ruth was thirty at the time of her parents' divorce, and her fourth child had just been born:

> I understood that my mother was very preoccupied, and I felt terrible for her. But it hurt so much that she showed so little interest in my new baby. I remember one afternoon — I'd just come home from the hospital with him, and my mother came over to visit. She sat way on the other side of the room from us, sunk in her chair, brooding. I wanted to shout, "Aren't you even going to *look* at him?"

Another young woman was in the midst of her own divorce when her father left her mother for another woman and moved to another state. Her overwhelming feeling at the time was, "The one time in my life that I really needed my father, he wasn't there."

## The Loss of Security

For most young children whose parents divorce, the world becomes less safe and predictable. Nightmares, fears, and phobias of all kinds become more common in children in the period surrounding their parents' divorce.

Grown children are not immune to this feeling of insecurity. Ours is an era when many young adults postpone settling down and making commitments until they are well into their twenties or early thirties. This means that for many young adults, much of the stability in their lives is linked to that of their parents. This link is often quite unconscious, surfacing only when it is ruptured. As one young man testified, "I was twenty-five and considered myself quite daring and adventurous. I traveled a lot, never lived in the same place long, had held a series of jobs. . . . When my parents split up, it was a total shock to realize how much I had counted on them for my own sense of grounding."

Following divorce, families frequently experience a financial decline. For women in particular, there is generally a substantial drop in standard of living. While men, with their greater earning power, are less vulnerable, their higher rate of remarriage means the addition of new financial responsibilities. Research has shown that the elderly divorced contribute less financially to their adult children than do their married counterparts.[3] Even under conditions of affluence, money often becomes the one remaining link between ex-spouses. Grown children, no less than young children, frequently feel caught in the midst of their parents' financial struggles.

Sarah was eighteen and on her way to college in New York City when her parents divorced. Her father, a wealthy lawyer, said he would pay her tuition and nothing else. Sarah felt shocked, hurt, and disappointed — especially because she and her father were so close in other respects. Her mother, deeply resentful of the divorce and "tired of being treated like a doormat," refused to help Sarah out, although she had an income of her own. Sarah went off to college "without so much as a new sweater" and with tremendous anxieties as to how she would keep up at a highly competitive school and at the same time earn enough money to pay expensive New York City rents.

What all of this means is that when parents divorce, they will never again be able to provide the same sense of security

that they have in the past. This is true on a purely material
level, and it is true on an emotional level as well. The two are
linked, of course: it is the rare family for whom economic decline does not have emotional consequences. Along with these
repercussions, most children discover other new vulnerabilities on the part of their parents, and many must assume a
caretaking role. At the most basic level, the divorce ruptures the
familiar and shatters the notions that what *has been, will be.*

## The Loss of the Family Home

Very often there is quite literally the abandonment of the
house in which one's family has lived, the painful division of
objects that, for as long as one can remember, have sat side by
side on the shelves. In the words of one young woman, "When
I first visited my mother and sister in their new house, I remember feeling as though the objects themselves were in
mourning for their lost mates."

Sometimes there's a tendency to focus on the loss of the
house — perhaps because it's actually less painful than the disruption of the family, or perhaps because it is the most tangible
symbol of the family. As one young woman said shortly after
her parents broke up, "I guess I'll get used to my parents being
apart — but I'll really miss that house. I always dreamed of
getting married in the garden." Diane's voice caught in her
throat when she talked about the house they used to live in:
"What a house: it was all wood, knotty cedar. There was a
walk-in fireplace, cathedral ceilings, and a pond surrounded by
willow trees. Now I visit my parents in their separate antisep-
tic apartments, and — along with everything else — it's just
not the same."

It is not just "happy" families, who have lost a house full of
happy memories, that feel this loss. Indeed, sometimes unhappy families are most attached to the house in which they've
lived. Sometimes it's clear that a house was purchased as a
last-ditch effort to make a marriage work and hold a family
together. Ericka was twenty-eight years old when her parents
divorced. Her parents' marriage had never been a happy one,
and she had often wished that they would part. During our

interview with her, she kept looking at a small cuckoo clock hanging on her wall. Finally she explained:

> That little clock came from the last house we had as a family. It was the most beautiful house my family ever had. It had these wonderful French doors that led into the kitchen and were great for making funny, dramatic entrances and exits. We were never really happy in that house, but in a way it represented what might have been — the beautiful possibility. And now all I have left is this clock on my wall.

## Anger

While grief may be the most enduring and all-encompassing emotion, anger is for many — after the initial shock of the news — the first and most keenly felt emotion.

Often, of course, the news of divorce comes as part of a whole package of disturbing revelations: "Your father has been having an affair," or "I'm moving in with another man." Such revelations naturally provoke anger and are intensified by feelings of having been betrayed, lied to, kept in the dark.

Even in the absence of such revelations, grown sons and daughters sometimes find themselves infuriated by the manner in which they are told. Though it had been three years since her parents' separation, Rebecca, twenty-nine, was still angry at the way they broke the news:

> They invited me over for Easter dinner, and then they told me that Mom would be moving out. After dinner I had to go to my job — I worked as a bar attendant at the time — and I remember feeling very angry. I felt that way for a week — as though I had lost my bearings — but mostly very, very angry. And I'm still angry about that incident. I don't really know why. I guess I felt manipulated. But maybe I'm just using that incident as a mask for other things.

It is easy to see why Rebecca, dressed in her new spring clothes and expecting an Easter dinner, might have felt ma-

nipulated by her parents, like a small child enticed with sweets
to take a bitter pill. At the same time, however, she was the
brunt of behavior that seems especially reserved for the adult
child: she was given the news in a way that precluded any
intense emotional response. Invited to a festive dinner, responsible for getting to work afterward — what could she do but act
"grown-up"? No wonder she found herself seething with anger.

Yet Rebecca is probably correct in suspecting that, if she
were to pull off the "mask" of this particular incident, she
would discover that the source of her anger was indeed far
more complex and deeply rooted.

At the most basic level, anger is a natural response to the
sense of being threatened. No matter how gently and tactfully
the news is presented, no matter how free it may be of gross
revelation and lurid detail, most sons and daughters experience it as threatening.

At the very least it signals change, a shift in the status
quo — and it is simply a principle of human existence that
change brings anxiety. However uncomfortable and unsatis-
fying things may have been, like Brer Rabbit we have grown
used to our briar patches. Furthermore, the news of our parents' divorce may make us acutely aware of life's unpredict-
ability. "This is not what I ever expected to happen," many
sons and daughters say. Kate, whose father began an affair
many years before he actually divorced her mother, said,
"I'm an orderly person. My father did everything out of order." For grown children there's an accompanying humiliation; they feel like young children again, being apprised of
major decisions over which they have no control: "We're
moving to a new town," "We're going to have a new baby,"
and now "We're getting a divorce."

Younger children, who are unaccustomed to thinking about
their parents as separate individuals, find the shift of focus
away from family and their own lives very disturbing. Adult
children, even when they can empathize with their parents'
need for change, may resent the intrusion of their parents' lives
into their own. For many adult children, the news of divorce
comes along with the plea, "Help me!" — whether it's "Help

me save this marriage," "Help me get through this divorce," or "Help me build a new life." Even when the plea is not put directly, many sons and daughters hear the news as a threat to whatever borders they may have tried to build around their lives.

This threat is a real one: just as young children find their lives significantly disrupted by their parents' divorce, so do grown children. This is particularly true in the first year or so, given the many difficult practical decisions that must be made, and given the dramatic conflicts, the mood swings, depression, excessive drinking, and erratic behaviors so frequently manifested by newly divorced people. Even under the best circumstances and over the long term, divorce generally makes life more complicated for all family members. For many adult children, this is one of the most long-lasting and intensely felt sources of aggravation.

Nick was twenty when his parents began the process of separating two years ago. Though he claimed to have accepted the fact that they are no longer together, his voice tightened with anger as he described his sense of being intruded upon. He was careful to explain that he has never minded doing things for his family — quite the contrary, the sense of mutual caretaking has always been at the core of their family life. What he resented was the sense of unnecessary complications crowding in on his life: having to drive across town from one house to another, becoming responsible for hundreds of practical details that his parents used to take care of for each other, the exhausting deliberations that surround each holiday. "What really burns me up," he said, "is that it's *their mess* that's overtaking *my life*. I didn't fail at their marriage — they did — yet I have to pay for it in so many ways."

Here Nick touched on a very significant aspect of divorce. There is a voluntary aspect, an element of choice that makes us feel that someone is to blame. Children of divorce perceive that their parents, who are supposed to be concerned for their children's welfare, are causing them pain instead. Although adult children often judge it as irrational, even shameful, still the feeling is "How could they do this to me?"

There's an old Chinese story called "The Empty Boat." A man is lying peacefully in a little boat on a tranquil lake when his boat is rammed by another. "How dare you?!" he shouts, but, as he stands up to see who has so inconsiderately disturbed him, his anger vanishes: he sees that there was no one in the boat. In just this way, it can be easier to accept what seem to us the natural disruptions of our lives — those brought about through illness, death, flood, or fire — than those that seem to us "manned."

Many sons and daughters feel angry at their parents for not having worked harder at their marriage. This seems to be particularly true for teenagers and young adults, like Nick, who have some understanding that relationships require effort, but who don't fully grasp just how difficult marriage can be. By the same token, however, adult children who have themselves been married for some time often feel: "We've worked through our crises — why can't you?"

Of course, what makes the voluntary aspect of divorce even harder to bear is that generally there is one partner who is initiating the divorce against the wishes of the other and in the hopes of a better life. It is common to feel that this parent is acting selfishly, thinking solely in terms of his or her own happiness at the expense of the family as a whole. There is particular bitterness and even outrage if such behavior conflicts with the values expressed by this parent over the years. This was true for one young woman, who wrote in an unsent letter to her father: "Our family has been built up in trust and faith. You have made a mockery of everything you taught us."

For Stan, who had patterned himself after his father, the "senator-hero," rage was a way of protecting himself. He had always been proud that he was so much like his father, but now — with the revelation of his father's years of infidelity — the similarities were threatening, both to Stan and his wife. Anger was a way of achieving distance, of breaking the identification.

Grown children are often shocked and disturbed by the intensity of the anger that arises. One way of trying to keep the anger to manageable proportions is to focus — sometimes quite obsessively — on what seem like the safe zones. Surely it is justifiable to resent the parent who initiated the divorce and to feel something close to hatred for any third party involved, the man or the woman who led one's parent astray.

Far more disturbing is the anger that erupts in unlikely places. Many report feeling angry at the parent being left — for not having been stronger or more attractive, or not having worked harder to keep the marriage intact. Laura reported feeling tremendously angry at her mother for having drawn them all into complicity with their father's years of infidelity. In her words, "I felt like she sold us all downriver." For Laura, too, anger helped her to distance herself from a painful identification. Rather than seeing herself as a passive victim like her mother, she became outraged and indignant.

Rafe, eighteen when his parents divorced, felt rage at both parents. He felt angry at his mother for being such a difficult person; for having, in effect, driven his father away. At the same time, he felt angry at his father for having left him alone to deal with this difficult woman. "I felt like — as impossible as she was — she was *his* responsibility, and he'd just abdicated and left it all to me."

Anger can be a deceptive emotion. It often feels primitive, elemental, like fire, yet frequently it disguises other, more threatening emotions. As unpleasant as anger may be, many people nonetheless experience it as an energizing, empowering emotion that impels them toward action. For adult children, anger may feel like the safest emotion, the one least compromising of their adult selves.[4] However, many adult children find themselves in the grips of other, equally intense — and often more frightening — emotions.

## Abandonment and Rejection

Divorcing parents often have to explain to their young children, "Mom and Dad aren't getting along anymore. But Dad still loves you. It's not you he's leaving."

It may be hard to imagine that an adult child might experience a parent's decision to divorce as a personal rejection. It may seem, even, like a logical error: "You haven't even been living with your parents for years. How could you possibly feel as though *you* were being left?"

Yet this is the experience of many adult children, and it is not so difficult to understand when we remember how very tightly a person's sense of self may be bound up with the family. Tess was twenty-three when her parents divorced; she is now thirty-five. During our interview she told us, "Even now — all these years later — my mother still asks the question, 'Why did he leave me?' " Tess's voice broke here. "And this is where it gets very emotional for me." "Why?" we asked her. "Because he left me too." Though the parents may have been living alone in the house together for years, what many adult children experience is that one parent is *leaving the family.*

Many factors contribute to the sense of abandonment, and fortunately some are relatively temporary. In the turmoil surrounding divorce, many parents become intensely preoccupied — to the point of forgetting birthdays and other occasions. Fathers may have relied on their wives to keep them emotionally in touch with their children; it may be some time before they are able to connect on their own.

Certain circumstances intensify and prolong the feeling of rejection. Some parents become frankly less interested in their identity as parents following divorce. Sometimes a parent is leaving to take up with a new partner or to adopt a new lifestyle that represents a shift away from what the family's values have been. And — particularly in the presence of their adult children — parents may be quite outspoken about their desire to reject the past and embrace the new.

Sometimes there is a strong identification with the parent being left. One woman told us: "People always said that I looked like my mother, and I talk like her. When my dad left her for another woman, someone who looked completely different from us — a petite blond, and we are all tall and dark — I felt as though *I* was the abandoned one."

Many adult children experience the reawakening of childhood fears of abandonment. For some, these reawakened fears are particularly powerful. This was the case for Noelle, whose father had left for a year when she was three. And it was also the case for Elizabeth, whose mother and stepfather divorced when she was twenty-five. Elizabeth's real father had died when she was an infant, and her mother remarried when Elizabeth was five, so her stepfather was the only father that Elizabeth had ever known. Though her mother and stepfather had already been separated for seven years, Elizabeth was, in her words, "devastated" when she learned they were actually going to divorce. When we asked her why, Elizabeth — who is forty-five and who gives the impression of being a very hardy, matter-of-fact woman — had difficulty speaking. Her eyes filled with tears, and after a while she said, "The only thing I can say to explain it is that from that moment on, I had recurring dreams of being abandoned."

## Guilt, Shame, Embarrassment

Young children sometimes feel that they are to blame when their parents divorce. If only they had not been so quarrelsome or had done better at school or had raked those leaves like Daddy asked, then surely, he would not be leaving. . . . Even adult children are not immune to such feelings.

Elizabeth told us in detail of the afternoon when her stepfather — whom she had always called her father — came to tell her of the divorce:

> I will never forget that afternoon. My father came over to the place where I was living and asked me if I would take a walk with him — so I knew something strange was happening. He told me they were going to get divorced, and I felt totally devastated. And this was the strange thing — what went through my head was, "But how can you get divorced when I haven't even been living with you for the last seven years?" In other words — I felt that if they were getting divorced, it had to be my fault.

Elizabeth claimed that as a child she was never conscious of being a strain on her parents' relationship. But what emerged when her stepfather gave her the news of the divorce was an overpowering feeling of having been a burden. After all, without her, her mother and stepfather would have been free to start an entirely new life, without any baggage from the past. Elizabeth's story provides a powerful example of how ancient childhood feelings may be awakened when parents divorce.

For the most part, of course, adult children are free of the exaggerated sense of omnipotence that makes some young children feel they are to blame when their parents divorce. This does not mean, however, that they are untouched by other feelings of guilt. Indeed, precisely because of their greater competence as adults, they frequently have very high expectations of themselves — and consequent feelings of failure.

In marriages that have been troubled for some time, adult children have often been drawn into the conflict: they've been asked for advice, or they've volunteered it. Often such advice has been given in moments of anger, without deep reflection — and now there's regret. Twenty-two-year-old Susanna told us:

> I was so sick of the tensions between my parents that when my mother asked me, "Should I leave your father?" I yelled at her, "I don't care what you do!" Now I feel bad about that. I know it's probably not true, but sometimes I think maybe things would be different if I hadn't been so hard-hearted.

When late divorce takes place after the last child has left home, it is not uncommon for this child to feel responsible for being the catalyst. "My last year of high school I felt like I was the one holding my parents together," one young woman said. "They broke up a few months after I got to college, and I felt that somehow I had failed the whole family."

Adult children are frequently in a position to help a parent in the process of transition — choosing and consulting a lawyer, lending money, helping with the move to a new house. Often this creates a double-bind situation: a son or a daughter feels compelled to help one parent, at the risk of alienating another. Over and over again, adult children speak of feeling like accomplices. For Rosie, the feeling was particularly acute.

Before her mother left her father for Fred, Fred used to send letters to Rosie to give to her mother. "He would sign them 'Uncle Harry,' " she told us. "It put me in a very awkward position. He thought that since my father was an alcoholic, I would be grateful that he was rescuing my mother."

While some express a sense of guilt over what they've done, others feel remorse at what they've failed to do. They lament that they should have seen the signs of trouble earlier, urged their parents to seek counseling, or stepped in themselves with some more drastic intervention.

Compounding all this is the fact that parents — lacking the same sense of restraint as they might have with a younger child — frequently blame their adult children: "You encouraged your father to leave me," "You could have convinced her to stay," or "You knew what was happening, yet you did nothing."

If some adult children are made to feel partially responsible for the failure of their parents' marriage, others experience a different guilt. Frequently the news of divorce comes with the rider, "We stuck this miserable marriage out so long for your sake." Like Rebecca at the Easter dinner, this is an example of parents' breaking the news in a way that forbids response. As one young man put it, "How could I have the gall to protest the divorce when she's telling me she's been miserable for our sake for twenty years?!"

Even without a sense of actual commission or omission of specific acts, many adult children feel a more diffuse, but nonetheless burdensome, sense of guilt. For some it may arise because, in spite of themselves, they sympathize with the parent who is leaving. For others, there's a sense of guilt that their own life is more stable, and there is something that seems unnatural about this equation. Question and turmoil are for the young; our elders are supposed to be constant.

What others experience is not so much guilt as a sense of shame or disgrace at their parents' divorce. In a letter to "Dear Abby," one grown daughter described herself as "absolutely beside myself" after she learned that her parents were ending their marriage of forty-four years. Though no hint of scandal appeared in her parents' situation, she was clearly distraught, and her letter ended with the question, "How can parents disgrace their families that way?" Alas, Abby's response did nothing to correct popular misconceptions about adult children and divorce. Reminding the daughter that "parents have a right to make their own decisions, for their own reasons," Abby asked flatly, "Where is the 'disgrace'?"[5]

As we've seen before, "parents," "children," "their marriage," "our lives," do not fall into such tidy units. The images we have of our parents' marriage and the nature of our family are intimately bound up with our sense of ourselves and are profoundly shaken when our parents divorce. And in many families, the very news of divorce is frequently accompanied by revelations that are themselves embarrassing.

There are other reasons, too, for the sense of shame and disgrace that so many adult children report. Most baby boomers grew up in the 1950s, when divorce was relatively rare and there were only one or two "kids from broken homes" in the classroom. Intellectually, they may hold a very liberal view of divorce: "What's the big deal? These days one out of two marriages ends in divorce." But what resonates are the layers of early memories. Kate, who was thirty when her parents separated, listed embarrassment as one of the emotions she felt most strongly. When we pressed her to tell us why, she hesitated for several moments and then said almost apologetically, "I guess that one of the ways in which I felt I was somewhat better than others was that my parents were still together."

If children of this generation feel a heightened sense of shame, their parents feel it even more intensely, and this in turn colors their children's experience. Rafe's mother was a first-generation Italian American with very "Old World values." She felt such shame at the separation that she forbade Rafe to tell anyone. Not only did he experience the discomfort of lying to friends and neighbors, but he was deprived of the consolation of sharing his burdens with sympathetic listeners.

The pain of shattered images is most acute for sons and daughters who have perceived themselves as coming from happy, stable families. Yet even in families that have been troubled for years, divorce brings with it a sense of going public with one's difficulties. Charles's father was an alcoholic and his parents' marriage had been miserable from as far back as he could remember. Yet he described the sense of shame he felt when they divorced. "It was like a huge banner was stuck on top of the house proclaiming, 'Look at this failure,' and that house — that failure — was where I come from."

Of course, for the adult child, there is the sense of guilt and embarrassment for having any intense feelings at all in the wake of one's parents' divorce. And here we touch on one of the most important themes of the next chapter.

# 5

## *The Unique Situation of the Adult Child of Divorce*

Of course, what is unique to the adult child cannot really be isolated, like a pure precipitate, from out of the mix of childlike responses. For one thing, what is unique to the adult child is the awareness of feeling *like a child* again. More than anything it is this complexity, this multidimensionality, that characterizes the adult child's experience of divorce.

### The Sense of Time

Nowhere is this more apparent than when we consider the adult child's necessarily different sense of time.

The older we are, the more likely it is that we have lived through other crises, that we have at least some inkling or experience of having emerged, mostly intact, from other dark tunnels. For this reason the adult child may be less vulnerable than younger children to the feeling of complete hopelessness.

But there is a shadow side. The older we are, the greater the wealth of memory reverberating around the experience of divorce. This means that whatever notes are struck will be rich in overtones, like complicated, shimmering chords. Along with the emotions associated with the divorce itself, there are years and years of a family's entire emotional history, resonating now like powerful, dissonant music. There is Laura's shock and grief and rage to learn that her father is leaving her mother for his young secretary. At the same time, there is the memory of that birthday party so long ago when she was scolded for asking, "Does that lady have to come too?" And there are memories from the years before and in between, long-buried memories, experiences too painful or confusing to process at the time, which now come crowding in upon her, many of them with the force of revelation.

The sheer volume of psychic material that is stirred up by divorce can be overwhelming for the adult son or daughter, and profoundly disorienting. A very young adult may have only recently emerged from the turmoil of adolescence. Now the fragile and still-emerging sense of self is overrun by powerful regressive forces, just when forward momentum is crucial to development. For an older adult, it may have been years and years since there was much thought or connection with childhood. Now suddenly comes this horde of memories — clamorous, unasked-for memories — knocking at the door, demanding to be reckoned with. Kate told us, "The divorce has affected my childhood. It's almost as though it happened in my childhood."

It is one thing to willingly undertake an intensive period of searching into the dark corners of one's past — it is quite another to have this task thrust on one. While some might welcome the opportunity, others do not. They feel invaded, interrupted, overpowered, thrown off course. Even if they choose not to explore the pieces of the past that now accost them, they feel that they are being forced to do so by others. Frequently this becomes a source of tension with other family members — with siblings, a parent, or even a spouse who is more eager to probe and expose.

The sheer number of years involved for adult children also means that the sense of loss and waste is tremendous. If much of the family history has been troubled and turbulent, there's the feeling, Why did we put up with it for so long, for nothing? If family life has been perceived as generally happy, suddenly there's the feeling, Where did it go? Did it ever truly exist? If so many years of seeming harmony could end in rupture — then what was the meaning of all those years?

Such questions plunge the adult child into an intensive period of revision. Some, it is true, find the process almost irresistible. "We felt like detectives," one woman said, speaking of herself and her siblings. "We went over and over, year by year, dredging up memories, piecing together clues, trying to figure out what really happened and what we'd imagined." For others, however, the process is involuntary; they feel they are being forced to acknowledge truths they would rather not see. For many, this is the most painful aspect of their parents' divorce. As one young man said, "You can cope with the present being a mess and you more or less expect the future to be uncertain, but the past — that's sacred."

The process is intensified by each parent's struggle to make sense of the past. If this struggle exists for any divorcing couple, it assumes giant proportions for the late-divorcing couple. Two people have spent their entire adult lives together. They stand on or near the threshold of old age. What stories, what explanations, will save them from vertigo? Some manage a moderate appraisal: "We had our good times. We raised a nice family. Now it's time to go our separate ways. . . ."

More often the process is not so temperate, and what makes it all the more painful is that parents and children may have such different needs and agendas. In order to ease the pain of separation and to justify leaving a marriage of twenty or thirty years, one partner may need to actively repudiate the past. The other — out of self-pity or rage or the need to express "I'm not simply a victim; I, too, can discard and reject and abandon" — may participate in the process. Diane described how upset she became when, not long after the divorce, her mother held a garage sale at their family home:

> There were all these dresses from the thirties and forties, and there was one especially that I didn't want her to sell. It was a plaid taffeta, with a peplum jacket and skirt. It wasn't even that pretty — but I got so upset, seeing it for

sale. My mother said, "What on earth would I need that for?" It wasn't that she was going around saying, "My whole life has gone down the drain" or anything that blatant — but still, she had kept these things for thirty years and only now had decided they weren't worth keeping.

When statements are made that challenge the past, whether overtly or indirectly, often there is little concern for their impact on an adult child: "After all, you're grown-up, you have a life of your own." But this "life of your own" is founded on the past — a past that is now being sorted out and sold at yard sales, a past no longer worth preserving, and sometimes even actively repudiated. Amanda told us, "Recently my father came to the house and gave me all the family albums. I was glad to have them, but it made me sad that they didn't mean more to him. It made me feel that I'm the only one who really values the family's history."

When so many years can be invalidated, or at least thrown into question, it is no wonder that some adult children find themselves in the midst of a full-blown identity crisis: Anna had believed that she was the product of a happy family; Stan knew himself as the son of a saintly man.

It is not just one's sense of identity that is thrown into question but also one's powers of perception — and this, too, has profound implications for the present. The frightening question arises: If I could have been so mistaken in the past, what am I not seeing now? As one woman said, "You begin looking for the flaw in everything — and, of course, when you look, you begin to see. . . ."

The ability to trust may be another casualty of the process of revision. Diane was only one of many who expressed the sense of having been betrayed. As she put it, "I felt I'd been tricked into thinking I had a happy childhood."

For adult children, painful questions of identity are rarely a matter of mere speculation. It is likely that important decisions have been made on the basis of values associated with the past. Perhaps one has made a marriage, chosen a career, started a family, on the model of one's parents. How is one to proceed, now that so much has been repudiated?

What makes these questions even more painful is the feeling that they are inappropriate. Once past adolescence, we're supposed to know who we are, how we got there, and where we're going.

## Self-criticism

For the adult child, then, there are not only the immediate reactions, the primal emotions, the stirred-up memories themselves. These are accompanied — or at least frequently interrupted — by an adult's complex self-awareness. Think of Elizabeth saying, "And this was the strange thing . . . I felt that if they were getting divorced, it had to be my fault." She experienced simultaneously — or nearly so — the infantile emotion *and* the adult's awareness of it as "strange."

For most, the awareness does not stop with the sensation of strangeness but becomes a highly self-critical and even self-condemning activity: "I can't believe I'm feeling this way," "I know this is really childish, but —," or "I know I shouldn't be letting it get to me like this." Over and over, we have heard these apologizing, self-deprecating remarks.

The adult child not only experiences the range of painful emotions generally associated with divorce, but also finds the very intensity of these emotions seriously damaging to self-esteem. "I am obviously not a very mature person," many conclude, "if I can be so shaken up by this event." Undoubtedly, this self-critical attitude is an important contributing factor to the prolonged depression that many in our study reported. It is difficult to set about the task of healing when there is so much denial and self-condemnation.

## Powers of Reasoning

Perhaps nowhere is the twofold nature of the adult child's position more apparent than when we consider an adult's powers of reasoning.

Though adults may vary tremendously in this capacity — and there are gifted children who exceed the abilities of many adults — overall it can be said that adults possess a greater ability to think abstractly, to grasp experience through general principles. Rather than being flooded with immediate impressions, the "booming, buzzing confusion" of the infant, as we grow older we are able to organize our experience conceptually. We can relate past to present and to future; we can anticipate, prepare, compare, place in perspective, analyze, explain, and draw conclusions. Where a young child might be completely overwhelmed with raw emotion, as adults we have more ways of coping with that emotion, more ways of drawing back and making *it* the object of our attention.

Clearly, these abilities — which are so linked to the very definition of what it is to *be* an adult — are among the chief advantages of the adult child. There is a flip side, however, for the ability to reason is not only an ability but also an important need for adults.

As we've seen, in the wake of divorce powerful feelings are stirred up and reawakened. Many experience a profound confusion and sense of disorientation in the midst of these feelings. For an adult the ability to make sense of experience is an important component of self-esteem; thus many grown children experience confusion itself plus confusion *as* personal failure, *as* reversion to childhood. Nina told us, "I can't believe that I felt that way and still do after six years. It seems so childish."

Other factors contribute to the sense of confusion. It is through their parents' divorce that many adult children first become aware of certain discrepancies, contradictions, and ironies in their family history. The result is that what might be a purely emotional sense of confusion in the young child may become an intellectual crisis for the adult child. Over and over we've heard adult children say: "The divorce made me feel everything was a lie," "I didn't know what was true anymore," and "I could no longer trust my own powers of judgment."

To speak of this as an intellectual crisis is in no way to minimize its intensity — in fact, quite the opposite. It is to point out what an important role intellect has in the life of adults. It is to underline that for an adult the ability to have a reasoned, coherent view of experience is a powerful and fundamental need. Witness the collapse of Laura's brother Stan, the predominant feature of which was the overpowering sensation that reality and appearance were out of sync.

Another young man told us:

> What made the divorce difficult was, armed with information about the world around me, I knew that my parents should be divorced. It was too painful to see them together. At the same time, the hope that they could reconcile their relationship and its conflicts and reunite was on my mind and in my heart for some time to come. I believe the experience of divorce for an adult child can be more painful, because the broadened mind that age brings does not prepare anyone for the feelings.

Unfortunately, some adult children may use their complex thinking skills to distance themselves from the pain of powerful and conflicting emotions. While a certain measure of distance is helpful and is, indeed, one of the chief advantages of the adult child, beyond a certain point it can become a defensive stance that prevents healing. So much energy is expended on pointing out contradictions and constructing explanations that serious wounds of the heart may go untended. The only healing path through grief is full experience of the mourning process. The process may take weeks, or it may take years. The only certain thing is that it must not be short-circuited.

## The Spiritual Dimension

Not surprisingly, the crisis sometimes takes on a spiritual dimension. This may lead to very positive results; some sons and daughters reported to us that their parents' divorce first activated their spiritual lives. Other listed their strong sense of religious values and the associated social supports as being among the chief advantages they felt they had as adults. There were those, however, for whom the divorce was very unsettling in precisely this dimension of their life.

Ruth, for example, had been raised as a Catholic. When her parents separated, her mother managed to obtain an annulment from the church. Her father, who had always leaned toward skepticism, became extremely embittered at this juncture. How could a marriage that had lasted so many years and produced both children and grandchildren be annulled? Were Ruth and her brother therefore illegitimate? His questions stirred up questions in Ruth's mind and contributed to a rift between her and her mother.

Kate had also been raised Catholic, and when she learned that her father had been living with another woman on and off for years, what she felt most acutely was a sense of hypocrisy. She told us, "Your religious values are so tied up with your parents and your past. When you have this kind of disillusionment with a parent, it can't help but shake you up on all kinds of levels."

For some adult children, it is the powerful negativity stirred up by divorce that challenges their notion of what it is to be spiritual. Rebecca very openly expressed to us her many angry and resentful feelings about her parents' divorce. Several times, however, she interrupted herself with the words, "I guess I'm just not a very spiritual person."

For Vivian, the conflicting feelings were particularly intense. She lived and worked at a Christian shelter for homeless and battered women. Many of the women who came to the shelter were alcohol or drug addicted, severely psychologically disturbed, and even violent. Vivian saw her vocation as learning to open her heart and to be at home, in the most literal sense, with society's most "unlovable" people. When her father left her mother to take up with, in her words, "a sleazy young chick," she became enraged. She felt hatred toward this woman as toward an enemy — but how could she, Vivian, have an enemy? It threatened the very core of her sense of herself and her purpose in life.

The intense negative emotions that arise in the wake of divorce make many adult children feel that they have failed *as* adults. This sense of failure is compounded when it is perceived as a spiritual failure. For some, it intensifies the sense of

loss: they now feel alienated from values that were most intimately bound to their family experience and that sustained
them from earliest childhood. This loss is even more difficult to
bear because what might have been a source of consolation
instead provides more fuel for the fires of self-condemnation.

Thus far, we've been looking primarily at the internal factors,
those qualities of adult consciousness that make the experience
of divorce unique for the adult child. There are a number of
external factors, however, which distinctly shape the adult
child's experience of divorce.

## Expectations

One such factor that has a crucial impact on the adult child's
experience is that of expectations. There is, first and foremost,
the general cultural assumption that divorce does not really
qualify as a significant event in the life of an adult child. The
role of the adult child is peripheral; the task is to be a sympathetic observer, confidant, and helpmate, all the while carrying
on with one's own life.

Underlying this assumption are other more fundamental
ones. Normal adult children no longer have intense relationships with their parents. They have resolved, or at least detached from, whatever major emotional issues may have
existed in relation to their parents and have evolved a strong,
autonomous sense of self.

Of course, the boundary between internal and external is
blurred here because most adult children have fully absorbed
these assumptions. And sadly, most of us are our own harshest
critics: if the culture at large has these expectations, adult children apply them to themselves with a vengeance.

### Parents and Adult Children

Nowhere is the impact of unrealistic expectations more intensely felt than in the relationship between divorcing parents
and their adult children. Late divorce challenges certain basic

assumptions that parents and adult children have about one another.

What many sons and daughters experience is a disturbingly abrupt transition. There is a fairy-tale quality to the stories they tell, as though in the blink of an eye or the wave of a wand they had experienced a radical transformation. "It was as though my mother went to bed one night and woke up treating me like a peer," one young woman said. Her experience is typical of many accounts; over and over we've heard adult children complain about having suddenly become their parents' confidants. For many it happens in the very moment of being told of the separation. It was then that Anna, twenty-five when her parents broke up, was told that her parents hadn't slept together for twenty years. In the space of a few minutes she had to absorb the news that they were breaking up, the realization that they had long been unhappy, and the fact that an intimate detail of their sex life was being shared with her.

Diane, likewise, complained that she got "all the gory details." When eight years later her father broke up with his second wife, she had to go through it all again. "I had to hear all about what they had tried to do to improve their sex life, all the fancy techniques, et cetera, and it was *not* what I wanted to hear." Another woman said, "I felt like the trash bin; everything was dumped on me." Revelations of past affairs were a common accompaniment to the news of divorce.

For many, this is one of the most painful aspects of their parents' divorce. It's not just that the material is intrinsically painful or distasteful. There is also the sense of a basic taboo being broken, and this collapse of many family rules is one of the more frightening aspects of divorce. Nor is it only sexual secrets that are disturbing. Rebecca learned that her father had long ago been diagnosed as manic-depressive. Bob learned that his mother had for years been a closet alcoholic. Secrets of any kind, revealed after so many years, bring with them an uncomfortable sense of shifting boundaries, uncertain ground — and a doubt as to one's own powers of perception.

It's the rare parent who fully realizes how deeply disturbed an adult child may be by these various assaults on the past.

The parent, after all, is in a state of acute distress, in the midst of a major life disruption. Such circumstances make anyone prone to self-centeredness, and where adult children are concerned, there are few checks in place. It is true that young children of divorce frequently suffer from being made privy to their parents' inner turmoil. Yet most parents with some degree of sensitivity understand that there are some things that their children should not have to see or hear. This sense of restraint is often absent in parents of adult children. Adult children with younger siblings have remarked to us about how differently parents treat them in this respect.

Not only is there little sense of restraint where adult children are concerned, but many parents seem positively impelled to unload on their grown sons and daughters. One woman told us:

> Two years after the divorce, my mother apologized to me for "dumping" on me. She explained that she was too desperate to get my father back to dump on him. And she knew she couldn't lay all that stuff on my younger brother and sister. And I understood the situation — I knew my dad — I knew what the scene was like at home, better than any of her friends or other relatives did, so naturally she picked on me.

To a grieving, raging parent, an adult child is someone who knows the family from the inside out yet is detached, invulnerable, leading a life of her own.

There are other factors that make an adult child seem, to a divorcing parent, like the perfect confidant. As we've seen, for many parents old enough to have adult children, divorce carries with it a powerful aura of shame. Rather than face the humiliation of sharing family secrets with a friend, a parent turns to a grown son or daughter. Diane said, "My mother belongs to a generation of stoic women who believe you don't air your dirty laundry in public."

Whatever the reasons, parents frequently expect their adult children to assume tasks that would not be so readily expected of a younger child. One young man had to break the news of his father's infidelity to his mother. Another had to telephone messages back and forth between his parents who, though living in the same house, refused to speak to each other. Again and again we have heard adult sons and daughters describe the difficulties of being messenger, confidant, mediator, or shuttle diplomat. While it is fair to expect that adult children have certain strengths, supports, and powers of understanding that make them capable of greater responsibility, there are some situations that no child, of any age, should have to handle.

## Ambiguous Status

Where there is restraint on the part of parents, frequently it is fitful and sporadic. Many adult children complain that they are treated in a way that is maddeningly ambiguous: now as a child, now as an adult. Secrets are half-told, alluded to, hinted at, as when Scott's mother referred to the "unspeakably terrible thing" that his father had done and then withheld the crucial piece of information. It is not hard to understand the frustration and resentment Scott felt. At the same time, it is likely that he participated in the process, with an adult's need to grasp the facts, and a child's fear and recoil.

Diane also acknowledged a certain complicity on her part:

> Though I was in my late twenties when my parents divorced, it was really the first time they had ever treated me as an adult. Sometimes I wanted to say "Stop! I don't want to hear about your lovers . . . !" but at the same time there was something very flattering about it — and that's what made it so insidious. Also — who can deny it? There's a certain prurient interest in such matters . . . I experienced it again with my father's second divorce, when I really got explicit details from his wife. I would come home so angry and disgusted, and my boyfriend would say, "Why don't you just tell her you don't want to know?" — but it's really not quite as simple as that.

Beyond the expectations that an adult child can handle intimate confidences, absorb negativity, validate, mediate, and arbitrate, there are still other expectations. Many parents expect their grown children to rescue them, in ways both practical and emotional. They may quite understandably feel, "I took care of you all those years. Now it's your turn to take care of me." Adult children themselves tend to feel this responsibility — but it is not so easy to assume, and parents sometimes forget this.

When it seems that overnight the parent-child relationship has become a relationship of peers, or even that of a reverse dependency, it is generally easier for parents to make the adjustment than for children. Though our parents might have been young and naive when we were born, it is we who were helpless infants in their arms and not the other way around. They have seen us through many dramatic changes; we have gone from little wriggling lumps of flesh to walking, talking toddlers, schoolchildren, adolescents, and young adults. We might have seen their hair grow gray and their wrinkles deepen, but generally the changes have not been so dramatic. Furthermore, as one woman said, "It is not the task of childhood to observe your parents, but it is the task of parents to observe their children." While our parents' view of us may be, objectively, the more appropriate one — we may have some very painful catching up to do.

## Parental Jealousy

There's a basic inequality that exists in our society: the bonds between parent and child are much more stable and permanent than those between spouses. This inequality may inspire jealousy on the part of parents, and guilt on the part of their children. While jealous feelings may be projected onto children of any age, an adult child is more likely to inspire feelings of rivalry and competition. Ruth, who was twenty-seven when her parents separated, said that one of the worst things for her was her mother's jealousy whenever she went to visit her father: "It got so I wouldn't even tell her that I'd been to see him — but she always knew, almost as though she could smell it on me. Even when he moved out of town and I went to visit him, I would feel guilty the whole time."

Jealousy often becomes or remains an issue when parents begin dating. Sophie told us:

> My mother had just started going out with this man. She wasn't really crazy about him, but he was very nice and he was very wealthy, and it was important to her. I was coming to visit her, and my mother had him pick me up at the train station. On the way back to the house, he began asking me whether or not I had a boyfriend. I tried to be casual and noncommittal, but he was very insistent. After that, he never called my mother again. My mother said to me, "What did you do to him on the way home from the train?" She said it sort of jokingly, but I knew there was an edge to it, and I really felt bad and somehow guilty.

An adult child is also more likely to lead a life that inspires the envy of a parent. Feeling that his own life lies in ruins, a father sees his grown son with an intact marriage, a lovely home, a promising career. According to one young woman:

> I was in my twenties when my parents divorced, and I had a really wonderful boyfriend at the time. He was tall and handsome, intelligent, and kind. He was the sort of person who just knows how to take care of things, in a very gracious way — and he was also very wealthy. Here was my mother feeling cast-off and abandoned in middle age — and sometimes I just couldn't bear the contrast.

It is always painful to be the object of jealousy, but it is especially painful to experience a parent's jealousy. One of the givens of being a child of any age is that our triumphs and joys will delight our parents. From the first crude crayon drawing all the way to graduation from college, we know our successes will make our parents happy. We are not prepared to be the object of envy.

Jealousy also implies that our life is full and rich, while our parents' life is lacking, and no matter how old we are, that's a difficult equation to handle. We want our parents to be strong and resourceful, the providers. When people are jealous of us, it suggests that our life is without pain or difficulty. In truth, nobody's life is as rosy as it may look from the outside to a bereft and needy person. When someone is jealous of us, we feel in some way caricatured, not truly seen in our own reality. It is especially painful when it is a parent who is seeing us in this distorted way.

## Phases of Adulthood

As we talk about parents and adult children, it is important to remember that the relationship is not a static one. At different phases of adult life we have different needs and expectations that strongly affect the experience of parental divorce. Until now, what little research existed on adult children and divorce has been focused on college students.

As we've seen, it is common for parents to wait with the news of divorce until the first or last child is off to college. Yet this is a very vulnerable moment for young men and women. They are just emerging from the turmoil of adolescence and do not yet have a life of their own. One young woman told us, "It's a very difficult age because you're sort of on the borderline. You're still financially dependent, and emotionally you haven't really had a chance to create your own life, yet you're expected to cope as an adult. So there're no privileges either way."

Some newly separated parents respond by becoming overly involved in their children's lives, forcing their adult children back into exaggerated dependence. At the other extreme, some parents behave like young adults — drinking, dating, engaging in reckless behavior. Both parental responses make separation and individuation all that much harder for their children.

Young people find the transition to college life stressful under the best of circumstances, and it is especially so when there is no sense of a stable homelife to back them up. As one young woman said, "I was away from my old friends, surrounded by unfamiliar people who'd never met my family and couldn't understand what I was going through — and even if they could, I didn't feel comfortable enough in front of them to let them see the pain." Vacations, rather than providing a much-needed rest from the intensity of college life, are draining and exhausting. Emotional turmoil makes it hard to concentrate on studies, to make new friends, to make the many decisions that will affect the course of the college years and beyond.

While parental divorce can be very disruptive in the life of a college student, one researcher observed that the intensity of college life makes it possible for some adult children to avoid facing the painful situation at home.[1] This may help to account for the delayed reaction that some older adults described to us.

As one research team pointed out, young adulthood is a critical time for making decisions that may affect the course of an entire lifetime; hence, parental divorce at this stage may have very long-term consequences.[2] One of our subjects was twenty when his parents divorced:

> It's been twenty-one years since the breakup. Overall, the impact has been far greater than I ever could have imagined. Personally, in my relationships; but also professionally. Because at a crucial time I lacked a secure emotional base, I made decisions that turned out to be limiting. Just one example: that first summer after the divorce, I was offered a fellowship to go on an underwater exploration in the South Pacific. Marine biology was my major and I would really like to have gone, but I had to come back home that summer and look after the four younger kids.

Most of the college-age participants in our study complained of financial pressures created by their parents' divorce. They felt very strongly that had their parents stayed married, they would have received more assistance. Susanna, twenty-two, told us:

> The money situation is so hard. Dad is supposed to pay for my tuition and my books. But whenever I ask him for the money, he always says, "I don't have my checkbook on me now." So I'm carrying this huge balance on my

credit card, and I really hate that I have to nag him all the time.

Such complaints are confirmed by other researchers.[3]

The research on adult children whose parents divorce stops here, but parental divorce is difficult at any stage of adult life. For those just out of college, there are new vulnerabilities. For all its pressures, college does provide a sense of structure and purpose. At the same time, it represents a kind of suspended state: for many people "real" life begins upon leaving college. This is when the question of commitment becomes relevant as never before, the stage when many take their first step toward marriage and a career. It is very difficult to move forward when the foundations are shaking. As Linda told us, "In your early twenties the world is a little scary because you're really just starting to make your own path, and it's a time you'd like your family to be your emotional support, not have to lead them through a dark tunnel."

Young adults in their twenties are still engrossed in the process of sorting out and separating from their families. Tess, who was twenty-three when her parents divorced, said: "As a young adult, you're just starting to let go of the fantasy of your family; you're starting to come to terms with the reality. For an adult whose parents divorce it's a double whammy — just as you're coming to terms with that reality, it no longer exists."

It might seem that the perfect time for parents to divorce is when one is well established in adult life, with a marriage, children, a home, and a career of one's own. Certainly such rootedness can provide a powerful counterbalance. However, as we examine later, this stage of life brings major responsibilities and the possibility of tremendous stress. And for some, the rootedness of their present life rests on what they thought was the firm ground of the past.

An added poignancy for some grown sons and daughters is that they have just begun to enjoy the relationship with their parents. They have emerged from the stormy years of adolescence and are looking forward to, or already enjoying, a more

relaxed and mutually satisfying relationship with their parents
when the upheaval of divorce occurs. As Diane said, "I had just
started to enjoy my parents as friends. We'd even started
double-dating — my husband and I and the two of them. And
then it was over almost before it began."

## Responsibilities

The many expectations that impinge on adult children do
not take place in a vacuum. Many grown sons and daughters
have very real and serious responsibilities to attend to. On the
one hand, these responsibilities constitute an advantage. They
provide a sense of structure and continuity that is not available
to the younger child. When one has children to look after and
a demanding job, there is simply no time to become entirely
submerged in one's parents' divorce.

On the other hand, the accumulated pressures can be overwhelming. Kate was thirty-one, and her parents were still in
the process of divorcing. Her mother had been in need of constant emotional support and practical advice. Nearly every day
there were troubling phone calls and difficult decisions to
struggle with. Each holiday involved intense negotiations and
considerable anxiety. In short, Kate's life was immensely complicated by her parents' divorce.

> Look at me. I'm six months pregnant, I have a three-year-
> old, and my husband and I both have brand-new full-time
> jobs. Our life is already very stressful: getting up every
> morning, schlepping Emily off to day care, all the days
> when she doesn't want to go, and I feel so torn. We've had
> a lot of financial insecurity. And now this mess. Some-
> times I just want to say, "Thanks a lot Mom and Dad.
> Great timing!"

Another young woman, Rebecca, provides an example of
just how complicated an adult's life can be. She has recently
married a divorced man who has joint custody of his two young
sons. He and his former wife are not on speaking terms.
Rebecca is struggling to gain the trust of her two little

stepsons — a difficult task, since their mother thinks of Rebecca as the enemy. On top of all this — her new marriage under difficult circumstances, her first full-time job as a social worker — Rebecca must cope with her parents' painful and protracted divorce. At the time we interviewed her, her parents were not speaking to each other, although many details of the divorce remained to be worked out. Her father has been in and out of a psychiatric hospital since the separation, and Rebecca has had to take over a great deal of responsibility for both parents.

Studies have shown that the sheer number of stress factors to which a person is exposed is an important predictor of both emotional and physical symptoms. Many grown sons and daughters are already leading very stressful lives, struggling to balance competing demands of marriage, parenthood, career. Parental divorce, with its welter of intense and confusing emotions and its added practical burdens, can tip the stress scale dangerously.

If most grown children manage to carry on under the weight of accumulated pressures, many live with the fear of imminent collapse. This fear is all the more intense when one has heavy responsibilities. We heard many variations of "How can I possibly collapse when I have three small children, a business to run, and mortgage payments to make?" And so it goes, in an ever-intensifying cycle of reactions: the many responsibilities lead to stress, the stress leads to fear of collapse, the fear of collapse leads to more stress.

An adult child simply does not have the freedom to act out or to withdraw the way a young child or teenager might. When reactive behavior does occur, the possible consequences are very serious: a failed year of college, a job or marriage jeopardized, a decline in the ability to parent.

For some, the many responsibilities have a positive effect, impelling them to mobilize their best energies and resourcefulness. But for others, the cost of carrying on is too high, and the stress seriously threatens their equilibrium. One woman wrote to us that she had developed lupus, a serious autoimmune disease, in the aftermath of her parents' divorce. Another man, now touring the country with a dramatic account of his struggle with cancer, felt that his disease was triggered by the stress of his parents' divorce. Those with stronger constitutions may manage to repress or deny the intense emotions. In this case, little emotional growth or insight can be achieved, and the entire process of adjustment is prolonged.

## Lack of Support

Young children rely on their parents as the primary source of emotional support. For them, one of the most difficult aspects of divorce is that just when they need their parents most, their parents may be physically and emotionally unavailable. Theoretically, adult children should have a great advantage in being able to find support outside their own first family.

Far too often, however, this support does not materialize. The general atmosphere surrounding the adult child's experience of divorce is one of denial. Friends, lovers, relatives, however sensitive, are frequently unaware of the depth of distress involved.

Imagine how this contributes to the stress of the experience. One is struggling each day to keep from going under. At the same time, one has deeply internalized the message, "Nothing has happened to make me feel this way." It is unusual for the adult child even to reach out for help and understanding. It is even more unusual to find that support forthcoming.

Those who responded to our printed questionnaire were only required to check off their answers. Yet many of them wrote very long letters. One ended by saying, "It has been very good to do this. It is the first time I have written all this down after ten years." Another, whose parents had been divorced eighteen years, wrote, "I appreciate being able to unburden myself to you, as I have never been able to discuss it with anyone at length."

# II

*The Journey*

# 6

## Coping with the Initial Phase

$S$cott sat on the side porch, tightly gripping the arms of his chair as he described the moment he first learned of his parents' divorce:

We were seated around the dinner table. We'd finished eating and my mother said, "Scott, we might as well tell you now —." The moment she said that, I had a flash of what she was going to say next. I felt as though my chair was rising up behind me, almost as if it was going to take off — it was the strangest sensation. Even though I felt like I knew what she was going to say, the moment she told me I was stunned. My reaction was so weird — it still surprises me when I think about it. All the time my mother was talking, I was looking at the fireplace, it was always my favorite thing in the house, and I was thinking how long after we'd all gone our separate ways, it would still be standing there. I remembered my dad saying, "In case of an earthquake, stand next to the fireplace. Everything else might be falling apart, but that thing is *solid*." My mother finished talking, and — it was like another voice came out of me, I had no intention of saying this — I opened my mouth and out came the words, "But I love our home at 123 Springdale Road!" and then I started to sob.

Vivian spoke of her initial reaction:

When my parents first told me, the only thing that came into my mind was the image of a huge tower of building blocks sent flying every which way in the air. For days, the first few weeks even, I felt completely disoriented. In fact, I felt so disoriented that I didn't even have a word for it. That was when I felt like I was cracking up. As soon as I could say, "That's what it is — I'm *disoriented* — " then I was basically all right, on my feet again. I had some idea of what was wrong with me — but those first days were *scary*.

Another woman said:

My parents had just told me, and I felt a strange kind of high. I know how odd that must sound — but I felt intoxicated — only things weren't blurry, they were intensely clear, focused, they felt incredibly real. It was night and I was driving home, and the stars looked so bright. I felt like I could reach out and touch them — I'll never forget that. Then when I woke up the next morning, that strange almost magic feeling had vanished. I felt like I'd been run over by a truck.

## Disorientation

News of any major change in our lives and in the lives of those close to us is disorienting. It disrupts the habitual daily flow and makes us realize the precariousness of so much that we take for granted. For young adults, the news of divorce may be the first serious crisis they've experienced.[1] As Penny told us. "My main feeling was, 'I can't believe this is happening to us . . . to me.' It was the first bad thing that ever happened to me. It was a dark mark on me. Like we had always had this good, stable, healthy existence and then suddenly this dark mark."

There are other reasons that make this particular news so disorienting. As children growing up, our parents are the foundation, the point of origin, the central reference in our lives. Even as adults, without our being aware of it, the internalized family serves this function. Especially if the surface has been calm, the image of the family intact, we give it little thought. Yet it flows below, the undercurrent of the self.

A young man said:

> When I was a kid, I thought other people's houses smelled funny, I thought they ate funny. Naturally I didn't think like this as an adult, but still my parents functioned as the ultimate standard for me, the central term of any comparison. When they split up, I felt at a loss, a complete loss.

One woman told us:

> The feeling I had when my parents divorced was the same as when I left California and went to college in the Midwest. My whole life I had lived on the Coast, and I measured everything in terms of how near or far it was to the ocean. Now, no matter how far I went in any direction, it didn't seem to make any difference. I felt this same loss of bearings when I first found out that my parents were splitting up.

As we've seen, the news of divorce often signals an abrupt change in the parent-child relationship. This, too, is disorienting, as Susan explained:

> I had just left home after the summer to return for my sophomore year of college. Two weeks later I called home for my parents' anniversary. That's when I learned that my dad was moving out. I flew home that weekend. My mom met me at the plane, crying. She was a basket case. She almost had a nervous breakdown. That was the hardest thing. Later, Dad took me out to lunch and told me, "A

lot of things are going to change. I want our relationship to change. I want you to be able to talk to me about everything, including men and sex." This was a big shock for me.

For many adult children, there's an added intensifier: the shock of being in shock. Until their family came apart, they didn't realize its central place in their lives.

## Revelations

The news "We are separating" is disquieting enough. Yet it is often accompanied by other, far more disturbing revelations.

For some children, just to realize how unhappy one or both parents have been is itself a shocking revelation. Along with the news of divorce, Julie's father told her, "Your mother and I have been unhappy for fifteen years." Julie was then twenty-one, but what went through her mind in that moment was, "That's my whole life!" Even when a child has known for a long time about a parent's unhappiness, a new piece of chronological information can be very upsetting. Marcelle told us:

> I'd known my mother had been very unhappy for a long time, but when she told me they were separating she said, "It's been miserable since the third year of marriage." I realized that would put it to the year of my birth! I asked her "Why did you have another baby if you were so unhappy?" — and that's when I learned I was an accident.

For some children, the information they learn at this time not only permanently changes their perception of a parent but drastically alters their own sense of themselves. Some have gone so far as to say they felt it was a different *world* from then on.

## Anger

As soon as the sense of shock subsides a bit, what many experience most intensely is anger. For some, the anger is simultaneous with the initial shock of the news. We encountered a number of adult children who were furious at the way they were first told — or rather, not told — of their parents' plans to divorce. Sarah was writing a check in the supermarket when she discovered what was happening. She was using her mother's checkbook, and she saw there'd been a check written out to the Divorce Mediation Center. There, with a line of impatient people behind her and the cashier handing her bags of groceries, she had to absorb the news that her family was coming apart.

When adult children are not told the news directly, they feel used and manipulated. One woman told us:

> I felt like I was tricked into discovering my father's plans, and then it was like my discovering it made it happen. If only I hadn't seen him getting out of the car with that woman, then it all would have just blown over, and my mother would have never even had to know.

Even worse is when it's left to the adult child to break the news to the other parent. Merely being possessed of such information places a terrible burden on the child and alters the parent-child dynamic. As one woman said:

> For five days I walked around with this secret in my head that my mother didn't know, even though it was really *her* secret. It made my mother seem so vulnerable to me, like a little child who doesn't know about some big, major thing that's about to happen to them, and it made me feel much more powerful than her in a way that was really uncomfortable.

Marcelle, too, complained of having been granted too much power:

> My mother told me she had been miserable for nearly twenty years, and that she wanted to divorce. But she gave me veto power. If I was opposed to the divorce, she would stay. Of course I told her she had a right to find her

own happiness. But it was very disturbing to me that she gave me this power; I felt magical.

Once they grant their permission or break the news, some adult children find that they become the brunt of a parent's anger: "a case of kill the messenger," as more than one person told us. Even if they aren't accused of complicity, they tend to feel it, as if in the telling they helped to bring the event about. Ron told us:

> When I saw my mom with this other guy, it put me in a weird position with my dad. I felt horrible. I felt like I should tell him. I thought my mom would tell him, but she didn't. She told me, "I was hoping you would tell him." Finally I told her that she should move out and not prolong the agony. I pretty much edged her out. Later I felt somewhat guilty. I thought maybe they would have stayed together if I hadn't forced Mom to leave so quickly.

If some parents prolong an agonizing silence, in other families the news comes spilling out in a way that is brutally direct. Steve spoke with obvious anger about the tactless way his mother had broken the news: "She called a meeting of the whole family, and right there in front of my dad she told us that she couldn't stand to live with him anymore. She even went so far as to say he was brain-dead."

Still others we encountered were angry because they were told in a way that precluded any intense response on their part: they were told at a fancy restaurant, in the midst of a formal event, or with the words, "We waited until it wouldn't be a problem for you anymore."

## The Cultural Vacuum

When there's an illness or death in the family, people have a much clearer sense of what to do: they visit, send cards, bring flowers, make meals. No such code of behavior exists to guide family and friends through the experience of divorce. As Susan said:

It was so traumatic. I was a mess. The year my parents split up I cried *every day*. I don't know what I would have done without the structure of school. I had to have some structure. I talked about it a lot. My friends and boyfriend were very supportive, but eventually they said, "You ought to get over this." People don't understand. Death would be easier to deal with because the person is *gone*. I felt that I'd been tossed aside. I was no longer a priority in my parents' lives.

Many described the initial phase as a confusing and isolating experience. One man said, "It's a major event and a non-event at the same time." A young woman wrote to us:

Something that I found very disturbing was the sense that a catastrophe had taken place, yet one that at first presented no outward signs, especially in my own life, given that I was not living at home. I felt stricken, as though there'd been a serious accident or even a death in the family — but on the surface, everything went on in such a normal sort of way. I still had classes to attend, papers to hand in. Even in my parents' lives, it was several months before the changes really became visible, before the moving out into different houses, the dividing of possessions, and so forth. I felt that we were on the brink of enormous changes, that radical adjustments would be called for, but I didn't know what they were. I felt the way I imagine I'd feel if I suddenly learned I had a serious illness. I felt as though some very powerful, threatening process had been unleashed within my family — but there were at first no symptoms. There was nothing to do but *wait* and see how the "disease" progressed.

## The Strangely Familiar

Despite the sense of shock and revelation, what many experience is an eerie mix of the strange and the familiar. Divorce does not generally come out of nowhere, but emerges from a long history of disappointments and resentments. Thus, the hurtful things that divorcing parents say and do to each other resonate with a deep reservoir of impressions in their children's minds. One woman told us:

> Throughout my parents' actual breakup, in the things they said to each other, in the looks that passed between them, and the feelings that came up in me, I felt a recurring sense of déjà vu. It was eerie — and it also made me feel guilty in a strange way, as though by some feeling of anticipation I had helped to bring the divorce about.

Another factor in the strange feeling of recognition is that in times of stress people exhibit regressive tendencies, a return to earlier modes of feeling and behaving. Adult children who think themselves quite mature and detached from old ways may suddenly have a rude awakening, as Scott did when he opened his mouth and a child's voice flew out, "But I love our home at 123 Springdale Road!" For those who've been living on their own for some time, the flood of intense feelings toward their parents is like a strange, regressive pull.

And, of course, simply to be in the old house again contributes powerfully to this sensation. As one thirty-five-year-old woman said, "There I was back in my childhood house, and everything was changing and yet all the smells, the furniture — everything was so familiar. I'd find myself back in my old room, sobbing on my little narrow bed with the pink quilt like when I was an eight-year-old."

## High-Stress Reactions

Much of what occurs during the initial phase of divorce is what goes on at any time of acute stress, and this includes a range of possible reactions: uncontrolled crying, sleeplessness or lethargy, difficulty eating or a compulsive desire to eat, headaches, backaches, and other psychosomatic symptoms.

Many of those we spoke with told us that they were not prepared for the degree of irritability that beset them at this time. One woman wrote:

I think I was braced for "the big stuff," the Nobler Emotions, and I was thrown off guard by the humbler fare. I remember taking my mother out to eat at a little restaurant, thinking it would "do her good." She took a first sip of coffee, grimaced, and proclaimed loudly, "This coffee's terrible!" I was embarrassed and annoyed. It was all right for her to sob and scream or rant and rave, but to proclaim loudly in a restaurant "This coffee's terrible" — that was hard for me to accept. Now I wish I'd set my margins wide enough for all the minor flare-ups that occurred. When my mother grimaced in the restaurant, maybe instead of seething with resentment, I would have understood: "Her marriage is over. I guess her coffee's going to taste lousy for a while."

Another woman told us, "One evening after a whole day of scraping and sanding the walls of my mother's new house, I decided to make a pizza to cheer us all up. I made it from scratch, the dough and all. After the first bite my brother said, 'I don't like the sauce this way —,' and I raced up to my room sobbing."

These incidents may seem too trivial to mention, but for many we spoke to they were a significant feature of the initial phase. As one woman said, "It's as though you take out enough emotional insurance to cover the big scenes and then keep falling apart over the little jabs."

Many agreed that in "the little things" they felt the pain of their parents' divorce most acutely. It was not so much the big scenes: the sobbing, the accusing, the dividing of possessions. In one woman's words, "The big scenes happened and they were terrible, but somehow I felt braced for them. They're the scenes that are written into every script, and in a funny way I think maybe I anticipated them." Of course, such scenes also have their own built-in catharsis: their very nature is to be highly expressive. For many people, what really hurts is the pain in the little moments between the big scenes, a pain so finely honed that one woman said it seemed "to have my name on it" — a look, a gesture, a subtle turn of phrase or peculiar inflection that goes right straight through to the rawest nerve. For years Noelle was haunted by the image of her mother's hand, arranging those little clay animals on her father's dresser.

This kind of pain is hard to deal with because it often comes so unexpectedly, seemingly out of nowhere, and because people feel very alone with it. Friends are geared for the big drama, the generic divorce scenes. They expect the sweeping statements: "It's been hell. My mother is completely shattered." But how can you really tell someone about a hand and little clay animals?

It is also in the little things that other members of the family seem most vulnerable. Laura said:

> It took some time for my mother — and for all of us — to realize that it was in the little things that she was going to feel the change most drastically. We'd all have finished an intense rap session with her, we'd be coming away feeling so pleased that some important plans had been made, some major breakthroughs achieved, and then — wham-o! Some little tiny thing would set her off. Once she fell apart after calling the florist to send a certain type of bouquet that she and my dad always used to send *together* to this one particular friend. Now it seems very understandable, but at the time it was very unsettling. You never knew what to expect.

### Seeing Parents Under Stress

Of course, the divorcing partners themselves are likely to exhibit the most extreme stress reactions at this time, for it is their lives that are most drastically disrupted. For many of those we spoke with, a very disturbing feature of the early phase was the behavior of one or both parents.

In the next chapter, we look more closely at the impact of some of these changes in parental behavior. For now, suffice it to say that at this time, more than any other, adult children often experience an alarming reversal of roles. What makes it especially hard to bear is that it comes in the midst of their own acute distress. Just as old fears and childhood vulnerabilities are reawakened, bringing a longing for guidance and reassurance, many adult children are called upon to parent their parents.

## The Global Effect

If the tensions were confined to those between children and their parents, things would already be difficult enough. Typically, grown-up children want to contain their reactions along very clearly marked boundaries. At most, they feel it is acceptable to be indignant at the parent who initiated the divorce and to offer wholehearted support to the other. But, alas, the reality is rarely so orderly.

As we've seen, there is often anger at the parent who did not want the divorce — for having been "in collusion," for having kept certain dark secrets, for not having been strong or attractive or wise enough to keep the departing parent. But tensions often spread to other family relationships as well.

### Siblings

Many of our respondents reported that a long-term positive benefit of their parents' divorce was a closer relationship with their siblings. Initially, however, many brothers and sisters experienced heightened tension with one another.

Sometimes, while all the children may openly express support of one parent, one child may be perceived as closely identified with the other, "the bad parent." For example, one young woman complained that she wanted to remain in a neutral position, but the rest of the family continued to regard her as "Daddy's girl."

In some families, certain natural affinities between a parent and one child become more visible in the wake of divorce, bringing a measure of hurt and resentment to the others. Mindy had always felt that her sister, Sarah, enjoyed a greater closeness to their father. After the divorce she felt this even more intensely as her father began to devote himself more fully to those interests that he and Sarah shared. The two of them were very interested in Eastern religions, something Mindy had no real connection to. When their father took up with a woman who was equally involved in meditation and yoga, Mindy felt even more excluded. It was as though a new little family had formed with two parents and a child — and no place for her.

Sometimes the tensions among siblings occur for purely logistical reasons. Perhaps one child happens to be living at home or close by and thus becomes far more involved than his or her brothers and sisters. When one child has to break the news, bear the burden of confidences, be the chief comforter, decision maker, and provider of practical support, this naturally leads to a certain resentment — and at the same time the other siblings may feel guilty and excluded.

For the most part, however, among our respondents the tensions seemed to have a deeper source in fundamental family patterns. The child, very often the eldest, who had always been "the responsible one," flipped into high gear, rushing around in frantic rescue activity, while others remained on the sidelines or withdrew. Sisters complained that their brothers remained emotionally uninvolved, and brothers complained that their sisters were overemotional. Sometimes such differing viewpoints became almost comical. If one member of a family told us, "The divorce really didn't affect me much," we learned to ask, "Do you have a brother or a sister?" Almost inevitably we would get the response, "Yes — and he [or she] had a *terrible* time of it."

Even in one of our best examples of a friendly divorce, there were wide disparities among sibling reactions. According to Claire, she and two of her siblings were not very upset by the divorce. Yet one of her sisters was "very upset, overly emotional, and still unhappy years later," and one brother was "very angry for a long time."

Just as siblings may have varying levels of awareness of family problems, the process of adjustment varies for each. Stan sensed the deep gap between appearance and reality long before his siblings; the resulting pain and confusion led to the emotional crisis for which he was hospitalized. By the time his parents actually separated, he felt relieved and vindicated. He was ready to rush ahead into the light of a new day, while his siblings were still groping around in the darkness of shock and disbelief.

Fortunately, the most exaggerated polarizations tend to subside after the acute, initial phase of divorce. Some siblings did report continuing conflicts over how to handle the holidays. And in a small percentage of families, a long-term rift developed between a parent and one child, which in turn placed a strain on sibling relationships.

It was clear, as we talked with people, that they were helped by learning to look at the family as a system. Often, we encountered one adult child who felt guilty or embarrassed by his or her reaction to the divorce. "I'm choked with rage and my younger sister is so calm," Julie told us. She'd been having a recurring nightmare that she was "the bad one" in the family. This is a pattern in many families: there is "the emotional one" who, like Julie, vents feelings for the other members. Julie's mother said, "I thought I was very calm, but when Julie went back to college I started to explode!" Understanding the intricate intermeshing of family relationships can help family members move beyond rigid, blaming notions of good and bad, responsible and irresponsible, mature and immature.

### The Pain of Grandparents

One woman wrote to us:

I made the great mistake in the midst of my parents' divorce of going to visit my grandmother. Actually, the mistake wasn't in visiting her, but in expecting her to be a refuge in the midst of the family upheaval. As I sat in the airplane on the way there, memories of childhood visits danced through my mind: mountains of blueberries for breakfast, my favorite landmarks in the city, the beautiful greenhouse, the riverboat. . . .

When I arrived, however, I found that my grandmother was nearly as devastated as I was by the whole affair and in no position to take care of me or anyone else. So there we were, two emotionally exhausted women, each wanting to be taken care of by the other. We ended up having the first and worst quarrel we ever had — which, needless to say, was not what either of us needed. I left behind an even sadder grandmother and arrived home more drained than ever.

This young woman, like others we spoke to, was not prepared for the intensity of a grandparent's reaction. She told us that she later realized that her grandmother felt guilty because it was her son who had initiated the divorce. We learned of many grandparents who felt such guilt. Older people, raised in a more traditional age, often see divorce as a moral and spiritual failure. For them, the model is sticking together, no matter how personally unhappy one partner may be. They have difficulty comprehending the decision to divorce, especially after so many years. If their child has chosen to divorce, this must be due to some lapse in upbringing.

One man told us, "My grandmother complained that she felt both responsible and helpless at the same time — a very difficult combination to handle. She kept going over and over the past, asking 'What did I do wrong that my son should treat his wife of twenty-five years this way?' "

Even more troubling are the grandparents who become defensive if their son or daughter initiates the divorce. In such cases, a grandparent often wants to look for evidence as to why "she drove my son away" or "my daughter had no choice but to leave him." The adult grandchildren often feel that they are being pressured to agree with a very one-sided story and that there is little understanding of their own desire to stay neutral.

When remarriage occurs, many grandparents have difficulty adjusting to the new partner. Some feel torn, as if accepting the new spouse means that they are betraying a son- or daughter-in-law of twentysome years. They feel forced to make difficult and awkward decisions, sometimes betraying their own values in order to appease their newly married child.

Beyond such issues of loyalty and right and wrong, there are other concerns for grandparents whose children divorce. Many have fears for their own security. They are at or near the age when they may need to depend on their middle-aged children. Grandparents may worry — quite realistically — that a son or daughter facing the upheaval of divorce may have less time, attention, money, and energy to share. Even if the grandparents' own physical and financial security is not an issue, they may have come to rely on children and grandchildren as the emotional center of their lives.

If the divorcing couple plans to sell the house, grandparents may feel the loss of the family home just as their grandchildren do. As they and their peers face the many difficult transitions of old age, they look to the younger generation to assure a sense of stability and provide the setting for happy family occasions. For them, the holidays may have been the high point of their lives; now they too will feel the loss and anxiety as each holiday brings up the question of who's going where.

Many grandparents who are old enough to have grown grandchildren feel acutely aware of being near the end of their own life. The prospect of leaving behind "a divided family," as a friend's grandmother kept repeating, is a great sorrow to them, and many experience it as a loss and a failure.

What this means for the adult grandchildren is that along with one or two depressed and needy parents, they may have one to four depressed and needy grandparents for whom they feel responsible. Indeed, several people we spoke with had assumed the primary responsibility for a grandparent following their parents' divorce. "I'm more settled now than my mother is," one woman told us, "so that's the way it worked out."

On a positive note, some reported that after the initial shock and sense of loss, their grandparent had become a unifying, connecting presence in the family. As one woman described it:

My grandmother keeps in touch with all of us, with my mother, my father and his new wife and her children, all the grandchildren and now the great-grandchildren. She's the matriarch, providing a sense of continuity and connectedness where there might have been fragmentation and rupture.

## The Lure of Absolutes

In all the pain and confusion, a powerful temptation exists to simplify, to see it all in black and white and adopt a simple code of action. This tendency manifests in a number of ways. One common pattern involves intense polarization within the family.

### Rigid Alliances

Divorce generally is a very unequal situation, and in late divorce the stakes are especially high. To see a mother "jettisoned" after thirty-five years as a hardworking homemaker, to see a seventy-year-old father "left all alone when he doesn't even know how to fry an egg," can easily inflame a sense of indignation and the desire to right the balance. For adult children, as other researchers confirm, the issue of taking sides is among the most anxiety producing of all.[2]

Among our own respondents, we found undeniable evidence of fierce alliances in the initial phase of divorce. For some of those we spoke with, there was no question that their role was to defend the "injured party." This was their task and their prerogative as adults. It seemed to them so obvious and appropriate that when questioned, they had difficulty even imagining that there might be alternative responses. When we asked one woman about her feelings for her father, who had recently gone off with a younger woman, she answered flatly, "*What* father?"

For their part, parents often take for granted that their adult children will assume this role. They do not feel a particular need to protect their children from "the terrible truth about your mom [or dad]." And given their adult capacities for reasoning and moral judgment, these adult children are intensely valued as allies — or resented as enemies. Ruth told us:

My mother had always almost idolized my father, at least outwardly. After the divorce, she did a complete reversal and suddenly my father was a ne'er-do-well. She told me all this awful stuff. I remember thinking, "She doesn't understand what she's doing. She's pushing me in the opposite direction."

Ruth resisted her mother's efforts, but many people we spoke with had allowed themselves to be swept up in one parent's hurt and rage. Almost inevitably, they eventually regretted the harsh, polarized stance they had adopted at the outset. As one daughter said, "Initially I was with Mom one hundred percent. I didn't allow myself to be angry with her — in fact not until after Dad died. But then I felt cheated; I felt I'd been so busy being loyal to her that I lost some precious years with him."

Scott gave us a vivid account of his own change of heart:

After that first night when my mother told me she was leaving my dad, I didn't see her for four months. I saw my dad regularly during that time and pretty much swallowed his side of the story whole. One night my mother called me, sobbing, from a phone booth, and told me she thought she'd lost me forever. You just don't leave your mother sobbing in some phone booth. On my way to get her, it suddenly hit me how alone she'd been. I think the pain was so unbearable at first that just to get some sort of handle on it, I needed things to be really clear and simple — and in the process I totally neglected her.

Scott's last comment says it all. It is indeed simpler to impose a right-and-wrong interpretation of things. Initially it may lessen anxiety, but in the long run it creates other problems: guilt and concern about "the bad parent," disturbing questions as to what really happened, a sense of not acting autonomously, of having been manipulated by "the good parent."

While it is true that generally one partner is much more shocked and hurt by the divorce than the other, it is also true that divorce is rarely a simple equation. As intimately as children may feel they understand their parents' relationship, there are undoubtedly many mysteries, many closed and secret doors beyond which they have never passed. One man we spoke with had himself been through a divorce shortly before his parents split up: "It was hell going through both crises at the same time. But what I learned from my own divorce is that there are no 'good guys' and 'bad guys.' Being unhappy in a marriage is not anyone's fault."

It *is* possible to remain neutral during the initial phase, but it *is* difficult — and often the adult child who tries will be subject to pressure. Ruth told us, "My mother just could not understand that loyalty to both parents might be the highest form of loyalty."

Shortly after Lisa's father announced that he had fallen in love with another woman, he moved out of the house. At first Lisa felt as though she never wanted to see him again, but a week or so later she recovered some composure. She went out to dinner and a movie with him, and when she got back to the house that night she told her mother, "I had such a good time." Her mother did not respond and Lisa repeated again, "I had such a good time." This time her mother burst into tears, and then Lisa did too. When they had both calmed down a bit Lisa explained to her mother, "If I see Dad, it's not because I approve of what he's doing. But I need to stay in touch with him. I can't bear the thought that something might happen to him and he might not even know where to find me."

This is a fine example of a young woman who was trying her hardest to act as an autonomous yet responsible and caring person.

### The Role of Rescuer

Along with the lure of simple right-and-wrong thinking, another temptation is to rush to the safety of a clearly defined role. One that exerts an especially strong pull on the adult child is that of rescuer.

Some adult children step in to take over the role of the departing parent. Diane told us, "The moment I learned my father was leaving, I just stepped right in to fill his shoes." Some attempt not just to compensate for the departing parent, but to be what he or she has never been able to be. And some attempt to be all things to all people: mediator, counselor, peacemaker. . . .

As with the role of ally and moral arbiter, the role of rescuer is one that adult children tend to see as natural and appropriate — a perception that their parents often reinforce. Of course, most adult children can be expected to be more reasonable and competent than young children. And divorcing parents *are* needy. So what's the problem if their adult children set out to save them?

It's not really the particular good deeds that are problematic but the underlying emotions from which they arise. Too often, adult children rush in to rescue their parents as a way of blunting their own pain. Being strong and helpful creates a positive self-image. This reinforces the sense of being in control and keeps those powerful and often frighteningly infantile emotions at bay. Anna said:

> My parents had a huge house, ten bedrooms, six bathrooms, stuffed with thirty-five years of belongings. My mother just left, taking only her clothing, a few paintings and pieces of furniture. She told me, "I just can't handle it." And my father is someone who just doesn't cope with things. So I took a plane down and single-handedly moved my father out.

"And how did you feel at the time?" we asked her. She smiled, with what is now an obvious sense of irony: "Magnificent! I felt magnificent!"

The risk of such "magnificent" rescue missions is that those threatening emotions, the pain and anger and disillusionment, go unexplored. And help — when it is coming from a welter of unexplored emotions — is, in the long run, usually not really helpful at all.

Often, such help has a hidden agenda. It comes with the message, "I am going to fix you up and make you better because I can't bear to see you vulnerable and in pain." Such help is sometimes a subtle form of aggression that easily turns into impatience and exasperation. One woman told us:

> I wanted to be there completely for my mother, but she was so petty and irritable during those first months that

I kept losing my patience. She wasn't responding the way I wanted her to — with dignity, like Jackie Kennedy at her husband's funeral. A couple of years later when my friend's parents divorced, I thought her mother was so gracious and stoical, the way I'd wanted my mother to be. But when her mother developed colon cancer within a year from the divorce, I thought to myself, "Maybe I'm glad my mother didn't try to hold it all in."

Family members often have a heightened sense of one another's vulnerabilities. In trying to help, they unwittingly give the message, "You're a basket case!" Such help does nothing to promote a parent's self-esteem and ability to function. Help that comes out of negative family patterns tends to reinforce negative family patterns. Susanna explained that, though her mother had initiated the divorce,

Those first weeks she was nearly paralyzed with depression. She sat in the living room, staring at the walls. I had to do everything for her. Buy food, take care of the house, make decisions. Then she started to get better — and that was very hard for me. It was hard for me to relinquish the control.

These are some of the reasons that such help so often proves ineffective and even backfires. A number of people told us that they rushed around trying to make everyone happy, and that in the end everyone just resented them. Many confessed that they ended up feeling unappreciated and taken for granted. One woman said, "From the very beginning I just rushed in and locked into this image that I created for myself of being everybody's savior and nurse. Then when I saw it wasn't working and got exhausted and wanted out, I had already created all these expectations and everyone was angry at me."

Both parents and children often have profound ambivalence about the role reversals that occur in the wake of divorce. Many parents want to be helped, yet feel guilty about burdening their children or humiliated by their own neediness. Their children want to help, yet often feel resentful or uneasy about the process.

As we've noted before, transitions are more difficult when they are perceived as untimely. Kate spoke for many adult children when she said, "You expect to take care of your parents when they're old. But this is happening twenty years ahead of time." If many adult children feel that it is too soon for reverse dependency, so do their parents.

For many of those we spoke with, one of the most important and hard-won lessons was that they had been far too ambitious in their rescue activity. Arising from anxiety and confusion, their efforts left them impatient and exhausted. More often than not, their rescue attempts proved ineffective and created more problems than they resolved. One woman said, "I finally came to the conclusion that I just wasn't the best person to help my mother. I was too close to the situation, and I was in too much pain and confusion myself." According to another woman:

> Something that really helped me was when one of my mother's friends, a woman who had already been through a divorce, said to me, "Whatever her need is right now, it's bottomless." That really clicked. If the need was bottomless — then no wonder I couldn't make everything all better. But the way she said, "*right now*, it's bottomless" made me realize that it wouldn't be that way forever.

All of this does *not* mean that adult children can't offer genuine and appropriate help to their parents, and in Chapter 13 we discuss a range of specific strategies.

Another very important qualification exists. For some adult children who have grown up in severely dysfunctional families, the role of rescuer may have served a very important function. As we saw earlier, Bill — whose father was an alcoholic and both verbally and physically abusive — assumed great responsibilities at an early age. Speaking of his six younger siblings he says, with justifiable pride, "I raised those kids." When his mother divorced, he supported her every step of the way.

Today, in his early forties, Bill works in a program for physically abusive men. Looking back at the divorce, he remains
proud of the active role he played. Clearly, the stance of rescuer
is at the core of Bill's self-image and has been central to his
psychic survival. It may be that at some future time, Bill will
want to examine the role it has played in his life. But for someone like Bill, such an examination would best be undertaken at
a relatively calm and stable point in life, not in the midst of a
crisis like parental divorce. Our cautionary comments about
rescue activity are directed to the great majority of adult children who are not dealing with such a long legacy of serious
family dysfunction.

We did meet other adult children who were coping with a
seriously impaired parent and who nonetheless had grown
skeptical of the rescuer role. For Rebecca, news of her parents'
divorce came with the revelation that her father was manic-
depressive. Shortly after her mother moved out of the house,
her father became suicidal and had to be hospitalized. He was
incapable of decision making at the very moment when many
decisions had to be made, and Rebecca had to be involved in
every aspect of her father's situation. She described the delicate process:

> In family therapy, my mother's long-term pattern as an
> enabler emerged. I have to be very careful not to walk
> right into that role. And yet my father has a real illness,
> and there's the constant risk of suicide. It's a balancing
> act, and I am constantly readjusting limits.

Another woman used almost the same words in describing
her struggle since the divorce to find the proper balance with
her alcoholic father: "Sometimes I feel like I'm inheriting my
mother's unfinished work. She was the enabler and she just
gave up and left the scene."

For both of these young women, the struggle is to give appropriate help in a way that doesn't sap their own strength or
perpetuate a negative family pattern of dependence. Both have
been helped by professional counseling, but there has been no
easy solution. Rather, it's a constant process of experimenting

and revising. And sometimes it means having to give up control in a way that is truly frightening. Rebecca told us:

> There are moments when I'm able to say to myself that even if my father were to kill himself, it would be better than the kind of dependency he has lived with for so long. These are the moments when I'm able to acknowledge that the most important thing for him is to have the chance to live his own life.

Ruth's mother began drinking heavily around the time of the divorce and was diagnosed with cancer soon after. Ruth's reaction was to put most of her own feelings on hold. "I made the decision to give her what she needed. I had to give up trying to get her to understand what I was feeling about the divorce. Between her alcoholism and the cancer, there was just no way to get through." Now, many years later, she said:

> If I could do it over again, I would let myself do more grieving. I would be less caught up in the fantasy of changing my mother. I would have sought professional help earlier, instead of focusing so much on trying to get my *parents* to get help. I've come to understand that children of alcoholics often grow up with a tremendous sense of being responsible for their parents. Now, after some very intensive therapy and lots of reading and soul-searching, I have a clear sense that I'm really powerless in other people's lives.

Some people will face the difficult kinds of decisions that these three women faced, and the balancing act between their parents' needs and their own will have high stakes indeed. But most adult children can rest assured that their parents are more resilient than either parent or child may think. This, for most of our respondents, was one of the most positive aspects of the divorce. As Anna told us, "I was sure my father would wither after my mother left. I thought she was his lifeline, that all the friends were hers. But I learned that he had all kinds of resources that I wasn't aware of. He'd never had to use them before. But they were there."

## The Role of Victim

At the other end of the spectrum from the role of rescuer is complete identification with the abandoned parent. Though we saw this less frequently than the rescuer role, it was a distinct pattern. As one research team observed:

> In providing empathy for troubled parents ... young adults may be placing themselves in a more vulnerable position. The emotions their parents share may become as real for the young adults, making it seem as if they were actually experiencing the divorce themselves.[3]

Of course, identification is strong between parent and child, and particularly between parent and child of the same sex. Many daughters told us *they* felt abandoned when their fathers left their mothers. When mothers left fathers, it was sons who often felt a crisis of self-confidence.

Occasionally, this natural identification becomes a serious loss of boundary between parent and child, and this can manifest in a variety of ways. Sometimes it's evident in speech patterns; where there should be "I" and "he" or "she," there is only "we": "I told Mom, we can't let this happen to us." Sometimes it erupts as an incapacitating illness or a form of self-sabotage: "I couldn't stand to have everything in my life be so smooth when my mom's was turned upside down, so I guess I sort of messed up my life for a while." Others told us stories of a strange kind of imitation: suddenly they would catch themselves acting out versions of their parents' dramas in their own love lives. Often they weren't aware of the underlying connection until *after* they'd picked a fight or thrown a scene.

Of course, it is also possible to alternate between the rescuer and victim roles — and indeed, what often motivates the rescuer role is the very fear of the pain that incapacitates the victim. In other cases, taking the role of victim is a way of refusing to become the rescuer, of making sure a parent stays safely in the parental role. "Look, Mom [and/or Dad]. You can't possibly fall apart right now because I'm in even worse shape than you."

Letting go of the victim role may be arduous, for when suffering is intense it is difficult to differentiate "my pain" from "yours." The problems with the victim role are obvious: while debilitating the child, it reinforces the worst possible self-image for the parent.

## The Way Through

What do we say, then, to the adult child who enters the dark woods of the initial phase?

The key to dealing successfully with your situation lies in the very words that describe your relationship to your parents: you are their *grown-up child*. This is the source of your special vulnerability and your unique advantage.

Be gentle with the child within you who grieves, who rages at the rupture of your family. Yet with all your adult powers of perception, with the freedom, the decision-making abilities that are yours, take responsibility for your own well-being. It *is* possible to be a responsible and caring child without drowning in your parents' divorce. When you take care of yourself, you will have more energy and clarity to give to others.

One woman wrote to us:

> Looking back now, I feel that I was hard on myself where I needed to be soft, and soft where I needed to be firm. I ruthlessly ignored my feelings of despair, anger, and exhaustion. In that sense, I was very hard on myself. Yet I allowed myself to be completely swept up in the commotion my parents' divorce created — and in that sense I now feel that I was spineless. Though I continued routinely in my daily activities, I lost my own center of gravity. I gave myself over completely to my parents and to the general family turmoil, and I lost touch with any source of strength and joy in my own life.

### Keep a Long Perspective

The current level of pain and confusion will not last forever. As much as possible, try to stay open, neutral, flexible. Without denying the intensity of your own feelings, you want to avoid words and deeds that will leave indelible scars. There's a world of difference between "I don't have any interest in your new life and I never will!" and "I'm not ready to visit your new apartment and meet your girlfriend [or boyfriend] right now, but I'll let you know when I am." The second example expresses your feelings while leaving the future open.

## The Right Confidant

Because everyone in the family is in a state of upheaval, it is important to find someone you can confide in who is not a member of the family and who can serve as a neutral sounding board. Though the temptation is strong to talk to someone who knows your family well, even a longtime family friend can pose problems. Paranoia and suspicion run high in the atmosphere around divorcing families, and you may find that on top of all your troubles you now have your mother or father accusing you of alienating the affections of their best friend!

## The Benefits of Professional Help

Because the initial phase is such a crucial one, a time when many habitual patterns of behavior are coming apart and when there is a danger of establishing unhealthy new ones, a trained and objective counselor may provide invaluable guidance.

For most of our subjects who sought help during the early phase, the benefits were clear. Seeing a therapist helped them to be less confused about their own feelings and made them feel less dependent on friends and family members for understanding. Several felt that an insightful counselor had helped them to see how their own behavior was heightening family tensions and had suggested more effective ways of coping. "It gave me some distance," "It gave me a handle on it," "It was my weekly refuge in the storm," and "It was my way of taking care of myself" — these were among the many positive comments we heard.

Several people told us that it was not until they felt reverberations in their own intimate relationships that they sought a counselor's help. One man added, "Somehow the fact that I was going in to talk about problems in my *own* marriage made it legitimate. I couldn't just go in as an adult to talk about my parents' divorce." A number of people said that they weren't able to seek out help until they felt that they had passed through the worst of the crisis. One woman explained:

> It was months after my parents separated that I finally began seeing someone, and then only for a very brief time. I think now that it mostly had to do with my basic state of denial: to see a therapist was to admit to myself how bad things were. Also, I couldn't bear for anyone to see me in such bad shape. Alas, if I had sought help earlier, I'm sure a number of difficulties could have been avoided.

Professional counseling is not for everyone. But it is sad to let pride stand in the way of what can be a source of genuine help — especially when such help can prevent further complications from developing.

### Self-Care

Of course, even the best professional cannot short-circuit the pain. *You* bear the ultimate responsibility for taking care of yourself. And as an adult, you have an enormous range of options.

Make use of them! Try to do something every day to reduce stress. For starters, eliminate any unnecessary commitments in your life. Too many adult children try to maintain the same level of functioning, while taking on the many added burdens of their parents' divorce. One woman wrote to us:

> High on my list of "If only I'd known" is: how I wish I'd done more in a very concrete, daily way to cope with the stress of the divorce! I was so busy denying that it was really affecting me that I couldn't allow myself any extra care — in fact, I came down harder on myself. I was in graduate school at the time, and I forced myself to keep up with what was, in the best of times, a grueling sched-

ule of work. I think I was afraid that if I paused even for a moment, I would be completely overpowered by the feelings. It didn't work, of course — the feelings came out as extreme depression.

Another woman told us:

I made a list of all the things I love to do that are both relaxing and renewing: I love to paint, I love to walk by the ocean, I love to ride my bike. I made sure I did at least half an hour of one of these things each day, and that's how I kept my sanity during those first few months after my parents split up.

As an adult, you don't have to wait around for Mom to set up your easel or for Dad to drive you to the beach. Use the freedom and the competence you have as an adult to take good care of yourself. Maintaining your own emotional balance is essential for you as well as for those whom you wish to help.

If you're not lucky enough to find an appropriate confidant, there are other safe ways to process the emotions. One young woman told us:

I had an hour's drive each way to and from work, and I just zoomed along in my little red car pouring out my heart to myself. I think that was a major factor in keeping my sanity those first months. I felt I had to be so careful about what I said around family members, and this was a real release for me.

This same young woman also found relief in writing. "Those first weeks and months I must have covered hundreds of long, yellow pages with my writing. It was a way to vent emotion, to grapple my way through to clarity safely — without running the risks of actually confronting my family with my raw emotions." Several days after she learned that her father was leaving her mother to marry a much younger woman, she feverishly scrawled out the following thoughts. The "you" she addresses is her father, although she never actually sent him these pages.

*How I See It*

*Us*

— Over 100 years invested in building a family. A family is a unit always there for the support of its members. You can walk out on that support, but then we are no longer a family — or rather, we are a family with a big hole.

*You*

— Deprived of rights and privileges of age.
   1. Gracefully growing old — not struggling to keep up with a young chick.
   2. Little debilities of age will be magnified by age difference.

*Her*

— What can she see in you? What is she running away from? If she can ditch one husband so easily, why not you a little further down the line?

*Me*

No promises — no threats — just how I see it now:
1. I hope to be a mother soon, and I don't think I will be proud or even eager to introduce my children to a man who could walk out after 30 years.
2. It will hurt me a lot — more than I'll let on, but at this point, if you walk out, I don't think I'll want to see you for a long, long time.
3. You will always have my forgiveness for what you are planning to do if you change your mind and stay.

The very form of this letter gives poignant expression to the adult child's experience: the welter of intense and conflicting emotions, the struggle to contain them through rational understanding — on lined paper, in outline form.


## What Is a Crisis?

For some family theorists, a family is in crisis when its habitual modes of coping are not adequate to meet the stress of a given situation. Under this definition, divorce might well be considered the quintessential crisis, since it threatens the very structure of the family itself. Certainly for many people, this is part of the horror of the initial phase: their family, the primal source of comfort in times of distress, is itself the source of distress and indeed no longer exists in the same way.

At its root, the word *crisis* expresses both the fear and the hope of the initial phase. It derives from the field of medicine, where it means "the turning point in an illness; the passage where the patient is both closest to death and closest to the possibility of healing."

We spoke with many people who expressed the fear of falling apart under the initial stress of their parents' divorce. Though the fear itself was vivid, they often had difficulty in defining just what "falling apart" would mean. Generally, there seemed to be the fear of losing control, being overpowered by emotions and thus unable to function.

As prevalent as these fears are, we encountered only one man whose psychological distress was such that he had required hospitalization. This was Stan, who "flipped out" before the news of the divorce, under the strain of all the contradictions he felt within his family. There were also the two people who believed that their serious physical illness had been triggered by the stress of their parents' divorce. But we did *not* meet anyone, who, through the stress of their parents' divorce, had been catapulted to the terrible point of no return that they so feared.

For most adult children, the greatest danger is not that they will fall apart but that they will prematurely bring the situation "under control" by denying its intensity, by oversimplifying its complexity, by managing it too efficiently.

There are moments in life when we pass through a dark and painful confusion. Old supports — the assumptions, habits, patterns of interrelating that have given our life meaning and order — fall away, and there is nothing yet to take their place. But if we keep on through this critical passage, we can break through to a higher degree of understanding, a clearer, more vital, and freer existence. These words may sound lofty and abstract, but we've encountered the reality of such transformations again and again. Here is one woman's account:

My parents' divorce was the beginning of a series of eye-opening experiences which have changed me so dramatically, I could almost believe the cells in my body are different.

I did truly believe all through my growing up that my parents had a wonderful marriage. This is what made the idea of their separation so shocking. To understand I had to ask questions, to grieve, get angry — and finally, in the end, see the depth of my own blindness.

For this woman now to go back to the time *before* the divorce would be a return to darkness.

# 7

## Adjusting to Parents as New People

For parents, there are visible and dramatic signs that their children are growing and changing. This is true even when children enter adulthood: there is graduation, marriage, the move to a new house, the birth of a baby. Because of the very nature of the parent-child relationship, and because parents' lives often appear more static on the surface, it is easy for grown children to preserve rather fixed, even childish, images of their parents.

Like so much else, these images get shaken in divorce, as parents change in profound and often startling ways. For many adult children, this is the most painfully long-lasting wound inflicted by the divorce. Long after they've adjusted to the fact that their parents are no longer together, many adult children still cannot accept the ways a parent has changed.

### The Early Signs: Seeing and Not Seeing

Usually an extended period of change in one or both parents precedes divorce. In perhaps rather subtle ways at first, one partner begins a process of pulling away, disassociating, planting seeds of a new life.₁ This helps to explain why many grown children look back and say, "Yes — now I see it — all the little clues begin to add up." Sometimes a grown child has been completely aware of, and even directly involved in, the process of change. But often it's not until the situation reaches crisis proportions that any sort of pattern is acknowledged.

Kristy was eighteen and on her way to college when her parents split up. Though she had been aware for two years that her father was "acting peculiar," it wasn't until much later that she could put it all together. She remembered:

> It began with dieting. My father had always been on the plump side, and suddenly he began going on these radical diets. His weight yo-yoed up and down, and his behavior changed. He seemed on the one hand very restless and speedy — and on the other, quite depressed. He was obsessed with the fact that he'd gotten past forty and hadn't reached his goal: to make a million dollars.

Looking on from the outside, it seems preposterous that Kristy could not have seen what her father was going through — it seems so blatant, a virtual caricature of a male midlife crisis. Still it came as a shock to her when her father announced he was leaving her mother and the West Coast to move in with a young woman in Florida. As we have seen, there are many reasons for *not* recognizing what, in hindsight, may seem obvious.

Adult children are particularly likely to feel intense remorse at having failed to read the signs, and it is not uncommon for parents to actually accuse their adult children of failure in this respect. One woman who was twenty-three at the time of her parents' divorce told us with particular bitterness, "My mother would never have expected my younger brother and sister to have noticed that anything was going on with our father — but she couldn't forgive me. She kept saying, 'You were always so close to him. You must have known.' "

Those children who are aware of the changes sometimes feel a different sense of guilt. Sarah was eighteen when she first noticed that her father was in a period of intense reevaluation of his life. He stopped going to the church where he and Sarah's mother had gone and became interested in Eastern religions. He and Sarah had always been close, but now they were becoming even closer. They went to yoga classes together, practiced their postures, traded books back and forth, and had long discussions. It was a happy time for Sarah, and she wasn't really thinking about the implications for her parents as a couple. When she learned they were divorcing, she was shocked and saddened. Her mother was very resentful of her, and it was hard for Sarah not to feel partly responsible for her father's departure. When he announced to Sarah that he was moving in with a woman he'd met at a meditation retreat, she felt "betrayed somehow." She felt as though she'd served as "a kind of bridge" and then been left behind — left behind to deal with her mother's anger and bitterness.

Sarah's metaphor of a bridge is an apt one. In a way that a younger child, whose life is still unformed, could not, a grown child may present a parent with an alternative way of life, in effect becoming a kind of role model. As young as Sarah was, she did serve this function for her father. As the parent is drawn closer to this new way of life, the child feels mixed emotions. There is happiness at the new areas of shared experience, a sense of validation, and — often belatedly — there is a sense of having been used, and guilt at having been an instrument of escape.

## Altered Perceptions

In some families, as in Laura's, the announcement of divorce comes simultaneously with a major revelation about one or both parents, a revelation that, in an instant, demands that the children drastically revise their perception of a parent. It is no wonder that, in describing the experience, many use metaphors of death. In the words of one young woman:

> The moment I learned that my father had been having affairs for years, it was as though someone had shot the father I loved before my very eyes. I felt tremendous rage toward the "murderer," yet it was my father himself — a

man who looked the same, and spoke the same — who had done this terrible deed.

The dramatic language others use makes one think of Adam and Eve biting the apple, of Oedipus discovering the truth of his parentage. However it's described, it's the experience of a kind of knowledge that permanently changes the world these adult children live in and that radically shakes the core of their own self-perception.

Nor is it the content alone that creates the impact of the revelation. The sheer fact of a revelation is powerful in and of itself. When Scott's mother said, "There's something I have never told you and never can tell you. But you should know that your father did an unspeakably terrible thing when you were small," those words permanently changed the nature of Scott's relationship with both of his parents. Prior to the divorce, his mother would never have shared such information. Thus, her telling him communicated that the ground rules of mother-son communication had altered. It introduced what was for Scott a frightening new level of intimacy with his mother. And, of course, it is impossible for him to relate to his father now without being aware of this "unspeakably terrible thing." This is also a prime example of the maddeningly mixed messages that so many grown children receive. On the one hand Scott is told, "You're an adult. You can handle this terrible thing." On the other hand, he's left in the dark like a child.

## Parents as Sexual Beings

For some adult children, it's the divorce that first makes them aware of their parents as sexual beings, and this in itself can be profoundly unsettling. In a culture in which few parents talk openly with their children about sexuality in even the most general terms, it often comes as a shock when parents begin sharing intimate details of their own sexual longings and frustrations. More than one person learned that their parents hadn't slept together for years; others were told by one parent that the other was "a terrible lover," "never satisfied," or "cold." Even if, as in these cases, the parents' sexual behavior has been strictly within the bounds of convention, simply to hear about it feels to some like the breaking of a primal taboo.

At the very least, such communication signals a radical change in the parent-child relationship. When parents begin confiding in their children about their own sexuality, it is clear that they're assuming a relationship of peers. Quite apart from the issue of sexuality, this assumption can provoke feelings of loss and unease in the child. In some cases the roles are actually reversed: we learned of several parents who turned to their children for advice on sexual matters.

Often, of course, in the wake of divorce the revelations go far beyond the mere fact of a parent's sexuality. For many children, the news of impending divorce comes along with the news of one parent's infidelity. In these cases, parents are rarely prepared for the depth of shock and indignation displayed by their adult children. The response of one father we spoke with was typical:

> My two children were grown up and living on their own when I broke the news that I'd been seeing another woman. Neither of my children were married to the people they were seeing. My daughter had been living with a fellow for two years. I was completely unprepared for their reaction to *my* nontraditional behavior — and, I have to say, I found it very unfair.

It is not uncommon for recently divorced or divorcing people to go through a phase of promiscuity. As the marriage dissolves, some of the restraints that were inherent in its structure give way, and some partners feel free to act out in a way they never have before.[2] For some, having a series of sexual adventures is a way of being assured that they are still attractive and desirable, a way of releasing anxiety or of burying depression and feelings of abandonment. For others, it is a way of compensating for years of emotional and sexual deprivation in a loveless marriage.

That adult children are capable of understanding such behavior does not mean that they can face it with equanimity.

Most find it deeply unsettling, the very essence of irresponsible, unparentlike behavior. Some feel betrayed by it: they see their parents acting in contradiction to the values they have always espoused. And some have basic fears about their parents' safety. As one twenty-year-old woman told us:

> I knew my mother was so naive. She had married my dad really young and hadn't really had any boyfriends before him. After the divorce it was like she went crazy, going out with all these guys, and I thought she had really strange taste. I mean, they weren't anything like my dad. They were guys she met in bars and it really made me nervous. I'd sit up at night waiting for her, just like she used to do for me.

## The Process of Revision

It is hard for some parents to realize the degree to which their adult children continue to hold idealized images of them. Parents often assume that their children have long since seen through to the fallible human beings they know themselves to be. And, of course, in most families, as children pass through adolescence there *is* a natural disenchantment that takes place, a move toward a more realistic vision of their parents. The process is not always complete, however; it may have been confined to rather peripheral issues, and in some families — like Laura's — the central family myth may have been so powerful that it was never really challenged at all. Kate observed, "Fathers are our heroes. When they fall, it's so much harder for us than for them." Tess told us, "As I realize that I've surpassed my parents, both spiritually and intellectually, it's very uncomfortable — even if it's good."

For some adult children, it is not until they themselves become parents that they are able to make peace with the new, diminished version of their one parent. As one young woman said:

> Now that I am a parent, I see how much *bluffing* there is in parenting — and I don't mean that in a cynical way.

My daughter is so dependent on me, she sees me as so powerful — and, of course, I try to be that for her. But inside, I feel that contradiction between who I really am and who I am *for her*. I don't intend to let that contradiction ever get as huge as it did for my dad and my vision of him — but nonetheless, it's helped me to understand what happened.

For some sons and daughters, there's a frank splitting off, a before-and-after story that preserves the image of the idealized parent. Kate told us, "I picture my father as a tragic Greek hero who was brought down by his one flaw: he doesn't want to get old." For others, the process of recovery involves a gradual reevaluation of the past, a careful sifting of memories, a piecing together of clues, which gradually paint a fuller, more realistic picture of their parents and their family life. Laura described the process in her family:

In the first months after we learned about my father's infidelities, most of the time we siblings spent together, we were like a pack of detectives, dredging up one occasion after another from our family's past, subjecting it to the harshest scrutiny. Sometimes we got almost giddy with a sense of destruction — at other times, it was unbearably painful. You'd think of an important event — Christmas, a graduation — and almost as though you were blowing a photograph up in full detail, you'd realize that — yes — one of those "ladies" had been there too.

Gradually, as Laura and others have experienced, the kaleidoscope of images comes into focus; reality and appearance are brought closer together. This process is an important one on the road to healing — but it is not joyful, and for some it leaves permanent scars.

The process is especially difficult when an authoritarian parent is involved. Particularly among the young men we've seen, when a demanding and highly idealized father is found to have transgressed, the result is a deep and long-lasting cynicism. As one man told us, "I know the task is for *me* to validate the

ideals I always associated with my father. I'm working on it —
but so much damage was done — it's going to take a long, long
time."

Certainly, younger children are equally susceptible to the
trauma of becoming disillusioned with a parent. What is different in the case of adult children, however, is that many
important life choices may already have been made on the
basis of values associated with the idealized parent. They have
made a marriage, chosen a career, gone about raising their
children in conformity with those perceived values — and now
it all seems a sham. A younger child, a teenager for example,
might be permitted a period of overt reaction to such a shaking
of the foundations, a prolonged phase of experimentation, trying out one set of values, rejecting it, trying out another. But no
such freedom exists for the grown child. In the words of one
man, thirty-four at the time of his parents' divorce:

> You wake up one morning and discover that everything
> you've built has been on sand. But you have to go on like
> it's all solid ground. You can't skip a beat. You've got to
> get up and feed the kids and go to work and tell the wife,
> "Yes of course I'll be home for dinner the same time as
> usual. . . ."

## Stress and Personality Change

Even if there have been no early warning signs or major
revelations, the initial period of high stress reveals parents in a
new light. Ron told us:

> My dad had always been such a rock. He had all the
> answers; he always knew what to do. Even though I dis-
> liked him in some ways, I looked up to him a great deal.
> I had only seen him cry once — when he was thirty-five
> and was curled up on the couch with appendicitis, wait-
> ing for the ambulance. After my mom left, my dad was a
> bowl of Jell-O. He was torn apart. I think I was oversen-
> sitized because my friend's father had committed suicide,
> and I was afraid that was a possibility.

Sometimes what takes place isn't so much new behavior as a heightening, or an exaggerating, of what has always been there. Laura's father had always insisted on the importance of being rational, but when he called for parliamentary procedure at their family powwow, he appeared as a caricature of himself. Paradoxically, in seeing an intensified version of a parent, some children feel as though they're seeing who he or she *really* is for the first time.

Often there is frankly new behavior on the part of one or both parents. In *Second Chances*, Judith Wallerstein described what she called the acute, or first, stage of divorce:

> This is the period when the stage is set for the spilling of anger and sexual impulses, depression and disorganization in the family. This behavior, which has been called "crazy-making," sheds light on the nature of marriage itself. Psychologically, the very structure of the marriage helps maintain adulthood. When the marriage collapses, many impulses are no longer contained.[3]

Many of those we spoke with saw their parents sink into depression. One woman's mother sat in a chair for weeks. Some parents alternated between paralyzed grief and frenetic activity that seemed designed to mask it. Others expressed and sometimes acted out a degree of rage and bitterness that their children had never witnessed before. Kate told us, "You have these two different people who shared things between themselves. Now suddenly these two individuals are letting loose with all this material." All too often, parents turned to drink, promiscuity, reckless driving, or other behavior that made their children worry about their safety.

At this time more than any other, adult children experience the tensions and contradictions inherent in being *adult children*. Seeing a parent vulnerable and in pain, they want to be the responsible grown-ups who can "make it all better." Yet at the same time, the child part of them is shocked, frightened, hurt, and sometimes also disgusted and enraged. Part of what makes it all so painful is unfortunate timing. A parent's time of greatest acting out, extreme reaction, and experimentation often occurs when a son or daughter is still reeling from the shock of the divorce, feeling most in need of reassurance and guidance.

Fortunately, much of the distortion and exaggeration of personality subsides once the high-stress phase is over. There are, however, certain things that — once glimpsed — can never be forgotten. It's like many myths of the underworld: though they may come back into the light again, those who have seen into certain dark, forbidden places remain permanently changed. In the words of one young woman, "Though gradually my mother settled down and stopped acting like a wild woman, our relationship will never be the same. I saw an edge of her personality that I'd never seen before. And now I'll always know that possibility is there."

## Divorce Changes the Parent-Child Relationship

Of course, it's not simply that parents change in the wake of divorce, but that the parent-child dynamic is altered. Parent and child begin to perceive each other in different ways; they take on new roles in relation to each other; they grow closer or further apart.

Based on her study of thirty college students, Katherine Stone Kaufmann wrote, "Whatever the nature of the parent-child relationship pre-separation, the marital break-up served to challenge that connection with at least one parent for almost every student."[4]

Even when such changes are positive, they are often initially felt as stressful.

### Different Needs and Agendas

A further strain on the parent-child relationship derives from their differing needs in the wake of divorce. As we've seen, children feel many of the same emotions that their parents do: grief, rage, abandonment, insecurity. They, too, must go through a loss in many ways akin to a death: the death of their family as they have known it and the rupture of many familiar patterns of existence.

But in some important ways, the emotional tasks that confront the child are very different from those that confront the divorcing parents. Children must go through the loss and the rupture and yet remain emotionally connected to both parents. This means that in some respects the children's task is more complex. They have to let go *and* hold on. This is a crucial difference. Husband and wife may become ex-husband and ex-wife, but children are always the children of their parents. It is not possible for children to reject a parent without rejecting a part of themselves.

One woman told us:

> My father and I were sitting around criticizing my mother, and my father said, "She'll probably be an intolerable old lady." He said it with a certain glee in his voice, as though he were getting out in the nick of time. That's when something clicked. I saw that we were coming from two completely different places. My mother might drive me crazy sometimes, but she's my mother and I'm with her through thick and thin.

Eventually, of course, all children must come to a more realistic assessment of their parents. But this process must come organically out of the *child's* development and not as part of the parent's transition.

As we've seen, the same dynamic holds true with respect to the family's past. At the very moment when the parents may need to move forward into the future, the adult children may feel that their childhood is being negated. Soon after Sarah's parents split up, the family dog, Biscuit, died, and Sarah's mother bought a new puppy. To Sarah's mother, no doubt, the playful new puppy represented an affirmation of her new life. She had made the decision to buy him on her own, she had picked him out, and he was to be her cuddly companion. But even though Sarah was no longer living with her mother, she greatly resented the demanding little intruder who had replaced her beloved childhood pet. To her he represented one more sign of loss and discontinuity. One day when she was visiting her mother, she saw the new puppy drinking from

Biscuit's old bowl. This was too much for Sarah, and she took the bowl home with her. Her mother was furious. Later she told Sarah, "Pay me back for that bowl."

Misunderstandings also arise because parents and children are suffering different dimensions of loss. A woman who feels she's had thirty lonely years with an uncommunicative husband may not understand how attached her children are to what they perceived as their stable and harmonious family. Or, as one young woman told us:

> I felt that my mother didn't really *love* my father as I did, and therefore it was hard for me to sympathize sometimes when she was so devastated after he left. But now that I'm older and married myself, I understand better how attached she was to being a *wife*, how frightened to face life on her own.

This kind of disparity may be especially great for adult children. A son who has been living away from home may be quite detached from the daily, practical sphere of family life yet emotionally attached to his parents as a unit. His mother may have trouble understanding the intensity of this attachment, "You're not even living at home!" And he, especially if he is still young and unmarried, may not understand the deep layers of habit that bind long-married couples and the pain his mother feels at being wrenched free.

## The Legacy of Divorce

Unfortunately, the very process of divorce leaves some parents with a residue of anger and bitterness that permanently mars the parent-child relationship. The general lack of social supports surrounding divorce and the adversarial approach fostered by the legal process do little to soften this tendency.

A number of our respondents described their parents as never having been able to get over the divorce. To be left alone after twentysome years of marriage was so far outside their values and expectations that they were never able to reconcile themselves to the reality. Years later, they were stuck in blame and denial. Tess told us, "Twelve years later, my mother is still focused on what she's lost."

In the process of divorce, old wounds reopen. A deep fear or grief or sense of insecurity that has been buried for years is reactivated — and in some parents it becomes a more or less permanent feature of their personality. Ruth felt that this is what happened to her mother:

> She was the child of an alcoholic. I think there were deep feelings of abandonment that surfaced during the divorce. Unfortunately, she couldn't really face them; she just began drinking more heavily herself. All her black-and-white thinking is so typical of alcoholic families. Even though she was the one who left, she worked it out in her mind that it was all my father's fault for not working on the marriage. When, after a certain point, I just didn't want to hear it anymore, she couldn't forgive me for not being on her side.

For Ruth, as for others we encountered, this transformation in a once-admired parent was the deepest loss associated with the divorce.

## Change and Late Divorce

Even if the initial phase does not produce radical behaviors, significant change is the very essence of late divorce. Divorce after many years happens not because a spouse was suddenly found to be intolerable but usually because of a profound desire — on the part of one partner at least — to live in a different way. While this is true to a degree of younger couples as well, it is experienced with particular urgency by the middle-aged. They know, as their younger counterparts may not, that time is not infinite. Their decision to divorce is often linked to milestones that are themselves occasions for significant change, such as the empty nest, retirement, or the loss of an aged parent. Furthermore, adults with grown children are freer to act out the desire for change. With no young children to support, a father can more readily leave his business behind and take up a freer, more footloose existence, a mother sees no reason to maintain the family home.

Generally, of course, it is the parent initiating the divorce who most keenly desires change. But even the partner who is content with the status quo is thrust into change by the other's shake-up. Diane told us that after her father left, her mother became "very unmotherly, very 'me' oriented." Sarah's mother, who was active as a social worker, had never complained particularly about her responsibilities as wife and mother. But after her husband left she became resentful of the ways in which she felt she'd been exploited. Both Sarah and her older sister, Mindy, experienced that their mother abruptly stopped being "motherly." In Sarah's words, "When we would go to visit, she would watch us like a hawk to make sure we weren't eating too much. When we did the laundry, she would charge us for it. She kept saying she wasn't going to be 'used' anymore, wasn't going to be treated 'like a doormat.' " Unlike Diane's mother, whose extremely me-oriented behavior was short-lived, the change in Sarah and Mindy's mother was longer lasting. Two years later, this remained the most painful issue in their relationship with her. Recently Sarah has been hospitalized for repeated bouts of bulimia. It is not hard to image how difficult it must have been for her to start her first year of college with no sense of a nurturing home behind her. "To have a mother who's watching you resentfully as you swallow one of her cookies. . . ." It is not surprising that she found herself in the painful cycle of uncontrollable eating and purging.

## The More Gradual Changes

In a very real sense, and quite apart from any spectacular new behavior, parents will become different people outside the marriage and family network.

When two people have spent most of their lives together, their personalities evolve in deeply complementary ways. Typically, a complex pattern of interlocking strengths and weaknesses emerges. This pattern of complementarities is a large part of what enables a marriage to function for a long time. And as we've seen, its disruption is part of what emerges as the profound disorientation of the acute, initial phase of divorce.

Parents of baby boomers typically established a marriage along clearly drawn lines: Father was breadwinner, and Mother was homemaker. For a long time, each may have appeared quite content within the balance. Now the two halves come apart, and it can be excruciatingly painful for a son or daughter to witness this fragmentation.

Some respond critically. A son who for years has shared household tasks with his own wife may find it difficult to comprehend his father's helplessness. A daughter who grew up with consciousness-raising and who has always worked to support herself may be exasperated by her mother's fear and panic.

But often, the feelings are more complex. Baby boomers represent the transitional generation. Their earliest, most formative experience was in the context of traditional male and female roles. Though they have lived through a radical shifting of ground and may have evolved different, more egalitarian patterns in their own lives, often there's a deep uneasiness or ambivalence at the core. Now the interdependence of their parents may be exposed in its most negative light, its shadow side — and the process resonates with some of their own deep fears and unresolved questions.

The task for each divorcing parent is to learn to compensate, gradually taking on some of the functions that the other has filled. At first, this can be an awkward, artificial process. But for many, this is one of the most positive outcomes that eventually does emerge from the rubble of divorce: seeing one's parent evolving as a more whole person. Steve, who was twenty-seven when his mother left his father, told us of the changes in his father:

> The horrible thing for us was the way that our mother told us about the divorce. Right in front of our father, she started talking about how boring he was. Of course, we knew there was a certain grain of truth in it. Dad had always been shy. And he doesn't hear so well, so he does tend to tune out of conversations sometimes. But after

Mom left, we realized how much of it had to do with the way she took charge of everything. She always did all the talking, she was always the life of the party, and he never had a chance. Of course, he *let* her do all the talking — but the point is, after a few months of being on his own, after he started to recover from the shock, he began to come out of himself. He began talking to us more, and looking up old friends. It's like a whole new person has emerged.

## The Newness of One-on-one

For some, it's the first time they've ever been alone with a parent for any length of time. This is frequently a source of considerable awkwardness in the early period of adjustment. One woman's mother was always the mediator of family relationships — now this woman finds she doesn't know how to begin a conversation with her father. Another finds that outside the bustle of family life, there's an uncomfortable feeling of "hollowness" when she visits each parent; the pauses between sentences seem so long.

Sometimes, of course, the experience is a pleasurable one, as one young woman told us:

Secretly, I had always felt that my father and I were so much happier when my mother wasn't around, banging pots, exuding anxiety. . . . We liked to sit quietly and sort of ruminate, and my mother was always charging around. That first year before my father remarried, it felt so special to go and visit my father in his little house. We would laugh. We'd have tea and all sorts of gushy sweets that my mother would never have bought.

In some cases, when there's been a very close relationship with a parent of the opposite sex, there's a sexual tension that arises. Until now, the commotion of family life and the presence of the same-sex parent may have served to defuse that tension, but now those buffers are gone. One woman spoke candidly:

In the months following my parents' divorce, I had these recurring dreams about "my father's penis" — no content really, just those words floating in my mind. I felt so shocked and disturbed by it, I finally went to see a therapist, and she told me, "Well — it's as though your father's penis is suddenly available, and that's frightening." It sure was.

Another young woman told of the first time she went to stay at her father's new place:

He had rented a small apartment, and the first time I went to visit I felt terribly self-conscious that my "female smell" was going to permeate the air. It was so weird — I mean, I've never even thought before about a "female smell" — but suddenly, it was such a powerful and uncomfortable feeling.

Just as marriage functions to restrain certain impulses, so does an intact family. When that structure dissolves, some people experience an uncomfortable feeling of anarchy, as though the lines around the forbidden and the permissible have grown fuzzy. This feeling tends to be particularly acute in the initial phase of divorce. As a new family structure is established, complete with its patterns and rules, most people find that it gradually subsides.

## Dating and Courtship

It is difficult for children — of any age — to witness their parents in dating and courtship behavior. Simply because such behavior is unfamiliar, it contributes to the sense of loss and disorientation surrounding the experience of divorce. New aspects of the parent are revealed, often making the parent seem more vulnerable, less reliable, less like a parent. Diane's mother, who had never even allowed toy guns in the house, took up target shooting, her new boyfriend's hobby. Diane told us that it was distressing to see that her mother was so "malleable," that "she displayed such a lack of personal integrity."

Another young woman felt embarrassed and irritated by "the little girl voice" her mother used on the phone with her male friends; it made her feel that her mother was acting "phony" and had "such an unsure sense of herself." For one young man, it was not phoniness or malleability but vulnerability that he saw as he watched his father anxiously check his thinning hair in the mirror before going out on a date.

None of us saw our parents courting, and it feels somehow inappropriate to witness a parent falling in love with another person. This feeling is complicated by concern for the other, still unattached parent. Merely to glimpse an embrace, an exchange of secret smiles, a love note lying on the kitchen counter, may bring about a feeling of complicity, as though one were possessed of a forbidden, secret knowledge. One young woman told us, "It's not like my mother set me up to spy or anything, but I saw with her eyes. I felt her pain." According to another woman, "It was hard to see my dad going out of his way to be affectionate and considerate of his girlfriend. I kept thinking 'How come he never treated Mom this way?' "

Of those we interviewed, it was the youngest adults, those in their late teens and early twenties, who had the most difficulty with their parents' dating. Susanna was twenty and still living at home when her parents broke up. Because the marriage had never been a happy one, Susanna had often fantasized about divorce. "I guess I saw it as a solution," she told us, "a trendy solution." When they actually did break up, she was shocked at her own reaction; she found the process of adjustment much more difficult than she had ever imagined. When we asked what had been most difficult about it, what instantly popped out of her mouth was, "My parents' dating." She explained:

> It was so hard the first time my mother brought a man into the house. He was from out of town, and I did not want him staying in our house. I was a brat. At the time I thought it was my moral conviction. Now I'd express it differently: he was a stranger, and it was our house, where we had lived with my father. Of course it was rather hypocritical — I'd had my young boyfriends over — but

that seemed different, because they were young. Now I think I'd accept it better.

Most of these young adults were struggling to define their own identities in love relationships; they had little psychic energy left over to consider their parents' love lives. Whether or not they were able to acknowledge it, clearly many of them still needed their parents to be the solid, authoritative backdrop for their own struggles and experimentation. Instead, just as they were attempting to separate, to forge their own adult identity, their parents' behavior began to resemble their own more closely, resulting in confusion and anxiety.

Further stress arises from the lack of appropriate norms surrounding a parent's dating behavior. What many expressed to us was a blankness, close to panic, a total confusion as to what to say or do. The first time Scott and his wife even knew that his dad had a girlfriend was when both couples met by accident in a movie theater. "There was my dad with this woman in a red dress, and what were we supposed to do?" Scott asked.

Often there is a sense of conflicting values: on the one hand Susanna felt a certain indignation when her mother first brought a man into the house. This is only natural; in the "normal" scheme of events, Susanna would be dating and her married parents would not be. Her mother's behavior seemed inappropriate and somehow illicit, yet at the same time, she described herself as a "brat" and her behavior as "hypocritical." Others expressed a similar conflict between their own mature and childlike selves. One woman told us, "It made me so uncomfortable when my mother first started going out with men. Sometimes I just wanted to run and hide in my room like a little kid. But at the same time, I had to be happy for her. I knew it was good for her to be getting some attention and getting out of the house."

### Basic Resistance

Even if purely objective onlookers were to report that two people had changed very little in the aftermath of their divorce, it is likely that their children would not agree. For the simple fact of relating to parents outside the familiar framework changes the ways in which a son or daughter sees them. And for most children, initially, there is resistance to change.

Parents frequently have little understanding of or patience with this resistance. Some bitterly resent being held to what they feel are unrealistic standards of behavior, standards that their sons and daughters should have relinquished long ago. In the words of one young woman, "I got so many *should*s. My father kept telling me: 'I'm happier now than I've ever been and you should be happy for me and rejoice in my new life.' "

But, as another woman said, "If it's all so great, how come I'm so unhappy?!" Even when the changes in their parents are felt as positive, there is loss involved — loss of the parent they knew as a child.

Late divorce challenges certain fundamental assumptions that parents and adult children have about one another. As one research team noted, "Children count on a period of strength — almost invulnerability — in their parents, up to old age. Events which upset such expectations represent more severe crises than when they come as expected, on time."[5]

For their part, when parents have waited "until the children are grown," this often means that they felt unable to attend to their own needs until their children had lives of their own. When adult children react intensely to the changes in their parents' lives, the parents are disappointed and disoriented. Any sense of timeliness they may have had about divorcing when the children were grown is shattered. The new freedom they felt entitled to is threatened. And sometimes, there's a sense of failure: "I must have done something wrong if my grown children are in such bad shape!" Often, what is happening on both sides is a failure to recognize how important parent and child remain to each other, throughout the duration of their relationship.

Yes, adult children do need to let go. Their parents must be allowed the freedom to grow and change, to seek new identities outside the familiar setting. All children, as their parents age, must let go of the layers of early images, of the deep desire for parents to remain immutable, invulnerable to change. Where aging is a natural, inevitable process, divorce is not, and in that sense it is more difficult to handle. But the important thing to realize is that the grief, the resistance to change, are perfectly natural feelings, and here no *shoulds* apply.

It is very difficult for grown children to acknowledge this grief. And it is difficult for parents — at the precise moment when their own energies need to be drawn forward, into the creation of a new life — to deal with their grown children's attachment to the past. But again and again we've seen that when sons and daughters try to bury or short-circuit the need to mourn, the whole process of adjustment is prolonged, and sometimes thwarted entirely.

# 8

## *Adjusting to Parents' New Partners*

It was one of the first visits to my father and his new wife. I had been very anxious the whole time, but things had gone well; we were leaving on good terms. Just as my husband was backing our car out of the driveway, my father's wife came running after us. "There's something I'd like to give you," she said, smiling warmly. She handed me a large paper bag through the window. Peering inside, I saw remnants of bright woven fabric. It was fabric from Spain, and though it was fifteen years ago that my mother had bought it, I remembered the day with absolute clarity.

It was the year we were living in France; I was fourteen, my brother seven, and we'd gone for a holiday in Spain. The trip had been difficult, hot and dusty, and the Spanish hours a strain: dinners at ten o'clock, bed at midnight. On this particular day, in a city whose name I don't remember, we had gone to a bullfight. My parents admired Picasso and Hemingway, those celebrators of the bullfight, and besides, it seemed the Spanish thing to do.

We were excited and nervous as we took our seats in the huge, crowded stadium. It was late morning, but it was already hot, and the light bouncing off the white walls of the stadium was glaring. The picadors came out on their horses, and then the toreador *himself. At first it seemed like a beautiful dance or parade, but gradually it grew more gruesome. My brother and I hadn't realized the bull would be killed, and the sight of that huge black body being dragged through the dirt, leaving a trail of blood, horrified us. It was my father who became ill, however. The heat and the glare and most of all the violence had been too much for him; he was getting one of his terrible headaches. We went back to our little motel room, feeling shaken and queasy. My father lay in bed with a cold cloth on his forehead, and my mother played quiet games on the floor with my brother and me.*

*Late in the afternoon, my father was somewhat better. By then we all felt cooped up in the motel room, so we went outside and found our way to a large department store. It was cool in the store and quiet. My mother found the fabric. It was beautiful — like fiery rainbows of strong Spanish colors, yellow, orange, and red. There was a magical quality about it — being in the store and finding it had somehow healed the day. And the day itself, in my memory, was the very quintessence of my family — our travels and adventurousness, my father's extreme sensitivity, my mother's creativity and vitality. When we returned to the States several months later, my mother made bedspreads for my brother. I remember how happy she was working on them, trimming them with black fringe. My brother had the bedspreads in his room until the day the house was sold and its contents divided.*

*. . . Sitting in the car next to my husband, I looked in the paper bag and saw the Spanish fabric. I said thank you to my father's wife and tried to mean it.*

This story of Noelle's exemplifies the fundamental difficulty and awkwardness in relating to a parent's new partner. This was a very minor incident, and there were good intentions on both sides, but the reverberations went far beyond the simple act of giving and receiving a bag of cloth. How could the new wife be expected to know the history of those old remnants? How could Noelle not feel that this new wife was intruding on her family's past, usurping her mother's place? She wanted to feel grateful, to acknowledge the warm gesture, but in the very moment of saying thank you, what went through her mind was "That's not yours to give."

### Facing the New Relationship

As we have seen, it is already difficult for adult children to accept their parents' dating and courtship behavior. In order to avoid the welter of intense and often conflicting feelings, many respond by ignoring the situation, pretending it doesn't exist or is merely a passing phase. When the new relationship becomes serious, when a parent moves in with a new love or remarries, it is no longer possible to ignore the situation. The reality of the new relationship must be acknowledged and the adult child's connection to it defined.

The statistics are clear: after the divorce, most adult children will experience the remarriage of at least one parent. In most cases, it will be the father who remarries; often, he will marry a younger woman.[1]

It is also clear that a parent's remarriage calls for an adjustment equal in intensity to the separation itself. A number of people find that it is not the end of their parents' marriage but one parent's remarriage that is the real family crisis. For others, just as they are gaining some equilibrium in the wake of the divorce, one parent's remarriage is a new upheaval.

Many of our respondents reported a marked deterioration in their parents' relationship after one parent remarried. A young man told us:

> Though my parents were living separately, they had come to some kind of an understanding. My father frequently went over to do things around the house for my mother, and sometimes he even stayed for dinner. They still related to us as a unit. All that changed when my dad remarried. His new wife resented his continued involvement with my mother — and my mom went into a real tailspin.

## The Built-in Difficulties
### The Shattered Ground

It is difficult whenever someone new is brought into the family circle: it alters the system, creating the need for adjustment on virtually everyone's part. Many parents find it difficult to incorporate a new girl- or boyfriend, a son- or daughter-in-law, into the family. These adjustments, while difficult, are safely within the natural scheme of things. When remarriage occurs following divorce, its very ground is rupture, disconnection, a failed marriage, and shattered family. For some it is the remarriage, not the divorce, that truly signals the end of the family as it was and completely extinguishes the hope for reconciliation between their parents.

Loss and rupture are the ground of all remarriages that follow divorce. This loss is all the greater after a marriage of many decades. In one recent study of divorce, the authors wrote that "the long history of marriage for the midlife divorced makes remarriage a particularly crisis-prone event."[2]

### The Sense of Betrayal, Abandonment

Many experience the sheer fact of a parent's departure as abandonment, as the act of "leaving the family." When another person enters the picture, these feelings are intensified. The parent seems to love someone else more than the child or the family.

One critical factor here, of course, is how the other parent responds. Typically, to be left for another person intensifies feelings of anger, hurt, humiliation, and jealousy. Such feelings are even more threatening for the parent who is already feeling daunted by the many challenges of growing older.

It is common for sons and daughters to identify with the parent being left, to feel rejected themselves. They, too, feel especially betrayed when an affair began prior to the separation. In such cases, there is often a deep and lasting resentment for the new partner. One woman told us, "This person knew something crucial about us before we did; she humiliated one parent, involved the other in a lie, and made my family's recent past somehow unreal: it was not what we thought it was."

Family members often become preoccupied with questions of timing. Julie was twenty-one when her father announced he was leaving for a new love:

The whole time frame is so disturbing. We keep thinking of things that we did as a family, knowing now that he was already in love with her. We took a family vacation last summer, and he took me aside and made a rather grand statement about his commitment to my mother, and when I think that the very next week he was going off to be with *her* — I just can't stand it.

Kate told us, "I can understand falling in love. But lying for five years? And then there was the circle of our old friends who knew and didn't tell us. We felt so duped."

Naturally, identification with the abandoned parent is most intense when there are strong similarities between this parent and the child. A woman who looks like her mother may find herself terribly insecure about her own appearance and very threatened by her father's new girlfriend. Is she, too, destined to be cast off in middle age?

For those who identify with the personality traits of the abandoned parent, there is a similar fear and questioning. Laura had been brought up to admire her mother's generosity and devotion to others. When her father took off with his young secretary, she felt betrayed and confused: "The divorce made it clear the white hats don't win." Why, then, should she follow in those footsteps? Diane had a similar reaction. She felt her mother had been the very model of what her father wanted in a wife and that she herself had tried to practice many of the same virtues: to be solicitous, faithful, putting others' needs before her own. Her father's new love was a very different kind of woman — glamorous, ambitious, much more self-centered. Like Laura, Diane felt a sense of betrayal and disorientation. Why should she continue to be such a hardworking, responsible, thoughtful person if that was not, in the end, what was valued? The eventual task for each of these women was to come to her own understanding of what values truly mattered *to her*. But this is not accomplished in the twinkling of an eye.

For some, the identification with the abandoned parent is so painful that they distance themselves in one way or another — literally or emotionally. One woman told us, "It was so painful for me to be near my mother at that time, to see what she was going through, that I left town. I moved to another state. But I still feel tremendous guilt — I handled my fear of abandonment by abandoning her."

For those who identify with "the bad parent," the one who has taken up with someone new, there is a different angst, a sense of guilt through association. Some feel considerable self-hatred and begin to doubt their own ability to be loyal. Some frantically exert themselves to rescue the rejected parent. Others expend their energy in fury at the parent who has gone off.

Of course, the new person is a convenient focus for rage. Many of those we spoke to recognized that they had used their parent's new partner as a scapegoat, a safe target. How much easier to direct their venom at the evil seductress who lured Dad away than to face the grief over his decision to discard the past and start a new life. Emotions have a logic of their own, and even when the new relationship has begun after the divorce, adult children may blame this third party for breaking up their family.

Eventually some realized that the new partner had been unaware there was a marriage and a family in the picture. "It made me feel better about her," one man said, "but worse about my dad that he could be such a liar."

Given the powerful emotions and the major adjustments involved, it seems clear that the longer the interval between divorce and remarriage, the less stress there will be for all family members. However, when a parent remains single for a while, many sons and daughters come to enjoy the private relationship with their parent. For some it fulfills a childhood fantasy. Sarah, who was eighteen when her parents divorced, had always dreamed of having her father all to herself, without her mother's censoring presence and her sister's jealousy. "For a few precious months I had that — and then *she* had to come along."

Children may feel they were used for the brief period when their parent was in need and then dropped for the new relationship. Amanda told us:

> After my parents split up and before my dad remarried was the closest that he and I had ever been. But as soon as he remarried, it was the same old story: he's just someone who needs to be totally subsumed in his marriage. When I told him that I missed the closeness between us, he told me he thought it was "unnatural." That really hurt.

Ron said:

> My dad had always been a very domineering person, not very in touch with his feelings. When he was alone and hurting, he really started to change. He started to put more stock in family, and I started to feel more appreciated. We got fairly close fairly quickly. Then he fell in love. His new woman just slipped into my mom's old role, and he went back to his old ways. I still love him, but like they say, "A tiger doesn't change his stripes."

When it comes to a parent's remarriage, most adult children would agree that there's just never a perfect time.

### Stepparent and Child: The Uncertain Bond

The relationship between stepparent and stepchild has always been represented as a difficult, complicated, ambiguous one, founded on uncertain ground, shrouded in distrust.

If the category is already ambiguous, it is all the more so when adult children are involved. "Step*parent*"? The term seems inappropriate: no parenting will take place here. What then? "My father's wife," "The man my mother lives with," "He," or "She" — the very way that adult children refer to these new members of their family betrays the deep unease, the lack of a sense of natural connection. As Cheryl put it, six years after her mother's remarriage, "I like and respect him. But he's not my *stepfather*. I have a *father*."

For the new stepparent, adult children are bound to represent a source of anxiety. They are a tangible sign of a partner's long and rich past, a past that the stepparent was not a part of and can never fully understand. The children's critical judgment, their loyalty to the other parent, their deep attachment to the family's past, are bound to be threatening. The intensity of their reactions is both unexpected and disturbing. Nor is it as easy, as with young children, to think of ways of winning them over. If there is no prospect for the new couple to have children of their own, then these adult children also represent a bond that the new couple will never share.

Of course, many of the difficult issues that confront stepparents and younger children will not arise at all. Adult children rarely live with the newly married couple; hence, there is no pressure of having to adjust to one another's daily habits. There is no need to work out a complicated visitation policy, and little or no struggle over discipline and authority. By the same token, however, there will be fewer opportunities to discover mutual interests and to forge bonds of trust and affection.

### Unrealistic Expectations

Parents' unrealistic expectations have a significant impact on the remarriage transition. Typically, parents overestimate the "adult" part of their children. They appeal to the rational, grown-up side and are not prepared for the intensity of their children's emotions. Amanda told us, "Because my mother had been mentally ill for a long time, my father just assumed that I would be unfailingly happy for him in his new relationship. He couldn't comprehend my grief."

Researchers consistently emphasize the dangers of trying to create an instant family. If parents of young children have a hard time realizing how long adjustment takes, this is all the more true of parents of adult children. "You won't even be living with us, so this will have very little effect on your life" is a common assumption. Many of those we interviewed complained that they were expected to adjust immediately to the new relationship, without the break-in period that would be granted to a younger child.

The weight of the past and the relative lack of flexibility on the part of adult children are also factors here. Adult children have had their family experience and are deeply attached to it, both consciously and unconsciously. Once they are living elsewhere, there is little incentive to participate in the creation of a new family. Sophie told us, "I can remember my father saying to me, 'You don't understand what we're trying to do. We're trying to create a *family*.' But I didn't want that family. I'd had a family — a family I loved — and he had destroyed it."

If some adult children feel pressured to become part of the new instant family, others have a different lament. More than one adult child complained of the new couple's exclusivity. "They just want to be in their own little world together," one young woman in her early twenties complained. "They think that since we're adults we don't need to be part of a family anymore. But it hurts."

Both extremes — expecting instant bonding or mature detachment — are unrealistic on the part of parents. The process of adjustment requires time and patience. Adult children, no less than young children, need the freedom to have negative reactions in the beginning and to absorb information about the new person little by little. Even when the new person is someone they know, they need time to react to the new relationship. Until they are ready to be with the new couple, they need to know that they can still see their parent alone. In the worst situations we learned of, parents had made the parent-child relationship contingent upon acceptance of the new partner.

Kate gave us an excellent example of how adult children can take responsibility for making their own needs known:

> We always had a big family celebration in August for our birthdays. But that first August after my parents split up, I wrote to my dad that I wasn't ready to go to the house and meet Shirley, but that I loved him and wanted to have some relationship with him. After he got it, he called. He came down and invited us out to dinner.

Some adult children were not as lucky as Kate. They, too, dared to write a letter or speak their thoughts but were met with silence or condemnation. Yet what seems most important here is the relief Kate felt simply upon *expressing* her feelings to her father. As she said, "I felt so relieved when I wrote that letter. It was so hard to do. But when I dropped it in the mailbox, I knew that he would receive that document and hear my thoughts uninterrupted."

### *The Riddle of* Why

Many of those we interviewed expressed puzzlement, even shock, at their parent's choice of a partner. "My father is so handsome and young-looking," Susanna said. "I couldn't understand why Mom would pick this old used-car salesman." Another young woman, who prides herself on her intellectual achievements, told us, "It's just hard for me to understand how my father could like me so much and then choose to spend the rest of his life with a woman who reads Tom Clancy novels and walks around in those wedgie slippers with the pom-poms."

Had we been able to view our parents' relationship with any objectivity, it might have seemed to us equally incongruous. But our primal familiarity with it creates an aura of necessity. Of course, there are those sons and daughters who, from as far back as they can remember, felt their parents were mismatched. Some told us that they had often fantasized an ideal partner for the parent they were more attached to. However, it was rare that the parent's actual choice of a new partner resembled that fantasy.

The process that draws one person to another is mysterious and complex. A father who encouraged his daughter to become a sophisticated intellectual like himself may choose to live with a simple woman who "walks around in those wedgie slippers with the pom-poms." Such attractions are hard to explain, since they usually arise out of deeply unconscious needs. The daughter is left feeling that her father has betrayed the very values he taught her to cherish, and there is little explanation that would satisfy.

## The Shoe That Never Quite Fits

The truth is that no matter who a parent takes up with, no matter what the circumstances, it's a difficult process of adjustment.

When a parent becomes involved with someone outside the family's circle, there's the forced recognition that this parent has been leading a life independent of the rest of the family, perhaps for a long time. Many sons and daughters have never really given much thought to what a parent does when away from home. It's almost as though the parent ceased to exist after stepping out the door. Now the awareness of this other life comes crashing in with painfully vivid reality. This in itself can give rise to a sense of shock or even betrayal.

When a parent takes up with an old family friend, there's a different kind of pain. This is often more humiliating for the abandoned parent and brings up feelings of betrayal and shattered trust. One woman told us, "I couldn't help but go back over the years and reinterpret. Suddenly all those visits and double family gatherings didn't seem so innocent anymore. I felt that, whether consciously or unconsciously, she was already inserting herself into my family, taking over my mother's role." In such cases there's often the assumption that the child's long-standing relationship with this person will easily translate into the new role. Even less time is granted for getting used to it. As one woman explained:

I had known this woman for years already as a family friend. It made for so many conflicting feelings. I found myself wishing she was a complete stranger, so I could just feel the anger and not the guilt. One of my friends kept saying, "Look. Right now you hate her on principle." And at the time, oddly enough, that was comforting.

When a parent's new partner seems very different from other family members, the sense of rejection is intensified. Diane told us:

I remember the first time my husband and I went over to a formal evening at Dad and June's. It was Christmas

Eve, and I was just so appalled at how much *stuff* she had — the silver settings, the Waterford crystal. . . . There were just heaps and heaps of fancy seafood, and curly lettuce on silver plates. It seemed so *unlike us*. Even my dad seemed kind of embarrassed by it, but still — just the fact that he had chosen her put him in a category that wasn't *us* anymore.

If, on the other hand, a son or daughter feels a strong resemblance to the new partner, there are other, conflicting emotions. It is easy to get along well; there's a comfortable understanding and the sense of being validated. That shadowy little Oedipus inside says, "See! Mom really did want to marry me all along, because she finally ended up with someone just like me!" But at the same time there's the sense of being replaced, of suddenly becoming superfluous. Emma liked her father's new wife, Abby, very much. She felt that they were very similar and compatible. "Whereas my mother is very lacking in self-confidence, Abby is much more like me — very assertive and independent." There was a relief in being around Abby and her dad; Emma didn't feel the anxious need to protect her as she did her mother. But at the same time, there were moments of piercing jealousy. "They'd dance in the living room together, and I'd feel like a third wheel."

Judith Wallerstein wrote, "Children who together with one parent had constituted a subgroup within the family, based on that parent's unhappiness in the marriage, suddenly [find] themselves displaced by a lover."[3] This was the case with Sarah, who had always felt a special bond with her father that excluded her mother. Sarah liked and admired her father's new love, Teresa, whom she felt much closer to in temperament than she did her mother. Like Sarah and her father, Teresa was interested in Eastern religions. One evening when Sarah visited her father in his apartment, he was telling her how he and Teresa had been meditating together. Suddenly the candle they had lit burst its glass container, and he had taken this as a marvelous sign. His old life was shattering; a new life was beginning. "And how did you feel when he told you this?"

we asked her. *"Bullshit!* is what went through my mind. *Bullshit!"*

### Older Parents and Young Loves

The confusion of roles is especially prevalent when a parent takes up with someone much younger, even close to the adult child's age. Then there's no question of being in a parent-child role, but "friend" doesn't name it either. As Ahrons and Rodgers observed:

> The issue, here . . . is not one of the stepmother "replacing" the biological mother. Rather, it is the inappropriateness of a mother-child relationship being established between two adults who are not very discrepant in age. Parent-child relationships do change when children reach maturity. They may become more peer-like, but they rarely become completely so. Even when "children" reach midlife, they are likely to maintain a different kind of relationship with their aging parents than they do with others of a similar age. While it may be possible to develop a peer relationship with their father's new spouse, this is complicated by their continuing parent-child relationship with him. Without any clear role models, the development of these relationships is likely to be stressful.[4]

Many of our respondents testified to the feeling of awkwardness, the sense that neither they nor the stepparent knew quite how to behave. Larry explained, "My dad married someone I'd gone to school with all my life — the fat girl, we always called her. She always wanted to be in the ball game, and we never wanted her to play. Now she was married to my dad!" Tess told us, "The first Christmas, my dad's wife, Sammi, gave me black lace lingerie. I guess that was her way of being intimate."

When the stepparent and child are close in age, the sense of being replaced is intensified: several daughters felt as though their father had taken on another daughter. Others described a sense of rivalry with the new partner. Pamela spoke of her physical discomfort when visiting her father and his wife:

"She's gotten very fat, and I know the fact that I'm so tall and skinny makes her feel inadequate. So I feel like I sort of have to slump and slink around."

In these situations, the sense of abandonment is intensified. There's more hurt for the other parent, the middle-aged mom who's been left for a fresh young woman in her twenties. But there's also the fact that in choosing someone much younger, a parent is clearly making a bid for youthfulness, and in that sense becoming less parentlike. Many adult children feel a kind of embarrassment, an unseemliness associated with the relationship, as evidenced in this portion of the young woman's unsent letter to her father:

> No one will ever look at your new relationship with anything other than a slight smirk. From the waiter to the business client, all will assume they understand just what you were after in marrying a woman twenty years younger. You will always cut a slightly ridiculous figure in public, very different from the admiration you now garner for your lovely wife of so many years.
>
> You gave me my name and for the first time I feel shame in keeping it, because you plan to squander it on someone else who can never be a part of our family. She hasn't gone the distance. She hasn't created us or grown up with us. She didn't even exist when you married Mom and started the family!

For Kristin, forty-two, it seemed almost like incest when her father, in his seventies, took up with her childhood friend. "In my teenage years I had lived with Sandra's family for a while, she was like a sister to me — and now she was living with my dad. It's very freaky — and my children are horrified. When they heard about it they just gasped and said, 'Grandpa?!' "

When a father marries a younger woman, there is the distinct possibility that she has young children who will be a part of the new household. A number of adult children expressed to us, often with embarrassment, the hurt and jealousy they felt. Tess said, "When my dad told me she had six kids, I started crying.

I felt like we were being replaced." Sarah told us wistfully, "My father's new girlfriend has a son — so now Dad's got everything he ever wanted."

Rita provided an interesting view from the other side. She and her brother, both in their thirties, get along well with the children of her mother's long-term partner. Initially, though, "his children were a little jealous of us." When we asked how old these children were, she told us, "In their fifties!"

When younger children are involved, it can make it harder for the adult children to work out the appropriate relationship with the new couple. One woman wrote:

> Because my father's wife had very young children who were living with them, it made it hard to figure out what my relationship to my dad and his wife was. They kept presenting themselves as The Parents, wanting to treat me and my siblings as The Children in this New Family — and it just wasn't where we were at.

Sometimes the new couple goes on to have their own child. In some families the new baby is a positive catalyst for healing, for now the stepparent and the adult child have a blood tie in common. However, other, more painful feelings may also arise. For one young woman there was the sense of an event outside the natural order of things: "The next baby in the family was supposed to be mine — my father's grandchild — not *his* baby." Diane told us, "My father asked me, 'Do you think I'm an old fool for wanting to have a baby in my life?' What went through my mind was, 'You'll probably do it a lot better this time, and I'm jealous.' "

Larry gave us an example of just how complex these new family arrangements can be. By the time his parents both remarried and had children with their new partners, Larry had children of his own. His father's son and his mother's daughter used to play with his children. "It did seem rather unnatural," he told us. "My children never adapted to it."

It is not just the addition of new children that makes blended families complicated. Remarriage introduces a whole network of new kinships into the family system. Suddenly there are stepgrandparents, stepaunts, -uncles, -cousins and old friends to contend with. While some may welcome the sense of a greatly extended family, others resent the complexity, the confusion of roles, the added familial pressures — "a zillion more birthdays to remember," as one man put it.

## Difficulties in the Initial Phase

Some relationships with a parent's new partner get off to a bad start because of the way the news is given — or not given. Sophie, twenty-eight, was very hurt when her father informed her after the fact that he had gotten married. When she expressed her hurt feelings, she was told, "We were waiting till the holidays when the younger children were together at our house. We thought we'd tell you all at the same time. We didn't see why you should be treated differently than the other children." Sophie was seventeen years older than the oldest of these children; she was not present at the occasion on which the little children were told. Furthermore, her role throughout her parents' separation and divorce had been entirely different from that of any of the other children. She had served as confidante to both parents, helped to relocate her mother and younger siblings to another state, spent many hours trying to help her mother through her deep depression and to relieve her youngest sibling's fears and anxieties. She felt that, at the very least, her rather complex role in the family might have been acknowledged:

> The fact is that my father took a major step in his life — a step that profoundly affected all of us — without telling me. That was very hurtful, just as I imagine he would have been hurt if I had married without telling him. I can understand their desire for privacy, to have a little wedding ceremony free of their children's doubts and complicated needs and resentments. But my hurt was never even acknowledged. Once he had informed me, I was expected to show up at a celebration — nearly six hundred miles from where I lived — with little more than a week's

notice. I feel this is typical of how an adult child gets treated like a child when it's convenient — "We didn't see why you should be treated differently than the other children" — yet in every other respect gets treated like an adult, in the kinds of responsibilities that are assumed, and in the sense that your hurt doesn't matter, you're too big to cry.

Most of those we spoke to had not attended their parent's wedding ceremony. Tess did, and found it awkward and uncomfortable. She said, "We really didn't know how to act. We'd never met her kids before, and we had imagined that we'd all sort of sit in the pews and elbow each other, but they really weren't very interested in relating to me and my sister at all." Diane told us, "I didn't go to the wedding. I just remember that my mother was very hurt that they got married in the same month that she and my Dad had. And I must say, I sure had a hard time remembering their anniversary."

In a PBS special on divorce, a group of teenagers was asked to talk about how they felt when their parents remarried. Many of them stressed how much they appreciated it when their parents not only informed them that they were going to be married, but asked them how they felt about it and were genuinely willing to listen. One young man went so far as to say that he was sure that if he and his siblings had not given their approval, his father would not have remarried.[5]

Few adult children expect their parents to ask permission to remarry, but they appreciate being told, and they appreciate the sense that their feelings can be expressed and will be taken seriously. One woman said, "I was old enough to know that my father had the need and the right to start his own new life. But at the very least he could have said, 'I know this will be hard for you. Please hang in there.' "

Some adult children find themselves in a classic double bind. On the one hand, the parent is saying, "This doesn't affect you. You won't even be living with us." And at the same time, the parent is saying, "Here's my new wife. Accept her. Love her. Validate my new life." A parent's need for validation tends to be especially intense where an adult child is involved; a six-year-old's disapproval is much easier to bear than that of a twenty-six-year-old. Unfortunately, some parents seem to feel that this validation can be assumed or, worse, demanded. A number of adult children complained that their parents made it clear that the children's feelings about the new relationship were not important but, at the same time, did not permit their children to be noncommittal or detached, much less upset or angry. In fact, they acted as if it were possible to establish by fiat what their children should feel. "You should be happy for me," Sophie's father told her, not realizing that *should* has no place in the realm of emotions; affection cannot be forced.

Parent and child tend to be quite out of sync in the initial phase of the new relationship. What a father experiences as a wonderful new addition to his life, the child experiences as a further reinforcement of loss. Just when a son or daughter is reeling in shock, the new partners are most in love. Just when the children would appreciate a little restraint, the new couple is overflowing with a sense of new beginnings. People who are in love tend to forget that the exhilaration they're experiencing is a private, subjective state shared only by the person they're in love with. They tend to think it's a state of the universe — or, at the very least, a contagious condition: "I'm so happy! Why aren't you happy too?" No wonder so many children feel pressured; so many parents and their new partners hurt and disappointed.

### Time Does Heal

Miraculously, given all the difficulties that lie in the path, most of those we interviewed acknowledged that, over time, they simply grew more used to the new relationships in their parents' lives. Even when the beginnings of this relationship had been quite traumatic, many felt they had been able to move on. Diane initially felt something close to hatred for June. But gradually, in her words, "It wasn't so much a matter of forgiveness, but of getting to the point where you say, 'OK — *this* is the reality.' "

When a prefab house is plunked down on a raw hill, it looks jarring and out of place at first. After a few years, the grass springs up around it, the shrubs fill out, the trees grow, and the house itself begins to look more naturally rooted to the spot. In the same way, after a few years of living together, the most seemingly incongruous of couples begin to look like they belong with each other. They create new habits, new routines, and in time, these cease to seem so strange to the apprehensively onlooking sons and daughters. The couple emerges from the initial period of infatuation and begins to settle into something more ordinary. What may have seemed the strange peculiarities of the new stepparent also grow more familiar.

Gradually the other parent begins to establish a new life. He or she need no longer be seen as "the abandoned parent," and sons and daughters are freed of some of the guilt and anxiety of "consorting with the enemy." If this other parent remarries, this can be a tremendous help in equalizing the situation. After a bitter divorce battle that went on for more than three years, Susan's parents each remarried *on the same day*. Susan told us, "Thank God my mom remarried, because she was so angry, it would be impossible if she didn't have a husband. She's still mad after five years, but her being married has helped a lot."

Researchers have concluded that the second parent's remarriage is not as traumatic as the first's, and that, indeed, it seems to restore some balance to the system.[6] Now it's not that an "evil outsider" has sundered the family but, rather, that both parents have gone on to new lives; a new era has begun. Several people told us that they wished their other parent would remarry. "It would be a relief," one woman said, "then I wouldn't feel so responsible for her. I would feel she had someone looking out for her."

Grown children, unlike very young children, will never forget the image of their parents as a unit. But gradually the sense of the absoluteness of that unit begins to fade. Sometimes, it's seeing a parent's greater ease with the new partner that brings this about, that finally clarifies and concretizes why the divorce had to be. As Liza described it:

> My father is very fun loving, and my mother is a very
> anxious person. My father's new wife is very exuberant
> and adventurous like him, and my mother's new husband
> is much more of a cautious homebody like her. It makes
> it clear that my parents just weren't suited to one another.

## Other Difficulties

If the passage of time heals some wounds, it can also bring other difficulties.

Some experience a kind of honeymoon period in the early phase, during which the new stepparent is gracious and accommodating, keeping a relatively low profile. As time goes by, he or she relaxes a bit and begins to assert a more forceful presence. Sometimes this means new areas of conflict arise.

### The Critical Factor

Most resented by many sons and daughters is the stepparent whom they perceive as taking over, or at least intruding upon or mediating, their relationship with their parent. Sadly, in our culture it is generally men who are more passive in relationships, women who do the "kin work." This is reflected in the fact that adult children most often complain of a father who has retreated behind his new wife.

By contrast, even when adult children are not especially fond of their mother's new mate, this does not have a major impact on the mother-child relationship. Larry told us, "I never liked my mother's husband. Nobody did. He was very abusive to my mother. But still, I was always welcome to come to the house. I didn't like to be around him, but I felt more welcome there than at Dad's. I could eat and sleep there and feel comfortable about it."

Adult children, just as younger children, are likely to resent the stepparent who signs both names to the birthday card and chooses the gift. Kate hated the invitations she got that said, "Your father would love to have you here with us." Once again, there's the unfortunate lack of synchronicity: just when a new stepmother is most anxious to please, a daughter feels most insecure in her relation to her father and most in need of *his* signs of concern and affection. Kate told us, "She's inviting us over to *our* family house, which they're completely remodeling. Give me a break!"

A number of people we spoke with felt extremely pressured by the new partner's attempts to woo them. An adult child is old enough to realize that the stepparent is trying to be friendly, trying to cope with the anxiety of a very difficult situation, and this gives rise to conflicting feelings. Some find it hard to acknowledge their resentment of the new partner's overtures. At the same time, such situations can easily contribute to a rift between parent and child: the parent sees the new partner bending over backward to be friendly, while the child remains stubborn and rejecting. Amanda told us, "My father said to me, 'You're not aware that Florence is so generous. She buys *all* the gifts.' But I am painfully aware that, one, he relinquished the task of choosing gifts and, two, the things she picks out are hideous!"

It is difficult enough when a stepparent takes over greeting cards, gifts, and basic keeping-in-touch. What is far more difficult is when a son or daughter feels that the new partner is actually changing their parent's feelings for them. Lily said, "We were all very close with my dad before he remarried. Then he started to be very judgmental of us, always comparing us to her children who were so ambitious and successful."

Over and over in interviews, it became clear that this is the most crucial factor of all. Just as a stepparent's attempts to mediate or actually change the parent-child relationship are what is most resented, the opposite is what is most appreciated. Diane, who had such a difficult time accepting June initially, explained how much she appreciated June's deference to her family: "A few times June called and said, 'Your father and your sister are having difficulties. What can I do to help?' " Clearly, it was the way that June posed her concern as a question, not assuming she knew the answers, not imposing solutions, that so impressed Diane.

Liza described her stepmother: "When I go to visit, she'll say, 'You and your Dad do whatever you want.' She let me come around to her. She hasn't tried to be a surrogate mother or a buddy-buddy. She has never tried to interfere in the relationship between us and my dad."

Another woman, Rita, had been fairly unemotional throughout our interview until she began describing the man her mother has lived with for the last seven years, a man she admires very much. "When I come to visit, he makes such an effort to let my mother and me be together. As he goes out the door he calls to us, 'I'm going out for the day. Have a nice time together. . . .' " This was the moment when tears came into her eyes and she found it difficult to speak.

Of course, mere gestures are not sufficient. Several sons and daughters told us that while their parent's new partner sometimes left parent and child alone for an hour or two, they nonetheless felt a hovering, possessive presence. Rosie said:

> My mother's husband is so jealous. After my dad died, I really needed my mom to stay with me. It was such a hard time for me, and I had to go through all his things. Fred didn't understand. He would call up and say to my mom, "We're losing money every day you're away. You have no business sorting through his old things with Rosie. You're *divorced*."

Another woman described her situation:

> I hadn't seen my father in two years. It was the second day of our visit to his house, and I was just starting to relax a little bit. My father and I were up in his room and he had just put on an old record that we used to love. I was just sinking into a chair, feeling a tiny glimmer of an old happiness. And all of a sudden his wife is having some emergency in the kitchen that he has to attend to. My sisters have had the same experience on numerous occasions. Her sense of timing is infallible.

Typically in these situations, the adult child blames the new partner for intruding on the parent-child relationship. It is harder to see and to acknowledge that the parent bears an equal responsibility for emotionally abdicating, for creating the vacuum that allows such a "takeover" to happen.

### Revision of the Past

An almost equally sensitive issue for some adult children has been the stepparent who they perceive is rewriting the family's history, engaging the parent in a revision of the past. One woman said:

> She told me that my father had never loved my mother; that they had never been happy together. I resented that terribly. I had witnessed their relationship for over twenty years. There were problems, yes. Serious problems — obviously. But there were all kinds of things I saw, loving gestures and happy times, that she wasn't around to see.

In any remarriage the new couple needs to sift through the past, looking for patterns, seeking validation and a sense of direction, sorting out what needs to be salvaged and what relinquished. This is especially important when the new relationship comes after a marriage of many decades.

It is natural for the new couple to set about this process of reinterpretation. It is equally natural for children — no matter what their age — to be attached to their own family's history. Judith Wallerstein has observed that children see themselves as keepers of the family history.[7] Adult children feel this just as intensely as young children, perhaps more so, because so many years are at stake and so much of themselves is bound up with those years.

The issue is not whose interpretation is right, but whose interpretation should be shared with whom — and how. Adult children will have to come to their own understanding, and it may be quite different. In searching for a "story" that makes sense of the past, the parents and the children — whatever their age — have very different needs. Furthermore, these different stories may be equally valid. A marriage that was debilitating for the parent may have nonetheless provided the stable back-drop for a happy childhood.

Divorce and remarriage often arise from a profound desire to start life afresh, to rebuild from ground zero. When divorce and remarriage occur later in life, this desire may have an even greater intensity, tempered as it is by the growing awareness that life is short and possibilities finite. Too often, the new couple uses the model of a first marriage and a nuclear family, as when Sophie's father told her, "You don't understand what we're trying to do. We're trying to create a *family*." But the long prior history of marriage and family cannot simply be swept out the door. Sadly, some people have found that any mention of the past is taboo. The hardest thing for Penny, eleven years after her parents' divorce and nine years after her father's remarriage, is that, "I'm supposed to pretend that my childhood doesn't exist. We aren't supposed to mention things from the past. So I don't know where I fit in. It just negates us ... as if we hadn't had twenty years of living together, with memories of picnics and fishing trips and parties."

To avoid such conflicts requires a stepparent who is secure enough to admit the existence of the past as the adult children remember it and to allow them to mention it freely when the occasion arises.

It may also require a son or daughter who is able to speak up, "This is how it was for me. You keep your story to yourself." It is fruitless, however, to engage in protracted argument: "You're wrong. My father really did love my mother — at least some of the time. I have this and this and this to prove it." What needs to be said is simply, "I really don't want to hear your new interpretation of my family's past."

Often the problem is that an adult child is still waiting for the "grown-ups'" validation. The true task of maturity is to come to one's own understanding, without needing to share it or to receive a stamp of approval from the parent or new partner. Such an act of autonomy not only brings greater peace of mind to the adult child, but it can also result in an easing of the relationship with the new couple.

## Financial Strains

Financial strains among family members, often a problem after divorce, may be intensified when a parent remarries. Though in some cases the new marriage results in greater affluence, more frequently it introduces a host of competing responsibilities. Where a father may have been content with a small apartment in the initial aftermath of divorce, upon remarriage it is likely that he and his new wife will want to set up a more substantial household. This may exacerbate the relationship with the other parent; several people told us that their parents had never fought about money until the remarriage.

If the new partner brings children into the family, resources are stretched further, and resentment is not uncommon. A number of people acknowledged, often guiltily, how resentful they were of the many added responsibilities a parent had taken on in remarrying. They had grown up anticipating a certain level of support from their parents in their adulthood, and these expectations had not been met. What made the situation more complicated in a number of cases was that these expectations had never been clearly articulated. Rather, there was a sense that certain unspoken agreements had been violated. One woman told us, "I just know that if my father had not remarried a woman with two young children, he would be able and willing to help me pay for my son's school. I don't feel I even have the right to ask, and yet I can't help feeling a certain resentment."

A number of sons and daughters acknowledged that they sometimes had bitter thoughts — what one woman called "small thoughts at dark moments" — about what would happen after their parent's death. One woman was sure that when her father died he would leave all of his money to his much younger wife. She, like many others, expressed guilt at having such thoughts. Yet, she explained, "It's not just the money. Your inheritance is emblematic of belonging to a lineage; it's symbolic of passing the torch. That's what hurts, the sense that your parent is selling out your place on the family tree." And sometimes, unfortunately, "the small thoughts at dark moments" do come true. Trina wrote:

> My dad died three years ago, and my stepmother produced a will which left her everything. We believe that he was too sick to know what he was signing and are currently fighting this in court. It is my belief that by producing this will, my stepmother was announcing to the family that he loved her the most. This whole ordeal has lasted over half my life (the divorce was twenty-three years ago) and has been very painful.

Several sons and daughters complained to us that a parent who had always been frugal, even penny-pinching, had now embraced an extravagant life-style. Rita told us:

> For years my mother had to struggle with her old broken-down washer and dryer that my father refused to replace. Every time she wanted to do a load of laundry, she had to fiddle with pipes and tubes. It's frustrating now to visit my dad and his wife in the old house and see all their lavish improvements.

Kate had a similar experience: "Even though my dad is a very successful doctor, he never spent any money on our house. Now they're fixing it all up, he invites us all over. I had this vision: it's like taking a toy away from a child, then waving it in front of their face." Another woman recounted, "In my family, we were always very simple with gifts, preferring homemade things to expensive store-bought items. With my dad and his wife everything has got to be Gucci and Calvin Klein, and suddenly I feel like my gifts are devalued."

### Negative Chemistry

In some sad cases, there is what could only be called incompatibility between stepparent and child. Such negative chemistry may seem fluky and even mysterious. Some people wonder, "Of all the people in the world, why did she have to pick the one man I find it impossible to get along with?" One or two adult children expressed an almost nightmarish feeling, as though a parent had been drawn to their own archetypal shadow.

In fact, it's quite possible that there's an underlying logic. In some cases, it is true, people marry a new version of their first spouse. But for many people, the very principle of remarriage is *change*. A father may have been drawn to his new wife precisely because she represents the polar opposite of his ex-spouse and because she lives in a completely different way. If his daughter has been made in the image of her mother, it's no wonder if she finds it next to impossible to adjust to the new wife. In fact, the new partner may represent a part of her father that she has never been able to acknowledge before. Several of our respondents found that what was painful and shocking about their parent's choice of a new partner was the realization, "So this is what my mother [or my father] is really like." Despite the initial shock and, in some cases, the continued discomfort that this realization brought, more than one person told us that what they had gained was a deeper, more realistic understanding of their parent.

## Happy Stories

There are some happy stories in all this. Jennifer, for one, felt that her parents had always been rather mismatched and that her father didn't really fit in with the rest of the family. Her mother's new husband is someone she feels much closer to in spirit than she does to her own father. During our interview, we noticed that his photograph is prominently displayed on her wall. Her mother seems a much happier, freer, more playful person, and as her father is comfortably remarried, she is not tormented with concern for him. She regrets that both remarriages have increased the distance between her and her father, but overall, there is the sense of a positive resolution to her parents' unhappy marriage.

Emma described her father's new wife: "Abby actually facilitated the relationship between me and my Dad. She talks a lot, and she made us feel comfortable with each other; she acted like a kind of cushion."

One young woman told us, "My father's new wife helped him learn how to communicate better. I feel he's actually more accessible to me, that we understand each other better than ever before."

Another said, "Now that my mother's remarried, I feel she's taken care of, and I can finally relax a bit."

Susanna felt she benefited from her mother's new relationship:

> It's just so good to see my mother being treated well. It's good for her, and it's good for me. I never saw my father treat her well, and that's been a problem for me in my own relationships. If a guy is nice to me, I've usually wanted to run the other way. I can feel that changing now.

Several others agreed that the new couple provided a positive model of marriage that they had never obtained from their parents. In each of these cases, it seems clear that the stepparent was able to compensate for something that the child had not received from the parent.


### And Yet . . .

Happy outcomes do exist, and if few people have actually experienced them, they do provide an inspiring model, a hopeful sense of what is possible. But we would not be truthful if we painted a brighter picture than actually exists. For the most part we found that when there was not outright discomfort and distrust, there was a rather restrained assessment of the new state of affairs. Those who felt they had an acceptable relationship with the new partner, tended to express it in mostly negative terms: "He didn't try to be buddy-buddy with me," "She doesn't try to interfere in my relationship with my dad," "At least he didn't come to my wedding," and "She's not after my father's money, and I can appreciate that." As Rosie explained, "There's a sort of neutral territory between me and Fred. I think we're both jealous of each other, but we don't go at each other. We have feelings that are better left unsaid. In truth, he doesn't mean enough to me to make an issue out of things."

Even in the best relationships, there's often the sense of something held in reserve. Joan told us, "I got along all right with my father's wife — but she was *not* my mother." Her emphasis was particularly striking, given that she had just described her mother to us as "a cold Swede" who "drove my father away."

Liza had one of the best relationships with a stepparent of anyone we met:

> I really respect my father's wife. She's a really neat person. She supports my dad. She would do anything for my brother and me. But she takes a backseat. She never interferes in our relationship with our dad. Yet even having said all this, I'd have to say that as much as I like and admire her, there's always something I hold back — my first loyalty will always be to my mother.

Some things seem to remain difficult, even under the best circumstances. One man could never get over the strangeness of seeing certain objects from his family home in his stepmother's house: "There are things she thinks are hers — like the painting my father and I did together when I was a kid. She has it hanging up in her room."

Diane said:

> One of the things I miss most about my family are the times, usually when my grandmother was visiting, when we'd tell stories about each other. There was the story about when my brother was a little boy, and he woke up in the middle of the night and peed in the laundry chute. There was the story about the night we camped out and my dad creeped out of the tent and slipped in the mud. There was no new information in these stories; telling them was just our way of celebrating being a family, this particular family together, and usually we laughed so hard we cried. Since my dad remarried, we haven't been able to do that. There's always been this "other person" there, and we haven't been able to cut loose in the same way.

## When It's Over

When the new relationship ends, through death or divorce, family dynamics shift profoundly once again. Rosie told us that it was not until her father died that she felt "finally released from the split loyalties" between her father and her stepfather. She loved her father deeply and had never warmed to her mother's husband, but she no longer had the feeling of being torn between different factions of her family.

Some of the most touching late-divorce stories we heard involved a parent and a stepparent whom the child had become very attached to early in life. Elizabeth's story comes to mind here. Her father died when she was an infant, and she had loved her stepfather from early childhood. Part of her anguish when her mother and stepfather divorced had to do with a deep insecurity about the stepparent-child bond. Would her stepfather continue to love her, since she was not his "real" child? Betsy, twenty-one, had lived through her parents' divorce when she was a young child. Her stepmother became the most important adult in her life. Now that her father and stepmother were divorcing, there was some anxiety as to what form her relationship with her stepmother would take. Given that increasing numbers of children grow up with stepparents and that remarriages are even more likely than first marriages to end in divorce, it seems that Betsy's and Elizabeth's situation will become ever more common — a profound attachment to a stepparent, held in place by an uncertain family tie.

Emma's was one of the more unusual stories. After her father's death, she and her stepmother — a woman not much older than herself — grieved together. In Emma's words, "It was a real bonding." Recently, Emma flew across the country to visit Abby. "It was a very good visit," she said. "And for the first time we talked of wanting to have a relationship on our own."

For the most part, however, when the new relationship ends through death or divorce, it seems to provide further evidence of just how fragile the bond can be between stepparent and adult child.

Over a span of eight years, Diane had worked out a reasonably good relationship with June, in spite of inauspicious beginnings. Since June and her father broke up a year ago, Diane said that June had disappeared from her life. Another woman, Joan, got along reasonably well with her father's wife, but after her father died there was some conflict about money, "And now, if I saw her, I'm not sure I would say hello."

If these relationships more or less evaporated, Rick had the opposite experience. What had been a relatively neutral relationship with his father's wife turned into a struggle after his father's death. Much to his horror, several weeks after the funeral Rick learned that his father's wife was arranging to have his father's body sent out of state to be buried near her new place of residence. Rick was shocked and enraged. He and his siblings had chosen to have their father buried in the veterans' cemetery not far from where they grew up because they felt that his time in the army had been the greatest source of pride in his life. Even worse, shortly before he died, Rick's father had confessed to him how miserable he was in the marriage. "When I thought of how unhappy my father had been with her, I just knew he wouldn't want to be there." He and his siblings stood their ground, and the wife eventually withdrew her claim. There was some satisfaction in that — but how difficult, in the very midst of mourning the loss of his father, to have to engage in such a bitter and unpleasant struggle.

## The One Irreducible

Of all the stories we heard, the happy ones, the sad ones, the in-between ones, it was clear that one irreducible factor always remains. Margaret put it best:

> Maybe our parents didn't get along so well. But what they both had in common is that they had known and loved us from infancy. There was some level on which they didn't question who we were and why we were the way we were. That's what I used to love about going home — that's what *home* meant to me — just basking in that. Now, at

each parent's home, there's this other person who doesn't know me like that. We get along all right, but it's not the same and never will be, and it's affected my relationship with my parents. It's just not natural in the same way, not even when we're alone.

### A Fragile Balance

Even at best, there is a tenuous, provisional quality about these relationships. Like hybrid, exotic plants, they can sometimes be brought to flower, but this requires very special conditions and a complicated, rather mysterious balance of tending and letting be.

What are the lessons, then, that can be learned?

Though the breakup of the old marriage and the start of the new relationship often occur simultaneously, they are better understood as two separate crises. Remarriage intensifies many of the feelings of loss, anger, and rejection associated with the divorce and introduces many new complications. Grown children, no less than young children, find it difficult to adjust to a parent's new partner. As with young children, the process is a gradual one, requiring patience and understanding. When parents don't pressure too hard for validation, and when stepparents don't try too hard to "woo," then tensions will naturally ease over time.

Grown children, like young children, appreciate being told in advance that a marriage is going to take place. They don't expect to be granted veto power, but they appreciate having their feelings taken into consideration.

More than anything, grown children appreciate it when this new person respects their own family's past and does not try to mediate, change, or otherwise interfere with the original parent-child relationship.

If these similarities exist between young and grown children, there are also some important differences.

Grown children, more than young children, are capable of appreciating the difficulty of the stepparent's role. They can more readily imagine — to paraphrase an old folk song — that "someday I might wake up and find I'm a stepparent too."

Indeed, some of those we interviewed were already stepparents themselves.

Grown children, more than young children, are capable of perceiving and appreciating that a parent is truly happier with the new partner. This, for many, is what finally tilts the balance, enabling them to let go of the welter of ambivalent feelings and, like Peter, to shrug their shoulders and say, "Hey — he's happy — what more can I ask?"

This moment of letting go is wonderful when it occurs, but it cannot be willed from within or imposed from without. When the special abilities of adult children are appealed to in an empathetic manner — not assumed, not taken for granted, not demanded in a forceful way — then the best conditions exist for building a positive relationship.

# 9

## *Serious Rifts and Long-term Estrangements*

**H**ow do you tell your father that you never want to see him again?" Lisa asked, days after learning that her father was leaving her mother to take up with another woman.

In the initial phase, people often feel that the bitter alliances and painful ruptures will go on forever. They feel that something irrevocable has happened. "When my parents divorced, life as we'd known it ceased to exist," one woman wrote. *Never* and *forever* are the words that spring to mind, but gradually, as family members begin to piece their lives back together and make some kind of sense of what has happened, most of the ultimatums soften a bit, most of the ruptures are healed. Unfortunately, in a significant minority of families, the rifts that arise in the wake of divorce are longer lasting. Though we did not learn of any long-term ruptures among siblings, we did learn of a number of parent-child relationships that — five, ten, and even fifteen years down the line — remained seriously damaged. Communication had been severely limited, reduced to impersonal holiday greetings or, in some cases, severed altogether.

As we've seen, parents and children perceive one another

differently in the wake of divorce, and sometimes the new perception is seriously damaging to the relationship. Just as marriage may serve to restrain certain hostile impulses between husband and wife, so the structure of the intact family may serve to restrain hostility between parent and child.[1]

## The Widening of an Old Gap

Joanne remembered her father as remote and uninvolved, but she said, "He was always there. He went to work; he came home; he watched TV." When she was twenty, he quite suddenly announced that he was leaving. Joanne wanted to ask him why, but couldn't. To this day, and in spite of a series of legal battles "over everything," Joanne and her three siblings have no idea why he left. After the divorce he moved to another state and cut off all contact and financial support, though he had a well-paying job. Joanne saw her father only twice in the past six years, visits that he initiated after he remarried and had a baby.

Joanne felt that her father had changed in the past few years, and she wanted to renew a relationship, but neither she nor her father know how to relate to each other. Though he was always there during her first twenty years, they remained strangers. What was perhaps most telling in Joanne's story was the apparent absence of emotion: in describing the father who had been remote all her life and then suddenly vanished, she expressed neither anger nor sorrow.

For Jennifer, the divorce — and, even more significantly, her father's remarriage — intensified the sense of estrangement that already existed.

> My father never could relate to us very well. He was always kind of formal and removed, a phantom. And his values are so different; he's very materialistic. In the last few years, since the divorce and his remarriage, I've had some basic realizations about who he is and what he will never be for me.

One of these realizations occurred on Jennifer's wedding day:

My father and his new wife came to the wedding, but about half an hour into the reception my dad told me, "We've got to go. There're some things we've got to do." Later I found out that they had gone to watch the sunset. That really hurt. I took it as a clue to what kind of a person he really is: someone who puts himself first. Since then, I deal with him in a different way.

This was by far the most common pattern that we observed. There was not necessarily a decisive breaking point or dramatic explosion. Rather, there was the sense that a preexisting gap had widened or that an old wound had been reopened.

## Father-Child: The Vulnerable Bond

Most, though not all, of the stories we heard in this vein involved the father-child relationship. Other studies on the impact of divorce revealed a similar trend.[2] Interestingly, an important finding in one study was that the father-child bond was much weaker for most of the subjects *prior* to the divorce.[3]

Many of those we spoke with may not have experienced an actual rupture with their father, but they did find that outside the context of an intact family — and, more specifically, without their mother's active intervention — the bond with their father, never strong to begin with, had weakened. One woman, reflecting on the difficulties between her father and her sister, told us, "They always had problems, but I'm quite sure that things would never have gotten this bad if my mother was there to smooth things over." Another woman was bitter: "The divorce just showed up my father as he is. He doesn't have my mother around anymore to help him remember our birthdays or remind him to think of us."

On the positive side, some respondents observed their father to be making a genuine effort. They were touched at their father's attempts to write letters, choose birthday gifts, extend invitations. Some experienced more ambivalent feelings. Rita said, "My father's begun writing letters to me, wanting to share his thoughts. It's hard. On the one hand I want to encourage it — but then I think of all the years of so little communication, and it's hard to just forget that. And I still don't see him making any effort to learn about *me*." Kate observed wryly, "My dad goes to all this trouble to call us up and arrange a time to come over. But then the whole time he's with us, he looks like he's sitting in the dentist chair."

At the very least, the knowledge that there are deep cultural and historical forces at work may give some disappointed children a broader perspective. According to one woman:

> It helps not to take it so much as a personal rejection when you realize that many men in our culture — especially the men of our fathers' generation — just grew up handicapped in the ·human relations department. There was always a woman around to take care of that for them, and without our mothers around, they just don't know how to go about it.

## Ruptures Between the Very Close

At the other end of the scale, we did learn of some serious breakdowns in communication between family members who had been very close. Typically as people spoke about such ruptures, they conveyed a sense of disbelief, a world gone topsy-turvy. One woman who had been extremely close to her father before her parents' divorce told us, "If you had asked me what was the thing least likely to happen in my life, I would have said it was this, that my father and I might one day not even be on speaking terms."

Yet from an objective point of view, it is not really surprising that such reversals take place. For one thing, family members who have always perceived themselves as very close may have had little practice in conflict resolution. Many of our respondents told us that they had grown up in families where there was little overt disagreement. For years, tensions had been smoothed over, buried, denied. The first genuine acknowledgment of conflict occurred in the form of "We're getting a divorce." Children who have grown up in such a household may have never learned the art of muddling through, of staying engaged in a struggle to reach agreement or compromise. With no practice in bending, the bough easily breaks.

A related problem is that two very close family members may reinforce each other's weaknesses. When a child is very similar to the parent, the result may be a lack of complementarity that reinforces the sense of impasse. When parent and child are equally stubborn, reticent, defensive, or unforgiving, there's a dangerous chemistry. The very qualities that once confirmed the sense of closeness now undermine the possibility of reconciliation.

When a child has functioned as a projection of the parent, there is little tolerance when the child diverges from the parent's point of view. Ruth told us:

> My mother always used to compare me with her: this meant that I was sensitive and caring and so forth. But after the divorce, when I couldn't completely endorse her point of view, I became "like my father": selfish and unconcerned. It's like there were only two people in the world.

There was no room for Ruth to be different from her mother without being completely *other*.

Often there is little sense of boundary, or poor differentiation, between close family members. Laurel, who has been estranged from her father for nearly ten years, described what she felt had been a major factor contributing to the rift:

> As I see it now, my father and I had a complete lack of detachment from one another. We'd had a mutual adoration society from my earliest childhood, and it fell apart after the divorce. He wanted and needed and demanded my validation for what he was doing, and at the time, I couldn't give it. I couldn't even see what he wanted from me. I was in too much pain; I had too much invested in my family as it was. He couldn't accept my having a reaction that wasn't the one he wanted, and I couldn't accept that he couldn't accept my reaction. We just kept

reacting to each other's reactions, until the whole thing reached critical mass.

Last and most important, as is evident in Laurel's words, is the intensity of such close relationships. Laurel's reactions mattered so intensely to her father that he was unable to let her adjust in her own time and in her own way. And his reactions mattered so intensely to Laurel that, as she later told us, she felt threatened to the point of emotional collapse when her father opposed her. Poor differentiation and high affect often go hand in hand. When emotionality is high between family members, there is little space or flexibility for the slow working-out of differences. The atmosphere is claustrophobic and overheated, and the most loving relationships can collapse under such pressure.

Of course, separation is the healthy resolution for both parent and child in an abnormally close relationship — but this does not make it any easier. What should have been a gradual process of separation and individuation, occurring in small steps throughout childhood and adolescence, instead happens abruptly, with stunning disillusionment. This accounts for the acute pain and dislocation so often reported in these extreme situations. Often it takes years for either parent or child to see how much they have gained from the rupture.

Some people who had experienced this type of rupture told us that in the aftermath of divorce, they felt that their parent had radically changed.

This was the case for Margo Howard, Ann Landers's daughter, who in her book, *Eppie: The Story of Ann Landers*, described the shock and loss she experienced when her parents divorced in her thirty-seventh year. Perhaps most moving is the account of the rupture she experienced with her once-adored father. Like others we have interviewed, Margo found herself in a maddening double bind. Her father virtually forced her to break the news to her mother that he'd been having an affair with a woman for three years and wanted to marry her — and then he resented Margo for doing so. He began to make increasingly hostile remarks about Margo, and finally insinuated one too many times that she was "only interested in his money."[4]

Looking on from a distance, it is easy to imagine that Margo's father feared being rejected by her. As his only child, with whom he had been very close, she was clearly one of the most important people in his life. On some level he must have known that he had behaved very badly — carrying on a secret affair for three years and then placing Margo in an untenable position. It is a common defense to strike first when we fear being struck, to accuse another of thinking the thought we most fear. Yet how devastating this must have been for Margo, to have the father-love she had felt from girlhood thrown into question, tainted with suspicion.

Sophie felt similarly shattered when her father first accused her of having lied to him:

> It was like the bottom fell out from under me in that moment. That he could even think that I would lie to him, when he had always been my soul mate, the one person in the world to whom I felt I showed my truest self — it just turned my world upside down. Even if we were able to piece together some kind of a relationship again, I don't think that I could ever get over that.

There are certain kinds of communication that can have devastating effects on a relationship, for they question the very nature of the relationship itself. They introduce doubt where before there has been implicit trust, the rock-bottom assumption that "We love each other and we're on each other's side." In so doing, they radically alter the field or context in which communication occurs. One can say, "No, I wasn't lying" — but that, too, is a statement that might be proved or disproved, where before there was not even a question of truth or falsity. How was Margo to respond to her father's accusations that she was only interested in his money? To express the anger that she felt at being falsely accused would only have confirmed his fear that she didn't love him. Yet a loving gesture — even if she had felt capable of it at the time — might have been taken as more "evidence" that she just wanted his money. It's no wonder that

Margo found it easier to cut off communication altogether and, at subsequent attempts to reconnect, the wounds had simply gone too deep to heal. Doubtless, the situation was extremely complex, but how different things might have been if her father had simply been able to say, "I'm afraid that you don't really love me." In one of the most poignant passages of the book, Margo described seeing her father from a distance:

> I was riding an escalator down in the Hancock Building, where he had his offices. He was riding up. I looked across at him, this sad familiar father, and felt faint. I held the moving rail tightly in order not to fall. I knew then that we would never fix it up. Stubbornness was part of me . . . and I got mine from him.[5]

Though Margo could still describe him as "this sad familiar father," her basic feeling was that her father had radically changed. "This once sweet, open, giving guy was now transformed into a suspicious and embittered middle-aged man. This was not the father I had known . . . this was someone else."[6]

As we have seen, significant personality change is often an accompanying feature of late divorce. It may be what precipitates the divorce in the first place, or it may arise in response to the upheaval of divorce, or both. Most people find that their parents eventually settle back down to a more familiar version of themselves. But some adult children, like Margo, do not; they experience an unbridgeable gap between their past and present parents. As Rosie told us, "My mom was Mrs. Cleaver. Then everything changed. I feel like I carry two different mothers inside." This kind of gap is especially hard to bear when there was such intense closeness in the past.

We learned of different ways that people had been helped to deal with the disparity between their before and after parents. Laurel's therapist encouraged her to sift through her memories of the past to see if there was anything that contradicted her glowing recollections:

> At first I was very resistant. I felt I had already lost my father in the present, so why should I lose the father I had

loved in the past, too? But my therapist insisted that it wasn't a matter of losing that father, but of "rounding out the picture." It was very hard work. I just did not want to see anything negative about my father. And I never did come up with anything really tangible. What I came up with was more like "negative space" — gaps, lapses — times he just wasn't *there* for me, times he was elusive, unavailable, absent. There weren't any earthshaking revelations, and it didn't damage the many very positive memories that I have of my father, but it did help me to see him as a bit more fallible, more human than I had before. It helped me to see that this wonderful father was in part my own creation. And it softened a little the "Jekyll and Hyde" image that I had come to have of him. I still feel that he has changed very radically from how he used to be, but I have a better sense of where the new personality came from. I have a better understanding of how his new personality has resolved certain problems for him — and created problems for me, and for us.

It is usually clearer to an outsider that the idealized parent is not quite so wonderful and that, however submerged or denied, certain lacks and faults are apparent. But the outsider's easy insight is the child's major challenge. To see a parent as a complex human being, as good and bad like oneself, is a major task of growing up. This realization, guided by the parents in the early years, also leads to a more realistic self-appraisal and to greater self-acceptance. In the end it permits the development of a new, more equal relationship between parent and child, one that has the flexibility to allow for differences, disappointments, and failures.

Before her parents' divorce, Ruth had always been very close to her mother. Their relationship had even survived one very serious challenge when Ruth was in her twenties and announced to her mother, a very devout Catholic, that she was leaving the church. But after the divorce, as Ruth sees it, her mother's tendency toward black-and-white thinking became more and more pronounced:

In the beginning, I let her say the terrible things about my dad because I thought she just needed to get it all off her chest. But it went on and on and got more and more obsessive until finally I just couldn't go along with it anymore. And then she began to treat me like a traitor.

Not long after the divorce, Ruth's mother was diagnosed with cancer. This thrust Ruth into a nurturing, caretaking role at precisely the moment that she felt most angry and conflicted with her mother. When it became clear that her mother was dying, Ruth experienced grief on many levels: she had to face the actual, physical loss of her mother at the same time as she was facing the emotional loss of the mother she had felt close to.

It was several years after her mother's death that Ruth went into therapy. Initially, much of the work involved acknowledging the depth of anger that she had felt toward her mother in the aftermath of the divorce. Once through that tunnel, however, Ruth's therapist encouraged her to go back and affirm the reality of the mother she had so loved and admired. This did not entail a "split personality" version of her mother. Ruth was able to look back and see early signs of her mother's very rigid thinking. But it was clear that her work with the therapist was healing. She felt validated in her perception that her mother really did change after the divorce. She was able to acknowledge the anger she had felt at that time. She did not minimize the loss: "For six years we really had no relationship to speak of, and then she died." However, therapy helped her to recover a sense of the mother she knew and loved.

One woman who is now almost completely estranged from her father made an interesting observation that may shed some light on ruptures between the very close:

I was so close to my father, and he is so different now, that in some ways it's easier for me not to see him at all. That allows me to preserve the image of how he used to be, and the grief is more like the big grief of going through a death. But if I see him, and he's not anymore the father that I used to love, then it's like having to go through the grief in small doses again and again and again. And I just find that too hard.

For some adult children it may help to remember that, like good nutrition, the good that was given to one as a child has become part of one's self and cannot be taken away or lost.

## Remarriage

The remarriage of a parent can reinforce any of these various tendencies, disrupting or perpetuating an old family pattern, widening a gap that was always there, or destabilizing a formerly close relationship.

For Jennifer it was her father's remarriage that consolidated the long-familiar sense of distance between them. She didn't mince words:

> I don't like my father's wife. She's very controlling, very sandpapery — and she rubs me the wrong way. To me she represents the complete opposite of my mother, and the dark side of my father. She's very materialistic. She's even admitted that she's a "princess" and that her daughter is a "princess in training." I always felt that my father was different from us, and now she's drawing him farther and farther away.

Wally, on the other hand, had always been very close to his mother:

> Because my mother and I had always been so close, she could not tolerate my initial difficulty in accepting her new husband. She applied such pressure — it was like trying to sprout a fragile seedling in a wind tunnel. And at the same time, my mother's husband is a very insecure and possessive man. As I see it, he was very threatened by the closeness between my mother and me. Rather than being able to help us through our difficulty or at least remain neutral, he further intensified it.

Another kind of difficulty arises when the new spouse introduces a different set of strategies for handling conflict. As Laurel explained:

> What made things so hard was that my father's new wife
> initiated him in a whole different language, a whole dif-
> ferent way of relating. Suddenly people were seen to be
> "conspiratorial" and "manipulative." My father began
> using expressions that had never been used in my family,
> like "It goes with the territory" or "The ball's in your
> court." In a way it was like a nightmare, when you're in
> danger, and you can't run. I felt this huge gap growing
> between us, and I couldn't speak. Words didn't have the
> same meaning anymore; everything was weighted in a
> different way.

Some people told us that their fathers became critical of
them in the wake of remarriage. To one woman's distress,
"within a few months of his remarriage, my father began writing me these very critical letters. I was pregnant and not married at the time, and the letters were really upsetting. I just
couldn't believe that he would do that to me."

Given the inherent vulnerability of the father-child bond, it
would seem that a father's choice of a new partner is most
likely to have a significant impact on the father-child relationship. Indeed, we found that when our respondents indicated
that a parent's new partner had significantly improved or significantly harmed the relationship, the parent in question was
most often the father. Even when adult children did not particularly like their mother's new husband, there was rarely the
sense that this had a significant impact on the mother-child
relationship. Susan is not fond of her stepfather and is not
comfortable around him when she visits, but she told us, "My
mom is just Mom; she'll always be Mom."

## The Mystery of Resilience

Overall, what is striking is that so many families survive the
very rocky early phase of divorce and are able to remain in

touch or to resume contact after relatively brief interruptions. Even when the initial circumstances are extremely disturbing and involve shocking revelations about a parent's behavior, this does not generally result in long-term estrangement. Yet in some cases where the initial circumstances are quite tame and the divorce on the whole quite civilized, a serious rupture later occurs. Just as individuals have been found to be more or less resilient to trauma, so it seems that certain families are more or less vulnerable to the stress of divorce.

## The Power of Family Patterns

Taking the broad perspective that systems theory allows us, we can see how some rifts evolve from the power of family patterns.

For instance, in some families the intense closeness between a parent and child has been held in place by the triangle involving the other parent. When Wally's mother finally left her alcoholic husband, the "rationale" for the closeness between Wally and his mother no longer existed. Without the father's insulating presence, they even began to feel somewhat uncomfortable around each other. Wally's concerns for his abandoned father, intensified no doubt by his own primal feelings of guilt at "having stolen Mom away" and fears of his father's jealousy, made it difficult for him to remain close to his mother now that she was a single woman. Gradually, Wally and his mother drifted further apart. Yet when Wally's mother remarried five years ago, Wally felt very hurt and "replaced." As might have been expected given the underlying intensity of their relationship, Wally's mother reacted strongly to her son's "lack of enthusiasm" about the changes in her life. Unable to find a new basis for their relationship, they have had very minimal contact since that time.

At the other end of the scale are the families in which a gap between two or more members has been smoothed over by the broader family dynamic. One mother we spoke with told us, "I was always there to soften the abrasiveness of my husband's personality for my children. Since I've gone, they've had some incredibly brutal confrontations."

In both of these examples, certain connecting patterns dissolved after divorce, resulting in a new or deepening estrangement. In quite a different way, however, some rifts arise from the strange persistence of certain patterns.

One young woman made this startling discovery:

> My father and I had always been very close, but a few years after my parents' divorce, he began writing me these terrible letters. At first I just couldn't understand the brutality of them, the cynicism and accusations were just beyond belief. I showed them to my mother, and she just shook her head and said, "Those are just like the letters he used to send me." It all finally dawned on me. My parents never worked out their relationship. They have nothing whatsoever to do with each other. But I believe that when you live together twenty-five years and have four children together, it doesn't just disappear. So the divorce — or the bad marriage — lives on, between me and my father. Sometimes he treats me with the loving concern of a father, but more often with the bitterness and rage of an ex-husband.

As painful as this discovery was, it has helped this young woman to free herself. "It still hurts, and there's still a lot of grief, but I don't take it all quite so personally anymore, and so I don't react with such intensity as I used to."

### Habits of Communication

Many of our respondents told us that they had grown up in families where there was little overt disagreement. The dominant values were harmony and homogeneity; differing opinions were not encouraged. For years, tensions were smoothed over, buried, denied. Not until the divorce occurred was there any acknowledgment of difficulty. Given this background, family members had few skills for coping effectively with conflict.

At the other end of the scale is the conflict-habituated family for whom the divorce, after decades of overt misery and hostility, represents the final splintering, the confirmation that resolution of differences is not possible. We learned of some families where there had been such a constant level of verbal abuse that, after the divorce, the adult child lost contact altogether with the abusive parent.

What both extremes — the "conflict hidden" and the "conflict ridden" — have in common is a lack of flexibility, a very limited range of options for working through stressful situations. It would take an entire book to provide a thorough account of the factors that contribute to estrangement between family members. What we wish to emphasize is that the divorce itself is not the sole cause of such ruptures. While it is likely that many of these ruptures would not have occurred if the divorce had not taken place, a close look reveals that the fault lines were present much earlier.

## The Cost of Disconnection

If the roots of rupture are extremely complex and somewhat mysterious, linked as they are to each family's unique history, one thing is strikingly clear: the cost of disconnection.

When people spoke of the loss of connection with an important family member, they most often likened it to a death. Some claimed to have "gotten through" the grief process: for one man, "It's as if my father is dead to me now, and it doesn't really affect me much anymore." For others, the process was unresolved, a continuing, open-ended grief. One woman told us, "I was watching a program about the families of POWs — and I realized that's what it's like. You feel cut off, and yet you can't be done with it, because you know they're out there somewhere." Another woman said, "It's like living with a low-grade infection. Most of the time I'm all right, but if I get tired or depressed or sick, or around the holidays or things that remind me of the past, then it flares up again." Many acknowledged that they were haunted by thoughts of their parents' death. Even the man who claimed that "it doesn't really affect me much anymore" added "sometimes I wonder what it will be like when he really does die." Here it may be helpful to remember Ruth's experience. It was years after her mother's death that she worked through her anger and grief with the help of a therapist. After that, she said, the anger was gone. She felt sadness and more understanding for her mother. Even after a parent has died, it is still possible to work through to a sense of reconciliation and recovered love.

Those who were relatively free of such ultimate concerns nonetheless described to us a nagging sense of something unnatural and unhealed at the core of their lives. Some laid the blame squarely at the feet of the parent. Others experienced it as their own failure, at least in part, and for some it was a failure that had a spiritual dimension. As one woman observed, "I keep telling myself that if I was a truly good person and really wise, this wouldn't have happened — or, at least, it wouldn't have lasted so long." Another woman said, "When we repeat the Ten Commandments at the synagogue, I get to 'Honor thy mother and thy father' and I just don't know what it means anymore."

If some people manage to block out the pain of disconnection from day to day, it nonetheless surfaces at holidays and special family events. On these occasions it also affects other family members, and this was a source of deep regret for several of those we interviewed. "It's bad enough that I have to go through this grief and the sense of loss that my father and I can't communicate," one woman told us. "But it really makes me feel bad to see the anxiety it causes other family members whenever something comes up, like a wedding or a graduation, that should be a happy event." Such regret is especially acute for those who are parents themselves. They feel partially responsible for their children's lack of connection with the grandparent and sometimes worry that they are not providing a good model of behavior for their children.

## Going Beyond

For all of these reasons, there is powerful motivation for getting beyond the impasse. Unfortunately, no simple set of strategies exists for getting past serious and long-term rupture. For a number of reasons, we strongly urge that people in this situation seek professional help.

First is the sheer complexity of the situation. Because such ruptures are intimately connected to the entire family history, it is helpful to have professional guidance in untangling such a deeply rooted weave of factors.

Second is the detachment that a trained professional, who helps family members to get beyond their own limited view, can bring.

And the third reason is that a professional counselor can be very helpful in suggesting strategies for getting beyond the impasse. A number of helpful books exist.[7]

We do offer these basic guidelines:

- However difficult it seems to approach your parent, when you can do so it is likely to yield some positive results. Parent and child both fear criticism and rejection, but behind the protective barriers each may have erected, there is almost always a yearning to heal the rift.
- Readiness is important. If a parent is still devastated by feelings of abandonment following the divorce, too much pressure from you may be unbearable. Proceed slowly. In a brief conversation or letter, you might try what one woman called "dropping a few pebbles." If the response is positive, you can go further. An immediate resolution would be wonderful, but tender feelings and painful wounds need to be handled with sensitivity. If you expect too much from the first contact, further disappointment is likely.
- Before you approach your parent, it is important to discern what the true issue is. Family members often get stuck on relatively superficial questions, when the real source of conflict is much deeper: the need for love and approval, excessive dependency, or inadequate differentiation. Writing an unsent letter, as in the earlier example, can provide catharsis and clarity.
- Learning effective communication skills is important. Often it is helpful to ask oneself: "What do I want to *result* from this communication?" Usually the answer

is not just release of pent-up emotions, but an actual improvement in the relationship. This means learning to listen effectively; avoiding blaming, accusatory language; steering clear of black-and-white thinking, of *always* and *never* statements. Understanding the complex roots of the rupture is important. In your communications, however, you would be wise to focus on what can actually be changed in the present.

- If the rupture has occurred between two parties, it is best for them to try to deal with it directly, without "triangling in" other members of the family. Third parties often make matters worse, as they try to interpret or explain secondhand.

- Expect anxiety. Anxiety always accompanies fundamental change. For this reason, the best course is to proceed slowly, to do what seems possible now. Remember that when stress is high, regressive tendencies and defensive tactics come to the fore. It is always best to cool off before acting.

- Lastly, it's important to remember that one can never change another person, one can only change oneself. Given the interwoven nature of family relationships, however, a change in oneself is often sufficient to bring about change in the wider dynamic. When an adult child says, "That's enough Dad-bashing, Mom!" Mom will have to suppress the anger or find another listener. A good thing to remember is that someone may hand you a package, but you do not have to reach out to take it. Of course, the relationship may not change in the way or at the time that you wish, but some new way of relating will have to occur.

We did hear some inspiring individual stories. Lorraine had never forgiven her father for breaking up the family and marrying another woman. Their rift continued for ten years until writing to us about the divorce led her to try to resolve her grief: "I really talked to my father for the first time since the divorce. I felt he was the only one who could answer all the questions I had; so I asked. He was, surprisingly, very willing to answer all my questions and resolve some of my feelings of rejection. He has helped a lot."

A number of other people told us that, like Lorraine, what had kept them feeling distant from a parent was that there was something very important related to the divorce that they had not been able to express. After talking with us, they were able for the first time to communicate to a parent how angered or how deeply hurt they had been by the divorce. Once they did so, they felt that something had cleared and they were ready to move on to a new phase of relationship. Of course, in these cases the parent was receptive to the adult child's communication. Alas, this is not always the case.

Others told us that though the underlying wound had not been healed, they had at least been able to reestablish some degree of normal connection. This was particularly important for those who had children of their own, and indeed it was typical that such reconciliations had come about "for the children's sake."

## Letting Go

Sadly, there are those cases where the only resolution is to let go of the struggle. Amanda had a particularly poignant story. She and her husband, George, recently moved back to their hometown to be close to family. They have three adopted children, and they felt it was important for them to have the expanded sense of connectedness that comes from having grandparents. George's father passed away some time ago, but they are very close to his mother. Shortly after their return, however, they learned that George's mother was terminally ill.

This left Amanda's side of the family, also living in the area. Amanda's mother is severely mentally ill and has refused to have anything to do with Amanda for the past six years, roughly the time since Amanda's father announced that he wanted to leave the marriage. Amanda's father is remarried, and though Amanda had never been comfortable with her father's wife, a woman not much older than herself, still, she was determined to establish a positive relationship.

Things went wrong almost as soon as Amanda and George returned. Amanda and George are vegetarians, for religious reasons. It was this that became the explosive issue. On several occasions when they went to her father's house, his wife insisted on serving them meat. One particular evening when they had been invited over to her father's house, emotions erupted and, in Amanda's words, "Some pretty terrible things were said on both sides."

Amanda went to a therapist for help in relinquishing her expectations of closeness with her father and his wife. The therapist suggested that this was premature; perhaps they could find ways to work through and resolve the conflict. Amanda contacted her father and found that he was willing to meet privately with the therapist. In this context, her father communicated that he and his wife would be willing to resume contact if Amanda and George would apologize for their behavior on that unfortunate evening. At this point, Amanda asked George to enter into therapy with her.

Together with the therapist, Amanda and George explored the issue. They both felt sincerely sorry for many of the things that they had said in the heat of emotion. They did not, however, feel any remorse regarding their request that their vegetarianism be honored. To the contrary, they felt that their quite reasonable request had been met with rigidity and a complete lack of empathy. Nonetheless, it was clear that only a blanket apology would do for Amanda's father and his wife.

At this point they asked themselves what could result from such a move on their part. The cost was clear: This meant apologizing for something they did not feel was wrong. It meant giving up any notion of receiving an apology for the wrong they felt had been done to them. It meant giving up ground, swallowing their pride, and, perhaps most important, settling for a relationship that was clearly less than honest.

On the positive side, however, they felt that they stood to gain two things. First, they would feel better about themselves "for having made our best effort." Second, they would gain a set of grandparents for their children. And, in Amanda's words, "Because our children are three abandoned, adopted children, that was the most important thing for us."

George and Amanda, as best they knew how, made their apology to Amanda's father and his wife. As Amanda described it, there were several days of waiting for the reply, during which time she felt very tense and preoccupied, found it difficult to concentrate, and had difficulty holding food down. Finally they heard through the therapist that their apology had been rejected. The father communicated that "from talking to other people," he and his wife had concluded that, while George and Amanda sincerely regretted what had happened, "they were not sufficiently remorseful."

Amanda has not yet given up on the relationship; she has made several attempts at connection since this incident. Because her mother-in-law is so ill and requires so much attention these days, she has temporarily suspended the struggle, but she is still hopeful that reconciliation with her father and his wife may be possible. Nonetheless, if things continue in this vein for much longer, she will have to disengage. As she described it, it is a question of energy and focus:

> Eventually, you have to put your energy where you're going to get something back. My mother-in-law is dying and yet still she gives so much to us. You have to make choices. I have a husband and three small children. For their sake and my own, I can't live indefinitely with the anxiety of waiting for a hopeful sign from my father.

When people feel that their best efforts are consistently ignored or rejected, when the relationship with a parent has become a continuing source of pain and anxiety and has negatively affected other key relationships for a significant length of time, then it may be time to let go. This may mean different things to different people: for some it may mean restricting the relationship to fairly formalized birthday and holiday greetings or encounters, for others it may mean a complete severing of ties.

Again, when such a step is being contemplated, we urge extreme caution. Ask yourself: Have I really gone as far as I can go? Have I really made my best effort and sought adequate help in the process? If my parent were to die tomorrow, could I live with myself, or would I be haunted by the feeling that I had left too many stones unturned?

If the answer to these questions is a firm — if painful — yes, then indeed it may be time for letting go. But even though there may be a need to relinquish expectations on the deepest level, still it is important not to do anything irrevocable. One woman told us that she tries to follow the adage, "Leave the door open — and don't want anything." Miracles can happen; the most hardened hearts can soften.

A serious rupture between a parent and child is nothing short of tragic. If after deep reflection, concerted effort, and professional help it still seems necessary — then it need not be seen as a total failure. There is no getting around the grief, but as one woman put it, "Sometimes the grief turns out to be a doorway."

Though Diane is not presently estranged from her father, she did experience what she described as "an internal rupture," the death of the relationship that she had loved and cherished. Not long after learning that her father intended to leave her mother for the woman with whom he'd been having an affair, she asked him, "Would you cut off from all of us rather than break with her?" Without hesitation, her father answered, "Yes."

Diane said:

In that moment I felt absolutely shattered, like I never existed. It felt as close as anyone could come to saying, "I wish you'd never been born." And he was the one who had always said, "When life gets you down, I'll always be in your corner." It made me feel like those fairy tales, where you have three wishes, and then in one horrible moment, you realize you've wasted them.

But the brutality of his response liberated me. Here was all the evidence — the four kids, all the memories, the beautiful house — of what a close family we were, yet he was willing to give us up for some woman I'd never even met. At first what he said made everything go black. I felt totally negated. But then I saw the absolute foolishness of it, and that freed me from something. It freed me from my awe of him, from the feeling that he could do no wrong. And that freed me from having to fulfill his expectations, to be his perfect little girl. So I can say in one breath: something was ruptured . . . and something was freed.

# 10

## *Their Own Love Lives*

Julie, twenty-one, was a senior in college and had come home for Christmas vacation. Her younger sister was also home from college, and the first days of the vacation were absorbed in the warmth of reconnection and holiday preparation. Christmas Day itself seemed normal and uneventful. Two days later, however, Julie's mother told them that their father was leaving to be with another woman.

Julie's initial reaction was shock and rage. One afternoon when she was home alone, her father — who had moved out of the house — knocked at the door and came in. She told us, "I just looked at him and stared. I didn't know what to do, so I did what I always do — I smiled. And then I felt so angry at myself. Finally I said to him, 'Who's going to leave, me or you?' "

In the following days, her rage remained intense, but as she described it, she alternated between hours of crying and of numbness, "feeling dead inside."

Julie and her mother are very close, and as her mother began to search for explanations, to clarify what had gone wrong in her marriage, she shared many of her thoughts with Julie.

Julie herself was involved in the first serious love relationship of her life. Suddenly she began to be afraid, to sense certain similarities between her father and her boyfriend.

After many hours of soul-searching, she decided that her boyfriend, though like her father in certain ways, was different in certain crucial respects. She was able to reaffirm her boyfriend's very positive qualities: he was a nurturing young man; he took her needs and desires seriously and, at certain crucial times, was even able to put hers before his own.

Though Julie had survived the initial crisis of doubt, it was clear that this particular relationship — and any other intimate relationship that might follow — would take place in a radically altered context. A certain innocence, a certain naïveté, was gone forever.

Many researchers have noted that parental divorce has a strong impact on younger children's views of committed relationships. As might be expected, children of divorce grow up with especially intense yearnings for a close and secure relationship, yet they are often deeply pessimistic about the possibility.

Recent studies of adult children confirmed a very similar pattern. Writing in the *New York Times Magazine*, Barbara Cain reported "radically altered attitudes toward love and marriage" on the part of fifty college students following their parents' divorce. She wrote:

> Some young women withdrew from boyfriends they suddenly suspected as being unfaithful, indifferent or increasingly remote. Others demanded premature commitments or promises thereof. And many abruptly aborted solid relationships in an effort to actively master what they believed they might otherwise helplessly endure.[1]

What is unique to adult children is the immediacy of their concerns. For Julie, the crisis of doubt over her boyfriend was nearly simultaneous with the news of her parents' divorce. For adult children, it is not a matter of some far-off future; it is a matter of *now*. And very often there is an actual relationship at stake. Jennifer said, "I was in a very bad relationship at the time of my parents' divorce. I really should have gotten out of it, but instead I became determined to make it work. And I really didn't deal with my parents' divorce — I just deflected it all into the relationship with my boyfriend."

In fact, the link between parental divorce and their own intimate relationships was so strong that several people we spoke with had difficulty making distinctions between one and the other; in conversation they slid back and forth as though no boundaries existed at all. When we asked Elizabeth what had been most difficult about her parents' divorce, she responded by telling us about the pain of her own first marriage. Clearly, the sense of abandonment she felt had been the same. Many others told us that the most difficult aspect of their parents' divorce had been the repercussions within their own marriages.

## The Sheer Stress

The sheer stress engendered by parental divorce puts an enormous strain on other key relationships. People may assume that stressful events bring couples closer together, but therapists and marriage counselors know that the opposite is just as often true: a death in the family, financial troubles, a sick or difficult child, all can lead to serious tensions between intimate partners.

When parents divorce, most adult children find their daily lives disrupted to a significant degree. There are long and painful phone calls, and sometimes a distraught parent visits for an extended period or actually moves into the household. There are difficult decisions to be made, and some adult children take a very active role in their parents' legal and financial affairs. All of this means that there is less time and energy for adult children to give to their own partner and children. Though many of these stresses do diminish after the acute initial phase of divorce, some remain a recurrent source of difficulty. Of these, the holidays were most frequently mentioned by adult children as placing an ongoing strain on their own family life.

## The Heightened Need for Understanding

More than anything, what threatens the relationships of adult children whose parents divorce is the welter of intense and often unexpected emotions. A number of those we interviewed complained that their partner did not properly understand or sympathize with the intensity of their distress. Several people's partners had been quite sympathetic initially, but they lost patience when the distress and disruption continued for more than a few weeks. Here, again, the popular misconception may be partially to blame: no one would be expected to bounce back so quickly after a death in the family.

Even when a partner is sympathetic, different styles of coping can result in serious tensions for the couple. When the rift evolved between Ruth and her mother, there were times when she longed for her husband to step in and take an active role in the conflict. But, as she described him, her husband is a man who "hates conflict." His style was to "sit back and see if it will all go away by itself." He was patient and willing to do what Ruth called "backup work." He would stay home and watch the children while she went out to face another episode with her mother, but he never actually confronted her mother, as Ruth at times intensely wished he would do. Ruth's frustration and disappointment eventually grew so great that she sought counseling in the form of a workshop for couples. She credited this workshop with having turned their marriage around, and it was clear when she spoke just how desperate the situation had become for her.

## Accentuated Male-Female Differences

When Scott's parents separated, one of the hardest things for his wife was Scott's lack of communicativeness. Other women voiced a similar frustration: they wanted to help their husbands or boyfriends deal with the pain of their parents' divorce, but felt shut out and excluded.

Interestingly, a number of men who were so reticent with their partner were very forthcoming with us. Sometimes it seemed that they had just been waiting for the right opportunity to unburden themselves of pent-up feelings. Perhaps the greater neutrality and detachment of the interview setting was the safe zone they required.

When asked why they had not wanted to share more with their partner, the men we spoke with gave a variety of replies. "It's just not my way to go on about things when I'm really upset," one man told us. Another said, "I think it was a kind of pride. Even though she's my wife, I just couldn't stand to talk about all these terrible things that were happening in my family in front of her. She'd start to rant and rave about what a bastard my father was, and then I would get all defensive." Several men expressed this protective attitude about their family; they felt their wife was far too eager to probe and expose the dark corners of their family history. One young man who had shared a lot with his girlfriend explained, "The divorce made me much more emotional in front of my girlfriend. That was hard. It made me feel weak. And it was hard to feel weak at a time when I was also feeling very insecure about relationships."

For their part, several wives expressed frustration with their husband's refusal to face facts, to come to an adequate understanding of what had happened. Deanna told us:

Sometimes it's so hard for me; I just have to bite my lip. He acts so shocked and surprised about his parents, yet it's clear to me that his father is — and has been for a long time — an alcoholic. When I try to point this out to him, however gently, he just shuts down completely or he gets angry at me.

These tensions reflect a phenomenon that is common to most families. Parents may criticize their own children but bristle and become defensive when someone else does. A member of the family may criticize and complain about another, but an outsider, even one's spouse, is not easily permitted such freedom. For this reason it is best for the spouse to listen and be supportive, but to limit criticisms to nonjudgmental suggestions, since anything more direct is likely to cause a defensive reaction.

Often there is failure on the part of both partners to understand each other's differing needs and agendas. Frequently the men we spoke with said that their wife or girlfriend was "going too fast" for them. They were just digesting the shock that their parents had not been happily married and would no longer be together, and their wife was racing far ahead — or far behind, delving back into family history, trying to get at the *why*. Especially when it was the father who had initiated the divorce, the men often felt threatened by the process, as though whatever dark facts were exposed might be equally true for them.

Several wives told us explicitly that what motivated their search for understanding was indeed the fear that the same fate might befall their own marriage. Few husbands seemed aware of their wife's anxiety on this score.

At the other end of the scale, some boyfriends and husbands find themselves overwhelmed with the intense emotionality of their partner's response.

Tess said:

> My parents divorced twelve years ago, in the first year of my relationship with Brian. I was in a state of extreme distress, yet because I was an adult, Brian felt that I didn't have a right to it. This set up a pattern that we've just now gone into therapy to resolve: his negation of my emotions, and my inability to trust him. This probably would have been the pattern anyway, but the divorce provided the platform.

Just recently, Tess told us, she had a glimpse of what she called "the tunnel-end light." In their most recent therapy session, Brian had a breakthrough: "He realized that what had often kept him from being able to be supportive of me was a fear of being inadequate." We suspect that the same is true for many of the men whose wives find them lacking in understanding: they are simply overwhelmed by the intensity of their partner's emotion. They might feel the same way if there was a death in the family, but at least then there would be a cultural framework for acknowledging the depth of feeling and the disruption of daily life. In the absence of any such framework, they are able to hide their fears behind the alibi, "You're an adult. What's the big deal if your parents divorce?"

## Fragile Beginnings

As Tess's story makes apparent, it is especially difficult when parental divorce occurs close to the beginning of a relationship. It takes a long time to build trust and security between partners. When a traumatic event occurs early on, particularly one that violates the very notion of trust and security, the delicate new roots of a relationship may be severely buffeted.

For one young woman, a serious divorce-related conflict with her father erupted — of all times — on her wedding day. In her words:

> Our marriage started out under the shadow of this conflict which later turned into a serious rupture with my father. I was in a severe depression for the first two years. My husband was very patient and supportive, but much of what was going on was beyond his — and my own — understanding. It placed enormous burdens on the marriage at a very delicate time. There's an energy and hopefulness that comes from being newlyweds, of course — and that's a certain strength you draw from. But there's so much you don't know about each other, and there are such unrealistic expectations. The other problem is that it establishes a pattern in the relationship — one person is "the basket case" and the other is "the strong, supportive one." We're just now, nearly ten years later, coming out of that. One thing that's very positive, though — when you make it past such a rocky beginning, what you get is a feeling of "we can make it through anything after this."

In marked contrast to these women, Kate had a very solid, long-term relationship before her parents' divorce: she and

Cliff had been married for six years and had lived together for five years before that. While the divorce was very stressful in and of itself, she felt that it had not had a significant impact on her own marriage:

> Cliff and I have a very strong relationship, and we'd already been together a long time. Even when things get very rough, there's the feeling that we're working toward a common goal, and we can tunnel out the other stuff. . . . And I'd learned by then not to expect Cliff to understand and be able to help me with everything that I'm going through. There're just some places where he's not there for me, where I have to go it alone.

Kate's last remark sheds light on what may be a special difficulty for newly formed couples. Early in a relationship, people typically expect their partner to be everything to them: friend, lover, playmate, parent, confidant, counselor. As the relationship continues, generally a more realistic set of expectations evolves; some needs must be met elsewhere — through other people or in solitude. When a crisis such as parental divorce occurs before such an adaptation has taken place, the disappointment and hurt are particularly intense and potentially damaging.

### The Sense of Loss

When parents divorce, this is a loss not simply for their children as individuals, but for their children's marriages as well. A marriage does not take place in a vacuum; there is truth to the saying that when we marry, we marry a family. Traditionally, marriage is a new beginning, a setting forth, but it is also a gathering in, being drawn into the fold of family history, sustained and supported by the solidity of family ties. What some experience when their parents divorce is that their own marriage — or future marriage — has been wrenched from its moorings, set uncomfortably free.

For Laura, who was twenty-seven and single when her parents divorced, the loss was experienced in a very immediate way, as a diminishing of her own self. She had always felt that her big family with its strong ties was one of her own greatest assets, an important part of what she had to offer as a future spouse. After the divorce she felt devalued as a potential partner.

For those whose parents have divorced before they themselves are married, there is sadness that their partner will never know their family "as it really was." One woman told us, "My husband says he can't even imagine my parents being together, and that's very hard for me to accept. I mean — they were together for twenty-two years, and that's most of my life."

For those who have been married for some time before their parents' divorce, there is the loss of whatever pleasure and comfort derived from being able to come together as two couples, younger and older. As Diane told us, she and her husband had just started being able to enjoy going out with her parents "as friends . . . double-dating" when the divorce took place.

Many of those we spoke with experienced a loss of "backing," as though their parents' long marriage had provided a kind of insurance for their own. Tess, who had been married three years, was emphatic in describing the degree of insecurity that her parents' divorce induced: "No one can tell me that my marriage is going to make it. Look at my parents: they were together twenty-five years!" Though this was a virtually universal theme, it had particular poignancy for the youngest of those we interviewed. Born in the mid-1960s through mid-1970s, they had grown up "in a sea of divorce," as one woman put it. "By seventh grade, nearly all my friends' parents were divorced, and everyone thought of my parents as the great exception, the living proof that marriage *is* possible." Another young man said, "I grew up with divorce all around me. All my friends' parents were divorced. I thought my parents were the one couple that it could never happen to."

As they described their anxieties, some used biological metaphors, expressing the fear that divorce in the family was "genetic" or "contagious." Others spoke of being "programmed" for divorce. What these metaphors have in common is the sense that divorce is an invidious process, outside of their own control. For adult children, recovery from their parents' divorce involves coming to terms with this fear.

### The Fear of Repetition

It is a fear that reverberates on many levels. And sometimes it is a fear that is actively promoted by parents. As Barbara Cain wrote of her college students:

> With rare exception, most in the study feared they were destined to repeat their parents' mistakes, a concern frequently reinforced by the parents themselves. "You're attracted to the same kind of charming Don Juan who did me in," one mother admonished. "Beware of the womanizer just like your father or you'll be dumped in your 40's, just like me." Many of the youngsters deeply resented these apocalyptic, cautionary tales. Others felt burdened by having to wrestle with the ghosts of their parents' past.[2]

Identification between parents and their children is a powerful psychological reality and often remains intense even when the children have become adults. Because adult children are often involved in their own intimate relationship, the stage is set for some potentially dangerous reenactments of their parents' drama. Ericka told us:

> Tom was completely unlike my father in all the obvious external ways. He was sloppy and disorganized, and my father is neat and orderly; he is emotional and my father is very rational. But the longer we were together, the more I realized how deep the similarities went. And when things were bad between us, it was just like reliving my parents' nightmare.

Of course, such a frightening sense of repetition might happen to any adult child who has grown up in a troubled family. What is different when parents divorce is the sense that conflict and difficulty inevitably lead to divorce.

One young woman described a frightening episode in the wake of her parents' divorce:

One afternoon I had an especially upsetting phone call from my mother. She was still feeling terribly abandoned and rejected by my father and had only just begun going out with a man — very much on the rebound. The night before, this man had told my mother that he was going to come over and take my mother out to dinner. She got herself all dressed up and waited and waited, but he never showed up. Finally, she told me, she just cried herself to sleep. The next morning he showed up bright and early, apologized profusely, and explained why, quite legitimately, he hadn't been able to make it and hadn't been able to call. He suggested they go out for breakfast, and he took her to a wonderful old hotel where they had pancakes. They had a great time, and my mother sounded happy and girlish as she described it to me.

Even though the story had a happy ending, it was very upsetting to this young woman to think of her mother as so dependent and abandoned by two men. She went on:

The evening after that phone call, I picked a terrible fight with my boyfriend. I'd set up this lovely romantic dinner over at my place, and then I just ruined it. I still have two tiny holes where something burned through the tablecloth that night, because everything got so out of hand. I went to bed sobbing, and my boyfriend stormed out the door.

The next morning I called him up and said: "Let's go out to breakfast!" We drove around town, and the place I picked was a hotel coffee shop, a place we'd never even noticed before. We sat down and I ordered pancakes, and just as I was beginning to feel really happy, it hit me. I was being my mother, going through the grief and then the release. That was very scary to me. I've always thought I was such an aware person, yet here I was, almost as if hypnotized.

It *is* frightening to feel that we are in the grip of such powerful and deeply hidden motives, not living our own lives but acting a role in someone else's script. Though few reported such obvious reenactments, many expressed similar feelings of identification. Here is the ray of hope: as soon as they are glimpsed, such powerful subconscious impulses begin to lose their power. Several people we spoke with had realized that there were certain things they needed to talk over with their parents. Once they were able to do so, they found that the spillover into their own relationships diminished.

## Heightened Insecurity

A number of people expressed deep fears of betrayal that they felt were directly linked to their parents' divorce. Kate told us:

> Cliff is really a very conscientious person, but I've gotten very sensitive to certain things. Last night he was two and a half hours late coming home from work, and I was livid. My dad never came home; he wouldn't be home till four or five A.M., and it wasn't until the divorce that we understood why: he had an apartment with this other woman. In the past, before that discovery, I never would have gotten that upset with Cliff.

Ron told us, "I'd been with my girlfriend for three and a half years, and in the beginning I was just a kid. I was very jealous all the time. I'd really begun to get over that, but then my parents divorced and my trust level was shattered." One woman's fear sometimes turned into a desire to sabotage the relationship. That way, at least, she would be the one in control.

For many of the women we spoke with, the fear of betrayal manifested as a financial fear. Both Kate and Tess emphasized how important it was to them to work and earn their own money. Kate, who had been pregnant during our first interview, told us, "I'm not working now, because my baby's small — and even though it's what I really want to do, it makes me feel very frightened and vulnerable right now."

Sophie said:

> Sometimes my husband can't understand why I get so
> anxious about money. He says, "You act as though you're
> all alone facing the world. We're married, remember?"
> But I feel that he doesn't understand how frightening it
> was for me to see my mother, abandoned at forty-six,
> never having worked in her life before and having no
> means of her own.

While many women expressed a deep fear of being abandoned, a number of men expressed the opposite fear. They worried that they, like the fathers they had so admired, would turn
out to be untrustworthy. Stan, who had identified so closely
with his father, the "great senator," became very anxious that
he himself was likely to betray his wife. Because his wife had
always perceived the strong resemblances between her husband and his father, she too became very anxious in the initial
aftermath of the divorce.

## Looking for the Flaw

For many of those who were already involved in an intimate
relationship, the immediate effect of their parents' divorce was
to make them more suspicious and distrustful of their partners.

As might be expected, such reactions were most intense for
those who had been taken by surprise by their parents' divorce.
Anna told us, "For years I thought my parents had a happy
marriage. When they divorced, I lost all faith in my own powers of perception. I began asking myself, 'What am I *not* seeing
in my own marriage?' For a while, it was incredibly difficult
and scary; everything was subjected to scrutiny."

Such doubts are painful enough when they occur among the
young single adults who, until now, have provided most of
what little research data exists. For those already involved in
long-term, committed relationships, the consequences can be
serious. Though Anna's marriage survived her doubting phase,
Diane's did not:

My parents' divorce happened when Loren and I had been married seven years, and there were things that I had already begun to question. But suddenly I began to look for the flaw in everything. I thought I had been so clever in choosing someone so different from my dad — but on a very fundamental level, I began to see the patterns of similarity. I began to see how Loren and I were both so absorbed in Loren, how nearly everything in the marriage revolved around his needs, his goals. This was very similar to the way my parents' marriage worked.

As Diane became first more aware of and then disenchanted with certain fundamental patterns in their way of relating, her husband grew increasingly anxious. The very foundation of their marriage was threatened — and it did not survive. Her parents' divorce did not cause her own divorce, but it did accelerate and intensify a process of questioning that was already under way. Several other people reported a similar chain of events: they or their siblings had divorced within a few years of their parents. As one woman explained, "My marriage was already in trouble, but I was so devastated when my father left, it made my own marital problems seem insurmountable."

## Marrying to Compensate

While Diane's marriage fell apart in the wake of her parents' divorce, Liza took the opposite route. Within months of her parents' divorce, she rushed into marriage. As she described it, "We were both very young. We were high school sweethearts. As I see it now, I wasn't in love with him — I was in love with his family." The marriage lasted about a year and a half, and Liza, now thirty-four, has been single since then.

Of course, when young adults rush into marriage without really having come to terms with their own family background, there's a danger that they will simply repeat the same patterns.

## Staying Single

As the various college studies have reported, the response of many young adults whose parents divorce is to insist that they themselves will remain single as long as possible, if not forever. Ron, now twenty-four, is typical:

> The major effect of my parents' divorcing in my twenty-second year has been to make me more cynical about marriage. Right now, I truly don't think that I will ever get married. I don't think that I could ever trust anyone. Everyone else's parents are divorced, and then the one couple you think will *never* divorce — your parents — end up doing it. It just doesn't seem that it can possibly work. One or the other person is bound to change in some way — and they're never going to change in the same way.

Though he spoke very adamantly, there was something hesitant in his manner, as though he was waiting for us to offer him some hopeful counterevidence. After a pause, he said, "Well, I guess if I would get married, I would pick someone I didn't really like. I mean — I would treat her well and everything, but that way I would know that if anyone was going to leave, it would be me."

Ron's parents' divorce was relatively recent, but his doubts may be long lasting. Susan, whose parents divorced eight years ago, has not yet married and is often worried that she will never succeed at marriage:

> I went through a very long period when every married couple I met I'd think, "Either they're unhappy, or it's never going to last." There's still a part of me that is disillusioned: What makes marriage work? *They* can't tell me. I'm still afraid that if I find someone I want to marry, it won't last.

Ten years after her parents' nonconflictual divorce, thirty-nine-year-old Lorraine told us, "I have to be more wary now. I'm always thinking, 'Oh, wow, I could never make marriage work.' The chief negative effect of my parents' divorce on me is that I find myself much more cynical about love and marriage."

Still others, like Liza and Diane, who are both in their thirties and have already been through a marriage and divorce, also link their present single status to their parents' divorce. Liza said, "I think a lot of the relationships I've been in have been just for security. I get into a relationship that's maybe not the best for me, and I put up with it, out of fear. That's changing now. I'm not as willing to compromise. But then," she sighed, "it makes it hard to find the right person."

Diane described her situation:

> The strange thing is — though my brother and sister are both married — I feel like I'm the one who really believed all those romantic notions about permanence and nurturing and commitment. I feel like I'm the keeper of the family that doesn't exist — and that may be why I resist starting a family. I take it so very seriously. I see it as too much work — and too much pain.

## Weddings

Several people told us that part of the initial loss they felt upon learning of their parents' divorce was that now they could never have the wedding they had always imagined. And a few told us they were staying single because they couldn't face having a wedding in the midst of their conflicted family! They were joking, perhaps, but weddings do indeed represent a source of spectacular tension for children whose parents divorce.

All the difficulties that are inherent in holidays are compounded when the special event is a wedding. Of course, what other event would be more likely to stir up so many longings and disappointments on the theme of family harmony?

When wedding plans are made shortly after parental divorce, many find it hard to let go and enjoy themselves. One woman observed, "I even had trouble telling my mother when I became engaged. And I picked a little tiny ring; I didn't want to be flaunting a big diamond in front of her." Another woman said:

> I went down by myself to pick out wedding invitations. At the table next to me was a young woman and her mother.

They were oohing and aahing over everything, and I hadn't even felt that I could ask my mother to come with me; I just thought it would be too hard for her, and all of a sudden it made me feel really sad.

Some, of course, find that planning their wedding is a wonderful antidote to their parents' divorce, a chance to exercise control, to do everything "absolutely perfect, from the very beginning," as one woman said. One year later, Rosie was still glowing about her wedding. It seemed very important to her that her wedding represented a significant departure from her own family's traditions:

I wasn't going to have Swedish meatballs and those silly little almond cups at my wedding. Everything was really *beautiful.* I had an antique wedding gown, and the food was exquisite. My in-laws live on the top floor of an old mansion, so I came down this incredible staircase, and we had this really classy band playing on the bottom floor. . . .

Others, however, feel that their parents' divorce haunts them like a shadow. One woman said, "I was trying on wedding rings, and I tried on one that was like my mother's — a plain gold band — and I just panicked. I couldn't get it off fast enough. I felt like it was going to sink into my skin and never let me get it off."

Many find that the plans themselves turn into a nightmare of complicated negotiations with conflicting family members. As Rory explained:

For me it started months before my wedding day: so-and-so wouldn't come if so-and-so came; so-and-so would never speak to me again if so-and-so weren't invited, and on it went. My father had only recently remarried — a woman who was much younger than my mother and who had been a close family friend. I didn't know how my mother would react at the wedding, and I knew it would make me very anxious. I felt I had been through so much with my parents' divorce, that my father basically split and left me to handle the emotional fallout. I felt I deserved to have this one day in my life as free from the shadow of their divorce as it could be. But my father insisted. After weeks and weeks of negotiations, we agreed that they would come to the wedding itself, but not to the reception afterward. Finally everything was settled, and when the time came, everything seemed to be going fine. We went out to dinner with him and his wife the night before and had a wonderful time. I went to bed that night feeling so happy. My mother was in fine spirits, there were so many old friends around. . . .

The morning of my wedding I was awakened by a phone call. It was my father, and in a voice of quiet rage he told me how terrible it was that he and his wife would not be coming to the reception. I was dumbstruck. I couldn't believe that he could be doing this to me — after so many months of negotiations — and on the morning of my wedding. And then, to top it off, he went around telling off other members of the family. I found my grandmother in tears . . . and then my sister.

I can't say that it ruined the wedding because — in spite of him — it was still a wonderful day. But it's something you don't ever forget — how could you? It's your wedding day.

Several other people had "terrible wedding stories" — some, in fact, so outrageous as to border on the comic. Rebecca told us:

At the time of my wedding, my mother was living in an apartment and my father was hospitalized with severe depression. My brother was living alone in the family house, and he had turned the house into a complete disaster. He was responsible for picking up both parents and getting them to the wedding. It got down to the final moment, and none of them were present. My brother had just never showed up. We finally managed to get my parents, and my mother got quite hysterical. She decided that my brother had killed himself — when actually, as we later found out, he had just overslept! Later that day my mother got totally drunk and actually told me to go to hell! All this anger came out. My father, who is never harsh, finally slapped her across the face. I think she was angry because her marriage had been disrupted, and mine seemed more promising. Neither she nor my brother ever apologized to me later.

Tess kept a tighter rein on her wedding, but it still had elements of the absurd:

I just left my parents out of it. They came, but I gave them no active role. That was my way of saying, "I'm not going to take any shit." My mother bought the dress and my father gave me money, but that was the extent of their participation. My mother came down with laryngitis, which was somehow so appropriate, as I had given her "no voice." The video we have is really hilarious, with my mother croaking away.

Tess, and even Rebecca — incredible as it may seem — both managed to have a very happy time, despite the many tensions and even outright explosions. Both felt that the key was in separating their parents' problems from their own. Tess, in particular, was very adamant that this was her day and she was going to be in charge:

I've sort of had to be the parent of the family, and I've finally learned that there are some advantages to that. If you know what you want and others don't, you can get it if you assert yourself. Brian was the one who wanted to get married. I didn't initially, but I'm glad we did. It was the happiest day of my life.

A wedding is, first and foremost, a day of celebration for the bride and groom. Ideally, all members of whatever extended and blended families are involved can come together, put aside their difficulties, and focus on the new couple's happiness.

But this is not always possible. If the divorce or a remarriage is recent, the wounds may be too fresh. Some might disagree, but we believe that a wedding is one day when the bride and groom have the right to insist that their desires come first. Though it is an important day for all family members, it is above all a milestone for the bride and groom. As one young fiancée told us, "I'm the one who's dreamed of this day since childhood, and who will remember it for the rest of my life."

In the traditional wedding, of course, the families of both bride and groom play a very important part. The past is honored and the future embraced: parents and grandparents take seats of honor, the father walks the bride down the aisle, the bride poses with her "old family," the groom with his, and then both clans together, happily united, smile into the camera. . . . These are the images we all grew up with; this is how a wedding is "supposed to be." But when one set of parents is divorced, tradition has already been broken in a most fundamental way. This is a source of pain and confusion at the deepest level, for it throws into question the very values of trust and commitment that a wedding is all about. It also infuses the entire practical process of planning a wedding with tremendous anxiety: Whose names will go on the invitation? Will Dad bring his wife? Who will sit where? Do the in-laws understand who goes with whom? Will Mom and Dad be photographed together?

But on the positive side, if tradition has been broken — then let freedom ring out! Let the bride and groom follow their own heart's desires. One woman told us, "I let myself get torn apart by so many family members' conflicting wants. I just wish I'd listened to my little sister who told me, 'Listen, this is *your* day.' "

Often, the real issues may be obscured. The young couple may not fully realize the many mixed emotions that divorced parents feel at their child's wedding. Parents often do not understand the depth of their adult children's anxieties, what it's like to take the leap into commitment when your parents' marriage has crumbled after so many years. Laurel said, "My father was so focused on whether or not his new wife was being accepted into the family fold that I don't think he really thought about what I was feeling at all." At the same time, she may not have been fully aware of her father's need for validation from her and from other family members. Researchers point out that there are few norms or guidelines to direct the remarried. Most of the remarriages we heard about were very private, and even somewhat secretive, affairs. Thus, a recently remarried parent may look forward to their child's wedding as an occasion for "coming out" with their new spouse. The child may not feel that this is appropriate, but it *is* possible to understand the motivation. A lot of tension and conflict surrounding weddings might be avoided if parents and children could communicate the deeper anxieties and longings that the event brings up. Laurel might have found a way of acknowledging her father's feelings, while remaining firm about what she wanted for her wedding.

Though several people told us that they had left things to chance, hoping that their alcoholic father just wouldn't show up or that Mom's boyfriend would have the tact not to come, others felt it was very important to establish clear guidelines from the beginning of making wedding preparations, even at the risk of seeming selfish and bossy. One woman told her parents, "Don't bother to come if you can't be civil with each other"; another told her father, "No drinking." Whatever the particulars, the guiding principle is for the bride and groom to ask themselves, What will ensure that this day is one we will happily remember for the rest of our lives? How much anxiety and uncertainty are we prepared to handle? It is one of the prerogatives of an adult child to take control, to shape the event, to take responsibility for saying, "Here's what we want. Please help us to realize it."

If it's been ten years since the divorce, and Mom still can't be in the same room with Dad and his wife, then maybe it's time to insist that she try. It's not a matter of external *should*s but of the bride's or groom's own sense that the time is ripe and that having Dad, his wife, and Mom all present will make for the happiest wedding day. One woman who didn't feel she was ready to have her father's new wife at her wedding was told several times that she should "rise to the occasion." We don't believe that the bride and groom should have to rise to the occasion of their own wedding day.

When you follow these guidelines, it's important to remember that whenever we try to create the "perfect occasion," we are setting ourselves up for disappointment. There are scores of people whose parents are not divorced and who nonetheless have "terrible wedding stories." The most you can do is to be clear from the beginning about what you want; to communicate it clearly and firmly without, if possible, alienating others; to plan for it as best you can. After that, there is nothing to do but relax . . . and have some champagne. If even Rebecca, with her brother who overslept, her hysterical mother and depressive father, can be radiantly happy on her wedding day — so can you!

### The Daily Task

What adult children lose when their parents divorce is the simple taking-for-grantedness of commitment, the comfortable belief that simply because a relationship has gone on for a long time, it will continue to do so.

If this is a loss, it is also the basis for a very positive insight.

Over and over again, adult children have stressed to us that one of the most important things they have learned is that a happy marriage is not a given. It takes work. When they were asked about the nature of this work, one theme was paramount: the need for open communication. Emma told us:

> When I look back now, the worst thing about my parents' relationship was the two-facedness, the lack of honesty. Shortly after my own wedding, my husband and I went to stay with his parents. Something came up that made them very angry about something we had done. But nobody said anything. We just walked around in this terri-

ble tension for a day or two, and then finally I said to my husband, "I can't stand this anymore. Either we sit down and talk to them about it or we leave." My husband was terrified; this was something very radical for his family, but I insisted. At the breakfast table I cleared my throat and said, "We have to talk about something," and we did. I can't say that it resulted in a miraculous breakthrough, but we did get them to listen, at least a little bit, to our point of view. And we started a whole new way of relating.

Kate said, "My parents never addressed the fact that they were having problems. It went too far too long." Tess used nearly the same words to describe what she felt was her parents' chief error: "letting things go too far." She expressed her determination to face problems: "This is a relationship that I went into therapy to maintain. That's how determined I am to stay with it and work through. My one fear is that at some point my husband won't be willing to keep working."

If they were determined to confront problems as they arise, these women were also aware of the need to exercise caution. As Kate explained:

I'm very careful about Cliff. Last night when he was out so late, I said all the horrible things to the mirror. I was so angry I was shaking. But when he came home, I chose my words carefully. I told him, "I don't mind that you stay out, but I really need you to call and let me know." That's how I do it. I don't let things sit. I express what's on my mind — but I'm careful not to just erupt.

Another woman told us:

I've learned that there's a lot you can do to make your life better without divorcing. I see around me so many people who think they have to divorce to grow. But I think there's this other way. It made me want to work harder on my marriage. And I have. We've changed a lot in eleven years together. We're learning how to be nice to each other. It's great.

## The Roots of It All

Parental divorce affords adult children an unparalleled opportunity for recognizing certain powerful patterns of family behavior. Often these are patterns that have been passed on from generation to generation, causing considerable suffering yet remaining hidden from consciousness.

The coming into consciousness of these primal patterns is inevitably frightening and dangerous. To call it an opportunity is not to underestimate its fearfulness, its potential threat to the status quo, to whatever measure of harmony and equilibrium an adult child has managed to establish. Ruth told us:

> My parents' divorce created a crisis in my own marriage. Things got so bad that I finally went to a couples' workshop. I went fully convinced of how right I was and how wrong my husband was. Something happened while I was there. I began to see that there were two sides to the story. In some ways it was horrible. I never cried so much in my whole life. But it really turned my marriage around. And it was a radical departure from how I'd been brought up to see things. It made me listen to my mother in a different way. I could no longer accept her black-and-white version of things.

Many of those we spoke with emphasized the need to seek professional counseling. One woman told us, "I needed help in order to see the patterns in the first place. I needed help to set about changing them. And I especially needed help sorting out what was old family stuff that I was projecting onto my husband, and what was really between him and me."

When the pain of parental divorce can be embraced as a healing crisis, the possibility of growth is tremendous. For awareness makes transformation possible. Now there is the chance to work through and resolve some of the deepest and oldest sources of pain in one's family. Adult children are in a position, as younger children are not, to question and to probe for understanding, to use their fully developed powers of reasoning to find the way through their family's particular maze of pain. The fact that adult children often have an actual relationship at stake adds pressure and anxiety, but also gives an added urgency and energy to their quest.

Sometimes — as in Diane's case — this work of untangling may loosen their own marriage ties. What Diane saw when her parents divorced was that she did not want to play out her mother's role of mute subservience anymore. She said, "We used to have a game we played, 'King Daddy.' I always thought it was a joke. But after my parents divorced and I began to look at my own marriage with a more critical eye, I saw it wasn't so funny." When her husband was not willing to adjust, the marriage failed. Though the experience was tremendously painful, Diane did not regard it as a tragedy. She continues to struggle with some of the same issues, but she is presently in a relationship that is based on far more realistic and mutual expectations.

## A Sense of Hope

Despite the fears and doubts, many adult children retain a sense of hope about the future. This was evident among our own group of respondents, and it was confirmed by other studies. As one researcher wrote of her subjects:

The breakup of their parents' marriages really unbalances them and makes them wonder about the viability of the institution of marriage in general and, in particular, of their own capacity to make and maintain long-term, intimate relationships. On the other hand, an overwhelming number express their intention to marry. They claim they have learned something about relationships from the failure of their parents' marriages and that they will avoid making the mistakes of the older generation. They are wonderfully optimistic, and we can only hope that their optimism is warranted![3]

## Paradox

A number of those we spoke with who already were married seemed to be living a kind of paradox, determined to make their marriages work and at the same time keeping themselves prepared for rupture. It is apparent in someone like Kate, who stated, "I *have* to make this work," and then — in almost the next breath — vowed: "I will never be one hundred percent financially dependent. I will always have my own friends and my own life. And I will never think I'm too good to start over."

Tess told us, "There are two equally powerful beliefs that have an impact on my marriage. One is that I truly believe that my marriage won't last. The other is that it simply must not fail."

As Tess continued speaking, it seemed that she had in fact found a way to live with the contradiction:

I've come to feel that the most negative thing about my parents' divorce — in terms of its impact on my own marriage — is also the most positive. On the one hand the divorce has made me feel, "I don't trust anyone. You can't prove to me that you're going to stay because look at my dad — he left after twenty-five years." But on the other side of that is, "So what?" The fact that there's no proof of forever doesn't mean that you stop working on it today.

# 11

## Parents Themselves

I *lay in my room in the hospital, my new baby girl beside me. In her tiny face I caught glimpses of other faces: I saw my mother's cheeks, my father's eyes. . . . It was eleven years since my parents' divorce, and by now I had grown thoroughly used to separate phone calls. But this time, picking up the phone, I felt — as I had so many years ago — a deep sense of refusal and incredulity, as though a voice inside me were saying, "No, this isn't how it's supposed to be." In that moment, the only thing that would have felt right was to tell them in one breath, "Mom-and-Dad, it's a girl!"*

*In the days that followed, I kept waiting to hear that some acknowledgment had passed between them, a phone call perhaps, or a note of mutual congratulation. It was only a small gesture that I expected, but it never took place. What surprised me more than anything was the depth of my own disappointment.*

### Reawakened Losses

As Noelle's story illustrates, the experience of becoming a parent can resensitize old wounds, awakening longings and sorrows that have lain dormant for years.

Having a child stirs up memories of one's own childhood, often kindling a desire to understand and reconnect with the past. New parents peer intently at old photographs, looking to find their child's smile or pout in their own baby face; they ferret out old toys and favorite books, and find new pleasure in the stories that begin, "I remember when you were a baby . . ."

Having a child also represents a step into the future, an embrace of what is to come. Exciting and hopeful as this is, it is also frightening, a leap into the unknown. There's a longing for the reassurance that comes from an unbroken past, a desire for wholeness, for touching one's roots: a fragmented family makes the process more difficult. One woman told us:

> Before my first baby was born, my mother came with boxes of my old baby things. There were tiny little night-gowns and flannel shirts that I had worn thirty years ago, all carefully washed and folded. It was the strangest feel-ing unpacking them. I felt as though all the little things had been so carefully preserved, but the big thing, the foundation, no longer existed.

Many experience, as Noelle did, the reawakened longing for parents to function again as the original pair. As children, they called, "Mom and Dad, look! Look at me! Look at what I've done!" Having a child feels like the penultimate achievement, and there's a longing to have it acknowledged in the primal way.

There's a longing, too, to have a united set of grandparents for one's children. Some feel this particular sense of loss even before a child arrives. For Diane, the thought that her parents would not be grandparents together was part of the initial grief she felt upon learning of their breakup. She did not yet have a child of her own, but what she lost was a particular vision of the future that she had cherished since childhood.

People commonly say that it is upon becoming parents themselves that they began to understand and to enjoy their parents as never before. Many who found their parents difficult as parents are able to appreciate them as grandparents to their own children. For their part, grandparents often say that one of the joys of grandparenting is the chance to reexperience all the best parts of being a parent — to be playful and supportive and encouraging — without the daily struggle and responsibility. For others, being grandparents means "getting to do it right this time," having a second chance to make up for what they were not able to give as parents. These kinds of resolutions cannot happen in the same way when parents divorce. Each parent may blossom individually as a grandparent, but there is not the same opportunity for the original pair of parents to reenact — or to discover for the first time — the joys of closeness with young children.

There is a broader dimension, too, to the sense of loss involved. Most parents want to bring their children into a perfect world. It is hard if even their own little piece of the world — the world within a world that is their family — is fragmented and conflict-ridden. The desire to create a placid, unruffled background for the new baby is particularly intense for expectant couples and new parents. Knowing that tensions still exist between the grandparents is distressing. Fantasies that the new baby will re-create harmony, perhaps bringing the parents together again, at least in their role as grandparents, may be very strong.

Though some told us that their parents' divorce had been part of what impelled them to create a family of their own, a surprising number of people told us quite the opposite. Though Rick now has two sons of his own, the decision to become a parent was much harder for him than the decision to marry. Though he was not able to explain why exactly, he links the difficulty to the unhappiness surrounding his parents' marriage. Another woman, Penny, was twenty-three when her parents divorced eleven years ago. She has been married five years, and still does not feel ready to have a child:

I remember thinking about how my parents' divorce hurt me so much. Parents hurt you and they don't even know it. I don't have children, but I'm afraid I'll do those kinds of things to my children. I've never felt qualified to be a parent. I don't know how my parents should have treated me. I don't know a better way.

Rosie said, "Children are so vulnerable to their parents. I'm afraid of having that kind of power."

### Pregnancy

Alas, for some the grief of parental divorce is experienced simultaneously with first becoming a parent.

We learned of one young woman who was pregnant with her first child when her parents' breakup occurred. Her own sense of joyful anticipation was frequently clouded over by the turmoil in her family. Added to the doubts and uncertainties associated with a first pregnancy were the intense emotions associated with parental divorce. At one point she became so anxious that she began to fear for her baby's health. "If anything's wrong with this baby it will be your fault!" she told her mother once in a particularly emotional outburst.

Kate was pregnant with her second child during the initial turmoil of her parents' separation. As a more experienced mother, she was less prone to panic than the first young woman, but still there were feelings of loss, sorrow, and bitterness. With an active three-year-old, a full-time job, and a husband who was very pressured himself, she would have appreciated some extra support from her parents. Instead, she found herself the daily outlet for her mother's grief and rage and was repeatedly drawn into complicated negotiations with her parents. Like the first young woman, she felt deprived of some of the natural joy of anticipating her baby's birth. For months before her due date, she fretted over plans for the baptism. Would she invite both parents? Would her father's new wife come too?

Pregnancy is a vulnerable phase in the life of a woman. It is common to be very emotionally sensitive during pregnancy, and fatigue is a nearly universal complaint. Many find it is a time of wanting to draw inward, a time of self-collection and preparing the nest. For all of these reasons, the upheaval of divorce in the family is precisely not what the doctor ordered.

The first pregnancy in particular is a time when many experience a deepening of the bond between mother and daughter. Now the daughter is crossing the threshold to stand, as a mother, beside her own mother. Simultaneously, it is the last time to be "Mother's girl," to be indulged in and doted upon before assuming the awesome responsibility of parenthood. This can be a very special time for mothers and daughters, and it can be a time of happy anticipation for the family as a whole. How sad when it is overwhelmed by the turmoil of divorce.

## A Sense of Guilt

If conflict persists after the divorce, some adult children feel guilty that they have not been able to resolve the family situation for their own children's sake.

For those whose parents are in the most tumultuous initial phase of divorce, the intensity of their own feelings undermines their sense of confidence and authority as parents. They find it hard to feel steady and convincing in their own parental role at a time when they are plunged into confusion, often reliving some of their own darkest childhood fears and anxieties. Many adult children already feel ashamed of the regressive tendencies that quite naturally arise when parents divorce. For adult children who have children of their own, such feelings are intensified by the sense of having faltered or failed just when they are supposed to be most mature — as parents.

Feelings of guilt may be especially intense when a rupture has occurred in the family. One young woman who became estranged from her father following her parents' divorce described the sense of personal failure she felt at not being able to resolve the conflict with her father:

This failure made me feel that I was not as wise or as good a person as I might otherwise have thought. And that made me feel less worthy of being a parent. I would think — I still think, "I've failed at this most fundamental relationship in my life. So what right will I have to tell my daughter how to conduct her life?"

She went on to describe how the estrangement had begun to affect her daughter, too:

> Lately, she's started asking, "Why doesn't Grandpa like us? Why doesn't he come see us?" She concocts these elaborate schemes for reconciliation. "Maybe if we all dressed up in funny clothes, then he wouldn't know it was us at first, and then he would find out that he really likes us. . . ." She says that sort of thing. And I've realized that — in part because of my inability to work things out — she's being deprived of a grandfather, of a relationship that's obviously very important to her, and naturally that's added to my sense of guilt.

Some adult children we spoke with confessed that they had hoped their children would "make it all better," becoming the bridge or providing the magic key to reconciliation. In some cases, of course, this does happen. When it doesn't, however, the pain of being estranged from a parent is intensified. One significant effect of such estrangements is to make adult children fearful that their relationship with their own children might one day suffer a similar rift. One man told us, "I look in my son's face and I can't imagine that anything could ever come between us. And yet, a few years ago, if you had asked me to imagine that I might one day not be on speaking terms with my father, I would have said, 'But that's impossible!' "

### The Sheer Stress Level

For those who have young children at the time of their parents' divorce, the sheer stress of it all is once again a critical issue. Here it is a stress that works in two directions: the stress of parental divorce makes it hard to function effectively as a parent, and the stress of parenting young children makes it hard to cope effectively with distraught and needy parents. Not uncommonly, a cycle of exhaustion and discouragement arises in which adult children feel they are letting everyone down, failing as children, failing as parents, and failing as spouses. One man told us, "It's a kind of desperate triage. You have to rescue your parents and care for your kids, so your own marriage just goes on hold."

It is important to remember, without being unduly alarmist, that the accumulation of stress factors in a parent's life can, in the extreme, lead to child abuse. Though Anna never lost control to that degree, she did become aware of a disturbing pattern: "At a certain point I realized that whenever I had one of these upsetting phone calls with my mother, I ended up spanking my kids. Finally I had to tell my mother, 'No phone calls! Let's write instead.' " It is imperative that adult children who are parents make every effort to get whatever added support they need in the wake of their own parents' divorce. In this way, they will be doing the best possible thing for their children, as well as for themselves.

### Unavailable Grandparents

When a new baby comes in the midst of divorce, grandparents may be too distressed and preoccupied to take notice. This brings hurt and disappointment to the baby's parents — as when Ruth, cradling her newborn son in her arms, wanted to shout across the room to her mother, "Aren't you even going to look at him?" It is easy to imagine the gulf that might arise between mother and daughter in such a situation. The mother is in a state of mourning, experiencing the many dimensions of loss that divorce involves. She is in the midst of endings, while her daughter cradles this new life in her arms. The contradiction may be too great for the mother: perhaps there is jealousy or resentment; or perhaps she simply assumes, "She's so absorbed in her new baby. She doesn't need me now." But most adult children do long for their parents' support and acknowledgment when a new baby comes. When parents are unable to respond with genuine interest and enthusiasm, their children feel cheated of one of the joys of bringing a child into the world — the joy of basking in their parents' pride and happiness.

Sadly, even after the initial turmoil of divorce calms down, some grandparents remain uninvolved. Ruth told us, "As my son got older, he started to look like my dad, and my mother just never let herself get close to him. I felt really sorry for him; he missed out on a relationship that was so important to my other children."

In some cases, a divorcing parent in the midst of midlife anxieties is simply not ready to face being a grandparent. The new child is not seen as a source of joy but as a symbol of the grandparent's own lost youth and impending old age. In fact, though it may never become fully conscious, this feeling is experienced by most new grandparents. Along with the joy of welcoming a grandchild is the inescapable realization of one's own changing place in the life cycle. Grandmothers, who are usually past the childbearing age, must acknowledge the passing of this capacity and all it implies. The more disrupted their own life, the more difficult it will be to ignore the poignancy of lost youth.

Another common scenario is the passive father who, without his former wife to keep him in touch with his children and grandchildren, simply drifts further and further away. Some divorced grandparents, of course, have acquired or begun a new family of their own. This in itself is a daunting process in middle age, and there may simply not be enough time and energy to go around. We interviewed many adult children whose remarried parents are involved with many acquired children and grandchildren. The logistics of having eight or ten children, their mates, and numerous grandchildren are mind-boggling and sometimes overwhelming. Even under the best of circumstances, adult children often find that they have to share their parent's attention with a stepfather or stepmother and numerous other children and grandchildren.

In still other cases, a divorced or divorcing grandparent may be disassociating from traditional family roles. This seems to be particularly true for women who, having been left by their husband, feel cast out and rejected in their lifelong role as nurturer and caretaker. Diane told us, "I can still feel surprised and hurt at how uninvolved my mother is as a grandmother." She went on to describe in detail how her mother's passion for ice skating keeps her twirling in a sequined skirt three evenings a week — clearly not conforming to Diane's childhood image of the sort of grandmother her mother would be.

As Diane spoke, there was a curious intensity in her voice — particularly curious as the children involved are not hers, but her sister's. She is very close to her nieces and nephew — but is it their loss or her own that she feels most acutely? Often the feelings are difficult to untangle. Undoubtedly Diane is concerned for what her sister's children may be missing out on. But she is also witnessing her mother as self-involved and unavailable — and this is a loss for her.

## My Child, Myself

It is clear that many adult children feel personally rejected when their parents seem uninvolved or unconcerned as grandparents. When early relations have been good, children naturally look forward to the extension of that same loving closeness between their parents and their own children. If it does not develop, disappointment and hurt are bound to occur. If the early relationship was more problematic, however, then a parent's behavior as a grandparent may remind an adult child of hurts and unresolved conflicts from the past. When a grown son disapproves of his father's detachment as a grandfather, he may be reexperiencing the pain he felt as a child at having an uninvolved father. A woman who sees her mother as a rejecting grandmother may be thinking, "So this is how you were: cold and critical."

A major factor here is the powerful identification between parents and children. It is especially intense when children are very young, when — because of their helplessness and undifferentiated sense of self — they really do exist as extensions of their parents. But it continues as children grow, and in some cases intensifies.

For some of those we interviewed, disappointment over a parent's behavior as a grandparent was the decisive factor in bringing about a rupture. Two women we spoke with were so hurt when their fathers ignored their children's birthdays that they subsequently became estranged. It is interesting to note that in both these cases, a somewhat problematic relationship with the father existed to begin with. In one case, the "father" was actually the woman's stepfather, and it seems likely that the divorce exposed a fragility in the relationship that had been there all along. In the other case, the daughter had long felt that her father did not really understand and appreciate her; his forgetfulness of her children's birthdays was the unbearable repetition of an old theme.

These examples illustrate just how close the identification between parent and child can be. A young mother may be acting to protect her child, announcing, "I don't want my son to be hurt by my father like I was." On the other hand, she may be projecting her own unresolved hurts onto her child, unwittingly pulling him into a conflict that began decades before his birth. It is tempting for adult children to deflect feelings of hurt and anger onto their children, expressing indignation on their behalf, as concerned parents, rather than facing their own vulnerability. We spoke with several adult children who told us that because of circumstances surrounding their parents' divorce — an extramarital affair, for example — they did not feel that their parents were "worthy" to be grandparents. One young man said he felt that his father was "no longer a good role model" for the grandson. Certainly, when parents feel that the grandparents are unreliable or hurtful, they have legitimate concerns for their children. But it is very important that they not live out their own unresolved conflicts through the children. One woman we spoke with used her children as her ultimate weapon against her father: "I told my father, 'If you don't do right by Mom, then you're never going to see your grandkids again.' "

The danger, obviously, is in ignoring the true source of pain, while unfairly burdening the youngest generation. Until she sees her mother distraught and enraged, a little girl may have been entirely unaware that her grandfather forgot to send her a birthday card. Worst of all, if she hears her mother describing the forgotten birthday as a reason for the rupture, she may conclude that she is to blame. She was not lovable enough to attract his attention, or she has done some irrevocably bad thing to alienate Grandfather from the family.

Because disruption and reevaluation are such an integral part of the process, parental divorce offers an extraordinary opportunity to explore boundaries, to see more clearly into the unconscious ways in which each individual's selfhood blurs — sometimes in inappropriate and unhealthy ways — with other members of the family. The same insights that arise for adult children in relation to their parents may be relevant in relation to their children as well. One woman told us:

> It was in the wake of my parents' divorce that I realized what an inappropriate closeness there had always been between me and my father. I've actually had several therapists tell me that it was a form of "emotional incest." Because of that, I'm very careful with my son. I try to make it very clear to him that his father and I have a very different kind of relationship than what he and I have. If I hadn't seen all the pieces of the puzzle come apart after my parents split up, I very likely would just have recreated a similar situation with my son, because that's what I grew up with, that's what I knew.

A great many of our respondents found that the divorce forced them into new ways of looking at their parents, new ways of relating to them. They didn't necessarily like those changes, but coming to terms often resulted in a new kind of closeness or, at least, a kind of peace within themselves. As Susan put it, "My relationship with my dad has improved a lot. We've really worked at it. We had a lot of trouble at first and we've had to renegotiate a whole new relationship. He's more of a contemporary now, though at times I still need his fatherliness."

When such renegotiation is possible between parent and adult child, there is a diminishment of the spillover into the grandparent-grandchild relationship. Difficult as it may be for adult children to challenge or even question their own parents, it is an essential task of the maturation process. The addition of a third generation, with its potential for both extending and complicating the issue of boundaries between people, provides yet another stage on which to reenact this drama.

### Overly Involved Grandparents

If some adult children find their parents distressingly aloof and disinterested as grandparents, others complain that in the aftermath of divorce one or both parents have become overly involved.

The scenario is not difficult to imagine: for a man or woman who feels bereft and abandoned in the wake of divorce, grandchildren may represent a bridge back to health, a new core of family. For the adult children involved, such expectations may be a source of conflict and confusion. A daughter may empathize deeply with her mother's sense of loss and longing for connection, yet feel stifled by her need for closeness. Such conflicts happen in intact families, of course — the difference divorce makes is that it may be harder for the adult child to set limits. As one woman told us, "I saw my mother divested of her role as wife after twenty-five years — how could I compound her loss by pushing her away from my family?"

Of course, in such circumstances, tact and sensitivity toward the suffering parent are required. But this problem is still basically one of parent–adult child separation. This daughter may be feeling overly responsible for her mother. Of course, she wants her mother to have a relationship with her children and the family unit. But she must also recognize her mother's need to develop other parts of her life. Allowing her mother to bury herself in the daughter's family will not be growth producing for any of its members. It would be wise for this daughter to encourage her mother in other activities and relationships as well as to include her sometimes with the family.

Achieving this kind of balance may not be possible in the acute initial phase of divorce, but adult children should recognize that extended support and sympathy often encourage dependency. Grandchildren cannot be offered up as compensation for the emptiness in a grandparent's life. Eventually some "tough love" may be required, just as it is often necessary for parents to push their children out of a too-comfortable nest.

## Competing, Conflictual Grandparents

Perhaps hardest to live with are the grandparents who openly compete for their grandchildren's time and attention. A few of those we interviewed complained that both parents insisted on being in on every special occasion — usually resulting in grandchildren who were frazzled and exhausted with two takes of each birthday and holiday.

Like parents who continue to wage their battles through their children, some grandparents seemed locked in their own version of a custody battle over the grandchildren. One son complained, "It seems like my parents are trying to score points with each other — who got to spend last weekend with the grandkids and who's going to spend this one. Sometimes I wonder if they ever stop long enough to really enjoy the children."

When young grandchildren become caught in a tug-of-war between perpetually conflictual grandparents, it is up to their parents to step in. It is not always easy, however, to determine when such a tug-of-war exists, and if the children are being showered with attention and gifts, it can be hard for parents to impose limits. One helpful gauge is to observe the children's behavior after returning from a visit with a grandparent. Does the child seem anxious, withdrawn, or in some way exhibiting unusual behavior? Is the child repeating negative remarks about one grandparent or suddenly showing a strong favoritism for one grandparent? If this occurs, then parents should find a way to observe what actually goes on during visits.

Even in the absence of such tangible symptoms, a parent's deep sense of unease should be taken seriously. If troubling questions and disturbing doubts continue, it would be wise to seek professional counseling in order to decide whether the nature and amount of contact between the grandchildren and grandparents need to be limited.

## Divorce in Two Generations

Sadly, for some children, their grandparents' divorce is a painful replay of their parents'.

Loreen was eighteen when her grandparents divorced. What hurt most was to relive, through her mother, the pain of her own parents' divorce ten years earlier. It created a strange role reversal for her, casting her in the role of the experienced one. Though her grandparents' divorce was painful in itself and stirred up many of her own saddest memories, she had to be the strong, supportive confidante for her mother and had little opportunity to work through her own loss.

Ericka's teenage daughter told her, "I'll probably get married and divorced a lot of times." Ericka told us, "It's very hard for me to hear her say that. Yet I guess it's better than having a completely unrealistic view of marriage."

## How to Cope with a Child's Anxieties

Older children who have grown attached to their grandparents as a pair are likely to be the most upset when divorce occurs. But children who are very young at the time of divorce will experience their own measure of distress. How best to respond to a child's anxieties when grandparents divorce?

Younger children are generally most concerned with their own immediate security. Most upsetting to them will be their parent's intense emotions in the wake of the grandparents' divorce. These emotions take focus and energy away from the children's needs, and they give the impression that a parent is vulnerable and not in control. Parents often worry about showing their feelings to their young children. However, children need to realize that grief and anger are emotions experienced by all human beings, old and young. Parents are humans, not gods. Seeing a parent weep will be momentarily upsetting, of course, but the world will not end. The parent will not shatter. Dad can still laugh, Mom can still play Candyland.

Because they experience deep, intense emotions, children can relate these easily to themselves. Too many intimate details of the grandparents' relationship is much more distressing to children because of their limited ability to process such information.

Of course, we are speaking about moderation, about occasional bouts of intense feelings. A mother who spends much of every day crying is not going to be available for parenting. If a father's major preoccupation is his parents' divorce, that is excessive. Emotions should help us to learn and to grow. If we are paralyzed or remain stuck in the same quagmire of feelings, it is time to seek professional help. And that, too — the fact that grown-ups sometimes need to reach for help — is something that children can learn from.

Parents who are very distraught have a responsibility *to their children* as well as to themselves to seek adequate help. Beyond this, children need to be reassured that while Mommy or Daddy is very upset right now, things will get better. They need to be reassured — if indeed it is the case — that their own mommy and daddy are still together and plan to stay that way. Lastly, they need to be told by both their parents and their grandparents that their grandparents will continue to love them, even though they will no longer be living together.

Older children will most likely want more in the way of explanation. A good rule of thumb is to keep explanations as general and nonaccusatory as possible: "Grandma wanted to explore and have adventures now that she's retired, and Grandpa just wanted to say home" or "You know Grandma and Grandpa have always had a hard time agreeing about things, and they finally decided they would both be happier on their own." More detailed information about the specific nature of the conflict, and especially details of sexual history, are likely to be very disturbing to children, even though they may insist on wanting to know. It is difficult to provide information without making them anxious about their own parents' marriage. Even to say something as neutral as "People sometimes grow apart over time" may make them fearful. The best approach is to say with sincerity, "It's very upsetting to all of us that Grandma and Grandpa won't be together anymore. I plan to try to learn from their difficulties so that it won't happen to us."

It is important to remember, however, that children overhear much more than adults realize. Hushed conversations in another room or on the phone are often picked up by children who seem to be busily playing or engrossed in their own affairs. Parents do need to encourage their children to talk about the situation, to ask questions, to find out what they think, and to express their concerns. It is surprising how often children have peculiar misconceptions that adults would never think of and hence cannot address unless they ask and listen.

## Healing Bond

In some families, children do become the catalyst for healing.

Peter was one of several who told us that it was when the grandchildren came along that his parents were at last able to put aside some of their ancient grievances and relate harmoniously as grandparents.

Stories like these represent the longing of most adult children who are parents themselves, the longing to see their own children greeted and supported by a loving and harmonious extended family. But once again, such happy endings cannot be forced. When they happen, it is because the underlying ground of the family is ready for such a transformation. Such readiness occurs when the adults involved, whether explicitly or at a more unconscious level, begin to let go of ancient griefs and anger and to move past rigid, habitual patterns of relating. Adult children cannot accomplish such transformations for their parents — and *their* children cannot do so for their grandparents. When the soil has been prepared, the coming of a grandchild can be like a tiny seed that bursts into flower. But when the ground is not ready, it is dangerous for adult children to try to cast their children into the role of peacemaker.

When divorced partners are not able to come together in their role as grandparents, this is yet another grief that adult children must face. On the other side of this grief is the realization that for adult children as parents, the crucial sphere of influence lies in their own nuclear family. Really all that adult children can alter significantly for the sake of their children is the quality of family life in their own home. It is here that we have heard the most positive stories from the widest spectrum of those we interviewed. These mothers and fathers want to make something good out of the pain by learning better ways of making a family, new ways of resolving conflict.

## A Clear Sense of Priorities

Despite the extraordinary stress, the complications and reawakened griefs, that accompanied parenting in the wake of their parents' divorce, nearly all of those we spoke with agreed that having children had been a source of comfort, strength, and inspiration. One woman told us that her husband and children were her "refuge." "I have to let go of my first family," she said, "but the love I get from my husband and children is really healing."

Others told us that having a family of their own had helped them to clarify what really mattered to them and to marshal their own best energies in that direction. It had also given them the courage to say no, to set limits when the needs of their parents threatened to engulf them. As one woman said, "There are things that I would go along with myself that I just wouldn't put up with when my children came along."

Some acknowledged that sometimes they felt pressured to have the "perfect family." One woman said, "My parents are divorced and now my sister is divorcing, so sometimes I feel that I have to provide the model family." Another woman echoed, "With my parents divorced and my husband's two siblings divorcing, sometimes I feel that we're the token family, that I have the full responsibility for being a family."

This pressure was felt most intensely when it came from within. One woman told us, "I want to be able to provide my daughter with a model family, but often I just don't know how to proceed." She was one of several people who told us that it was only in the aftermath of their parents' divorce that they realized what a tense and unhealthy atmosphere they had grown up in. They felt they had been given very few skills in communication, and sometimes they felt very handicapped in dealing with their own children. As Tess observed:

> I feel that the breakdown between my parents came about because of the total lack of communication in our family. Sometimes it is incredibly difficult and painful for me with my husband, and sometimes I feel so bad in front of my daughter that I can't provide her with a better model. But recently I had what seemed like a very important realization: I can only do the best I can.

The good news here is that parental divorce can provide adult children with a powerful impetus to tend their own hearth, to keep their own marriage and family life healthy and vital. One woman expressed a view that was echoed by many others:

> If your parents divorced, it's likely that their marriage always had problems. In my family, we never could communicate well. But with my children I feel a greater openness than I've ever felt before in my life. In my family we were always very repressed about anger, but with my children I find I can get angry in a very simple, direct way. I express what's on my mind — and then it just dissolves. This is such a revelation to me — that it's possible to get angry and still be in touch with the love and the trust. I feel it's a wonderful secret that my children have taught me.

Fortunately, a united pair of grandparents is not necessary to the development of a healthy and happy child. What *is* necessary is a parent who is able to work through the grief of his or her own parents' divorce. During the acute initial phase, sometimes it may seem impossible to function adequately as a parent. At such times, it is part of being a good parent to seek adequate support for oneself. It is when parents deny their own pain, forcing themselves to live up to unrealistic expectations, that they risk harming their children.

More important than anything is perspective: the extreme sense of loss and disorientation will not last forever. It is imperative to work through the grief, so that unconscious cycles of suffering will not be passed on through the generations. Ultimately, the kinds of revelations and restructured relationships that come out of divorce may be, for the grandchildren, the most valuable inheritance of all.

# 12

## *Holidays and Special Events*

Months before each holiday season, the barrage of images begins, defining the "perfect day," exhorting us to attain it. If it's Christmas, then it's red and green, the sparkle of gold, the scent of pine. It's snow falling gently outside the windowpanes, while inside, a multigenerational family is blissfully opening presents. . . . From all sides comes the message: On this day you shall experience intense pleasure of the senses, happy reunion with family and friends, the joy of giving and receiving, the reenactment of cherished traditions.

No wonder that so many experience anxiety and disappointment instead. Popular magazines abound with articles on coping with holiday stress, and it is common knowledge that both depression and suicide rates peak at the holiday season.

Intensifying the media blitz from without, there is the powerful storehouse of memories that each of us carries within. Every holiday is the anniversary of a previous holiday, inviting comparison with other, perhaps happier times. Some mourn the lost magic of childhood, the passing of youth, the relatives no longer present.

Because holidays are so closely linked to the past, it is common to revert to an earlier, more infantile self. Uncle throws a

238

tantrum because the roast is overdone; Grandmother sulks because the sweater wasn't quite what she wanted. Emotions are close to the surface, and there is little room for escape or privacy. Visiting relatives come, and living space is cramped. Familiar routines are broken: people live out of suitcases, overeat, drink too much, and don't find time for the morning jog or the late-night bath that usually restores composure.

All of this means that when each big holiday arrives, the emotional background is already very loaded. Add divorce to the equation, and the stress increases exponentially. As more than one person put it, "Since my parents divorced, being home for the holidays feels like tiptoeing through a minefield."

One of the reasons that holidays remain such a pivotal issue in the minds of many adult children is that they seem to reveal the very essence of what the family has become. As one young man told us:

In between the big events, you can sort of forget about things or remember how they used to be. But then Christmas or graduation or a wedding comes around, and it's all there staring you in the face: *this* is what my family is. This collection of individuals who live in different houses and require complicated seating arrangements.

Indeed, some researchers use holidays and special events as an important index of a family's postdivorce adjustment.[1]

In some families, the holiday stress begins months in advance when plans must be made as to how the time will be divided, given that traditional ways of celebrating can no longer be assumed. In place of the glow of anticipation, there are tense negotiations about the holiday itself and often a renewal of old conflicts surrounding the divorce.

No matter how carefully plans are laid, when the big day rolls around, there's often anger at both parents, guilt at neglecting one of them, or the exhaustion of running back and forth between both. For those lucky enough to have parents who can be in the same room together, there's the strangeness and strain of carrying on as though everything were just the same.

Underneath it all is the pain of loss. There's an acute awareness that the family is not what it used to be, and there's the feeling of having lost the holiday itself. The two are inextricably linked. For many people, particularly in our secular age when many of the religious associations have faded, the meaning of each holiday lies in connection with family. At the same time, holidays are one of the primary ways that families define themselves: "Our family opens up presents on Christmas Eve, *never* on Christmas morning" or "We always spend the holidays at my grandmother's house up in the mountains." The very essence of holidays is repetition, continuity, unbroken tradition, and our attachments to the smallest details run deep.

There is a special sadness when the holidays of young children are clouded by the pain of divorce: they're being deprived of an enchantment that, once lost or never experienced, cannot be retrieved. But there is also a special sadness for adult children. Many grown children see their parents and siblings only on holidays; the rest of the year they relate through telephone and correspondence. This means that even in intact families, the holidays are emotionally charged. There is readjustment to living under a single roof, confusion as to parent-child roles, pressure to store up a year's worth of togetherness. Divorce intensifies these pressures immeasurably.

Imagine how it is for the young man who has just gone off to college. He's made it through the first tumultuous months, adjusting to dorm life, dining-hall food, hordes of new faces, new academic pressures. He's made it through September . . . October . . . most of November. . . . Then Thanksgiving comes along, the first big holiday since he's been away. The students around him are packing their bags in excited anticipation. He, too, longs to go home, to be greeted at the door and wrapped in the familiar: to be in his old room, see his old friends, taste his mother's cooking. But he is full of anxiety — he is going home to adjustments even more difficult than those he has just faced. Family members will be tense, if not openly grieving or raging;

the house will be half-empty or full of packing boxes: his family and his past no longer exist in the same way.

He comes back to school depleted, emotionally burdened, knowing that along with the papers and final exams that mark the semester's end, he must brace himself for the really big holidays ahead. One student told her parents, "I'm spending Thanksgiving at McDonald's. Then you'll both miss me."[2] Some in our study complained that their parents had saved up their grievances and their most difficult decisions for their child's return. "I walked in the door and my mother just burst," one young woman told us. "I didn't even have time to put my suitcase down."

For the young woman who is already out in the world but still unattached and unsettled, the situation is not much better. She does not yet have a home or a family of her own, and her friends go off to be with their parents. Where the holidays might have provided a sense of reconnection with the past and reintegration with the family — a welcome respite from the struggles of her own life — now they intensify the sense of uncertainty and fragmentation.

For young married couples, there is already the tremendous adjustment of sharing holidays together. Do we go to his family or mine? Do we practice her family's traditions or mine? When one set of parents is divorced, there seems no end to the questions, the decisions, the complicated negotiations that arise. Marcy said, "It was shortly after our parents' divorce that my sister and I both married. It was so difficult and awkward to try to incorporate two new sons-in-law into a family that was falling apart."

For married couples with children, there's another kind of pain. Often it is the experience of becoming a parent that first awakens the longing for family tradition. Many grown children lament that at the very moment they began to cherish that tradition, it was extinguished. They had eagerly looked forward to lighting the menorah or decorating the Christmas tree as an extended family, drawing their children into a sense of history and reliving vicariously the magic of their own childhood. Holiday times make them feel with special sadness and sometimes bitterness that the legacy for their children is a broken one.

## Dealing with Anxiety

Anticipation and memory are built into the very structure of holidays and special events. This helps to explain the obsessive, even phobic nature of the anxiety that some people feel. As one woman told us, "The constant, dread-filled thoughts begin months before each family gathering. And when something does go wrong, it's so hard for me to forget about it. It's in my mind like a full-color Kodak moment. Here's Mom snarling at Dad on Easter Sunday."

There are different ways of handling such intense and persistent anxiety. Because some families avoid any meaningful contact throughout most of the year, significant issues are buried and repressed, surfacing only when the family comes together at special events. This places far too much pressure on occasions that are already highly charged. When underlying losses and conflicts are faced with greater openness in the context of daily living, anxiety surrounding special events will lessen.

On a less fundamental level, there are certain specific techniques that may be helpful. Some people suggest setting aside a certain amount of time — fifteen minutes in the morning, for example — that is devoted entirely to worrying. When they find themselves dreading the upcoming event, they remind themselves to worry about it during the specific time that has been set aside. As contrived as this may sound, it's a way to face the dark thoughts without letting them color the entire day.

Another technique is to question the underlying thoughts that are feeding the fear. One woman told us, "I ask myself, 'What is it I'm so afraid of?' And often I find it's something really irrational, like 'I'm afraid that when I look at my father's wife I'm going to die.' When I say it like that, and especially if I write it down, I see how irrational it is, and then I can let go." Once one faces the question, What is the worst thing that can happen? — even if the answer is not irrational — it loses some of its power to frighten.

Others find it helpful to imagine the event moment by moment, actually rehearsing a plan for each contingency. "And if my father's girlfriend and I should happen to rub elbows, I'll just look her right in the eye and say, 'Hello. How are you doing?' and then I'll move on."

A word of obvious advice is to do something deeply relaxing before arriving at the event: strenuous exercise, meditation, or a long walk through the woods. It can also be helpful to plan something very pleasurable and stress free for right after the event. This then becomes a happy, alternate focus for those anxious, anticipatory thoughts.

## Practical Solutions

For those who've come to some kind of truce with the holidays, the secret lies in what one man described as "figuring out the formula." In the examples that follow, we provide a spectrum of possible "formulas," as well as some of the difficulties inherent in each one. As whenever we suggest practical strategies in this book, one family's solution can't simply be borrowed as is. What each family eventually arrives at must evolve organically from its own unique history, its own special mix of needs and expectations. Also, a solution that works at one point in time may no longer be viable a few years later. As parents remarry, as grown children form their own intimate relationships, as grandchildren arrive, new ways of coming together will have to evolve. The search for the holiday solution is best seen as an ongoing, constantly changing process.

### One Parent Becomes the Center

In many families, whether by conscious choice or tacit assumption, one parent becomes designated as the holiday parent. The obvious advantage of this solution is its simplicity. It is much less tiring and confusing to be rooted in one spot than to shuttle back and forth between two households. If one parent has retained the family home, then this solution offers the best possibility of keeping up family traditions. When the divorce itself has been perceived as an unequal situation, then this seems like the easy choice and the just response. As one young man told us, "Mom dumped Dad and moved in with her boyfriend, so there was never any question as to where we'd go for the holidays — we went to Dad's."

Often, alas, the situation is more complicated, the emotions more ambivalent. Even when one parent has clearly been wronged, still there are feelings for the other parent. Often in these situations there's a silent message being sent to the absent parent: "You deserted us, but we're still a family; we can carry on without you." But for the first year or more, it doesn't feel like a family when one parent is missing. People describe it as "an ache," "an emptiness," "a huge crater in the middle of my family." One man said it reminded him of those records called "Music Minus One." Another woman told us:

> That first Christmas without my father, it felt like a phantom limb. I had all these "impulses" that went towards him, like coming down the stairs and expecting to see him, lighting the fire as he always did on Christmas morning, or opening up some funny gift and wanting to show him . . . and he wasn't there.

Even to acknowledge such feelings for the absent, often deserting parent seems like a betrayal: several people described sneaking upstairs or to a back bedroom to place a secretive phone call to the other parent. Along with the guilt, there are other conflicting emotions. As one woman described it: "I'd call my dad, and if he was lonely, then I'd feel sad and like I was letting him down. But if he had told me he was doing just great without us, then I would have felt hurt and angry." Even the simple act of opening a gift may become fraught with tension. If your father has sent a gift to you at your mother's house, do you open it in front of her? One woman said:

> After the divorce, my father began to give me gifts of really beautiful clothing for my birthday and at Christmas. In the past, my mother had always bought me such

gifts, so I had never really had an opportunity to see what he might choose for me, and I was really very touched and flattered. But at the same time, it made me uncomfortable. The gifts seemed more like what he used to give my mother, and actually, what he picked out tended to be *her* colors, not mine. My mother would see me wearing something he'd given me, and she would say, "How beautiful. Where did you get that?"

Some experience a conflict between their own adult sense of responsibility and the childish desires that holidays stir up. If Dad is alone, who will make the holiday bright for him? If Mom is alone, how will she cope with the empty day? One woman told us, "I knew I had to be with my mother over the holiday, because she was the really needy one, but I knew we'd be having much more fun at my dad's — and, of course, I felt guilty for even having such a thought." Meanwhile, those who stick with Dad sometimes complain that the atmosphere is bleak and bereft; in our culture, it is more often mothers who deck the halls, bake the sweets, and exude the holiday aura.

Concerns for parents are powerful feelings in adult children, yet holidays bring up longings for the treasures of the past, the desire to be a child again, coming down the stairs on Christmas morning. Adults know this cannot be but have adapted to the gradual change, aided by the yearly reenactment of family rituals. When these are lost through divorce, the longings are intensified. This is another situation that makes adult children feel ashamed of their own needs, often labeling them as childish or selfish: "How can I feel this way at twenty-six?" or "I should be thinking about how awful this is for Mom, not worrying about myself."

A further sense of fragmentation occurs when siblings are divided in their loyalties: Brother always goes to Mother's house, Sister to Father's. As one woman described it, "My brother was much younger than me and still lived at home with our mother. On holidays, according to custody arrangements, he generally went to my dad's. That would have left my mother completely alone, so I always went to her house, but then I had a double loss of both my father and my brother."

Some adult children feel that they are being used as pawns when the holidays come. In the absence of the custody battles that plague families with young children, holidays often become the prime source of contention in late-divorce families, especially when grandchildren are involved. "I felt that my mother was using us to punish my father," one woman told us, "and though I felt very sorry for her, I felt very resentful, too — and it really darkened the holidays for us."

What others feel is somewhat more subtle; not so much that they're being used to get revenge as to shore up one parent's fantasy that the family is still intact. For newly single parents, struggling with anger, grief, and loneliness, the reenactment of familiar holiday rituals is a way of holding on to the past, both for themselves and for "the children." Those "children," meanwhile, may feel compelled to participate in keeping that fantasy alive for themselves as well as for the parent. Thus the holiday celebration is overburdened by multiple needs and feelings.

Diane remembered:

The first Christmas was terrible because my dad was leaving. The second Christmas was terrible because my sister, who was married and had a new baby by then, wanted to have Christmas at her house. That was her way of coming to terms with the change — but my mother wanted to continue being the matriarch, and she was devastated.

In some families the one-parent pattern is established early on, when one parent seems clearly more vulnerable, or when the other parent has not yet had time to set up a separate household. As the years go by, this pattern begins to feel less appropriate. One man told us:

We fell into the thing of always going to my mom's for the holidays. She was the one who had been left, and besides — it seems like it's usually more the mom who does the holiday thing. But then things changed. They both got remarried, and now Dad had a house and a wife, and he started to want us to come there, too.

There's the sense that a new solution is needed, but the very prospect stirs up anxiety. One woman said:

Three years after my mom left, we told my dad that we thought we shouldn't *always* be at his place on the holidays. It was terrible — almost like going through certain parts of the divorce again — with all his feelings of being abandoned and rage at my mother — and so we just gave up on the idea.

Two suggestions for those whose parents have recently divorced are to remember that the first year's solution may not necessarily provide the blueprint for all future holidays and to be flexible as circumstances change over the years.

### Equal Shares

The other solution most often favored by families involves some method of divvying up the holidays. The obvious advantage here is a greater sense of balance and equitableness, and once the method has been decided upon it can proceed relatively smoothly.

Families that live in the same area often divide the day itself: Christmas brunch at Mom's, supper at Dad's. The major disadvantage of this solution is the frantic sense of rushing back and forth: "You eat one huge meal at one house, and then before you've even digested it, you're off to eat another huge meal on the other side of town." "You can't ever relax." "I used to love to linger around the Christmas tree after opening presents, but now we have to pack up the car and move on." "It reminds me of those progressive dinners you hear about in L.A. You eat the main course at one house, then pile into the car and drive on the freeway for an hour to reach dessert. Real relaxing!" These are a few in the long litany of complaints we heard. Parents with children were especially emphatic about how exhausting this arrangement was. Oddly, though, families who had chosen this formula seemed least able to imagine any other possibility. It seemed unthinkable to not see both parents on each major holiday.

What other families find just as equitable and less exhausting is to alternate holidays: Dad's for Thanksgiving, Mom's for Chanukah. Next year, it can be Mom's for Thanksgiving, Dad's for Chanukah. The sadness here is that, as one woman put it, "On each holiday, there's one parent whom you miss and feel sorry for." Another woman told us that a solution she and her brother had come up with was to make a Christmas video for the absent parent.

### Grand Mixer

In a smaller percentage of families, everyone, including both parents and sometimes even new spouses and grandparents from both sides, manages to get together for the holidays. While some testify to a certain amount of strain, others insist that — given enough rum in the eggnog and general commotion — holidays feel "almost like old times."

Elizabeth comes from a truly unusual clan. When she first began to describe her family, she laughed almost apologetically and said,

> If I were to try and explain to you all the connections in my family, you would think it was almost incestuous. Every few years my family seems to break up and re-group, and the holidays reflect that. Both my parents come with their spouses and my grandparents are there with their new spouses, and there are ex-spouses — and it's basically the same set of people, but in different arrangements.

It is tempting to see Elizabeth's family as a kind of cheerful, polymorphous family of the future, freed of neurotic attachments, wonderfully flexible and forgiving. However, even as she painted a picture of happy holiday "regrouping," it was hard not to remember the tears that came earlier in the interview when she spoke of her recurring dreams of abandonment.

A more realistic description of "a grand mixer" was given us by Peter. He told us that once a year, the extended family comes together — including both parents and their new spouses. His mother's current husband actually refers to her ex-husband as his brother-in-law. "And how is it for everyone?" we asked in astonishment. "Well," he said, sighing deeply, "we work at it."

## The Adult Child as the Center

For those who tire of difficult negotiations and harried shuttling back and forth, a viable solution is to make one's own home the center for holiday activities.

Tess told us:

> I got so sick of the whole complicated business, never knowing who was going where and feeling guilty wherever we went, that I just decided: I'm going to do it. I'm just going to have a kind of open house, and whoever wants to come, can come. It's up to them to behave — and since it's my house and I feel like I'm doing most of the work, it makes it easier for me to say, "Stop drinking, Dad," or "Quit yelling, Mom."

For this solution to work, there must be some minimal ability on the part of all family members to get along, or at least the willingness to try. It is important to remember that family members are rarely at the same state of openness or ease in relating to one another. Serious conflicts arise when one member of the family insists that everyone should be able to get along. One sibling's invitation to an open house may be perceived by others as a dare or test: "Are you mature enough to be in the same room together?" In such cases, it is not doors or hearts that are opened, but old wounds and battlefields.

Where the willingness does exist, however, this solution can be a very satisfying one. It works best for adult children who are settled enough to have created their own sense of home, especially those who have children of their own.

## When All Else Fails

In some families, even years after the divorce, tensions in general, and at holiday times in particular, are so great that a very different kind of solution has to be reached.

One man, after five years of struggle, gave up on his own family and chose to spend holidays with his in-laws. One woman declared that the holidays would just be for her, her husband, and their two young children. Another woman, who at thirty-two is living alone and unattached, says she uses the holidays as her private retreat time. "I work very hard all year and I have lots of friends. When holidays come, it's my special time to be alone."

There are few adult children who do not remember the anguish of the first important holiday following their parents' divorce. Some have memories that evoke nothing so much as the Last Supper. Susanna told us about the Christmas her family spent just before her father moved out of the house. Her mother sat silently in her chair as they took turns opening presents; every now and again she got up to take a photograph of their "last Christmas" as a family.

When we asked adult children to think back to this time, many refused, saying it was too painful. Some said that for several years after the divorce, each big holiday seemed like a reenactment of the divorce. An added pain for many was that the news of divorce had first been given on a holiday, when all the family was gathered together; for a long time after, that holiday was remembered as the anniversary of the divorce.

Almost all agree that the acute pain subsides after a year or two. Sadly, however, holidays remain a recurring source of tension for many families, even ten and fifteen years later.

When parents remarry, new tensions are introduced. As one woman said following her father's remarriage, "The family traditions are all changed. I'm sentimental and when we don't keep them somewhat the same, it says that what we did before was the wrong way."[3]

On a positive note, some find that their parents' divorce, in this as in many other ways, allows them to break with patterns that have become rather empty and confining. Several people told us that it was in the rubble of their parents' divorce that they were able to discover the lost spiritual meaning of such holidays as Christmas, Passover, or Easter.

Laura said:

That first Christmas we were all gathered around the tree with my mother, feeling totally strange and disoriented without my dad. We started singing the little songs we always sang, going through the motions of our familiar childhood Christmas. But it felt really hollow. Finally one of us said, "Hey, we don't want to go through this charade. Things have changed. We need to create some new rituals." And we have.

## Special Events

Birthdays, weddings, graduations, anniversaries: these are like holidays in that they come charged with a sense of tradition and they stir up powerful expectations of happiness and family harmony. They bring other pressures, too. While Thanksgiving and Christmas are general cultural holidays, birthdays and graduations belong to a single family member. There's a sense of unfairness when parental divorce overshadows one person's special occasion. Other events, such as weddings, are meant to be once-in-a-lifetime recurrences. When divorce clouds over such an event, there's the sense of something irrevocably lost.

Just as many adult children first receive the news of divorce on a holiday, for others the news breaks on a special occasion. Sometimes it's the milestone event in the life of a child that triggers a crisis in the parent. It was on Joan's graduation from high school that her father left the family. "He told my mother he was going to get a package of flashcubes, and he just never came back." Joan was eighteen at the time; she is now in her fifties. Even today, the pain of that memory is intense: "I just couldn't believe that he could do that to me on such an important day of my life."

Unfortunately, we heard many stories of personal celebratory events that required weeks of negotiations with parents and that still ended in minor or major confrontations between the parents or between parents and the adult child — the one who was to be the honoree. All too often, one person's special event becomes a forum for family members to struggle with the unfinished business of the divorce.

Kate was struggling in anticipation of her baby's baptism. Would she invite both parents? What if they couldn't get along? Did she have to invite her father's new wife, too? Could she invite her in-laws and not her own parents? Finally, after reaching a peak of anxiety, she decided, "I had to focus on the *baptism* itself. And that helped me realize that the ceremony was for our new baby; for us, the parents; and for the godparents. That helped me put it into perspective."

Kate's insight provides a helpful clue for dealing with virtually any holiday or special event. The pain of such occasions is to feel the rupture with the past, the fragmentation of one's family, the clash between expectations and reality. In being painfully uprooted from some of our deepest attachments, we are simultaneously freed to ask, "What *is* the real meaning of this occasion?" For some this will bring the discovery of new and ultimately more fulfilling traditions. At the very least, it suggests that we can learn to adjust our focus. If tensions and conflict persist between our parents or other family members, they don't have to be in the foreground of each holiday; we can learn to let them recede. No matter what our family dynamics, Easter is still a celebration of springtime and renewal; New Year a time for letting go and moving on.

# 13

## *What to Do? Emotional and Practical Strategies*

**W**e've seen the dangers involved when children attempt an all-out rescue of their parents. Such attempts tend to reinforce negative family patterns, to exhaust and deplete the rescuer, while promoting an unhealthy dependence and crippling the self-esteem of the "rescuee." Yet most children want to be of help to their parents, at least to the parent whom they perceive to be most hurt by the divorce. In what follows, then, we address the adult child who asks, What kind of help can I appropriately and realistically give?

Of course, the range of possibilities is nearly infinite. The needs and resources of different families vary so greatly that no simple blueprint of dos and don'ts is possible. One of the most important things to remember is to try to keep your own needs separate, to be sure that you're not fixing up a parent's life in order to bury your own pain, boost your own self-esteem, or show up your other parent.

An important first step is to assess realistically how much you can give — an assessment that may vary from day to day. If all last week you helped your mother move, a brief telephone conversation may be all you can manage today. You cannot be

253

genuinely helpful when your own reserves are depleted. These are the moments when your anguish and anger will burst forth and intensify the pain of your needy parent. There are times, of course, when you will cry together — but not when you are trying to be of practical help.

Second, it is important to assess your own emotional support system. Is there a good listener in your life, someone whose presence is comforting and renewing? Darcy told us, "Every night when my fiancé picked me up at home, I would cry in his arms for half an hour or so, telling him about the latest scene between my parents who were still both living in the house. I could never have gotten through that time without him." If you are feeling well supported, you will have more to give your parents and will feel less resentful of the times when they seem lost in their own pain.

Before launching into action on any front, the following questions can serve as a useful touchstone:

What can I do for my parents
1. that will best help them to catalyze their own strength and preserve their self-esteem;
2. that does not reinforce negative family patterns;
3. that makes good use of my own best skills;
4. that will not create a serious, long-term disruption in my own life?

Of course, in the first months after separation a parent may be so distraught and disorganized that it is necessary to step in and play a very active role: serving as an emotional first line of defense, making and actually carrying out some of the practical decisions, watching over health and diet, taking care of basic household needs, and making sure the bills are paid. But even in the midst of such total immersion, it's important to keep a sense of perspective and to prepare the ground for greater independence in the future: "Here are your groceries, Dad. When you're feeling a little better, we'll go to the store together so you can learn where things are." "I've taken care of all your bills this month, Mom. For next month, I've made out a schedule that shows you when each bill needs to be paid."

It is difficult to keep a sense of perspective without imposing an agenda: "It's been six months; you should be over your depression by now." The real issue here concerns the *boundaries* between parent and child, not the time frame of healing. The acute initial phase may last six months or much longer; what is important is that during this time, the adult child helps the parent in a way that fosters *mutual* independence, that honors the separate being of both parent and child and acknowledges the parent's inner strength and capacity for healing. Of course, this is much more easily said than done.

Impatience sometimes comes from the fear that a parent's current state of misery will go on forever. It won't — but recovery may take much longer than the child imagines. Even a sensitive adult child may have trouble understanding the complexity of late divorce, the profound interdependence that exists between the long married, the difficulty of forging a new, separate self.

## Should You Try to Reconcile Your Parents?

Some children wonder whether they should try to prevent their parents' divorce. As adults, they may feel it is their responsibility to do so. Among others a common complaint is that they were told too late: "If only I'd known earlier. I would have convinced them to work things out."

It is true that some couples do come to regret the decision to divorce and feel they did so for the wrong reasons. In such situations, it's understandable that their children feel a deep frustration that so much pain and disruption might have been prevented.

But how to tell if your parents are potentially such a couple? Professionals in the divorce field sometimes speak of a *reactive divorce*. This is a divorce that comes not out of deep and abiding marital unhappiness but rather as a response to external stress or to one partner's temporary internal crisis.

Some professional counselors do strongly attempt to discourage divorce in such cases. But should this be your role as a child? Remember that you are *not* an objective observer or a disinterested party. Remember that many adult children — especially those from stable and reasonably harmonious families — are not fully aware of the depth of their parents' unhappiness. It may seem to you like the divorce is "coming out of the blue" when in fact one or both parents have been suffering for years.

If you feel strongly, and on the basis of good evidence, that your parents are on the brink of a reactive divorce that they will later come to regret, then communicate this fact to them. Urge them to seek counseling. If you yourself are married and have weathered a similar crisis, then share your experience with them. But do not engage in the emotional blackmail of your parents. They must make a decision based on an honest assessment of their genuine, long-term needs — not on your pain at first hearing the news.

We did speak with one woman who, along with her siblings, had persuaded her parents to stay together. "Are you glad you did?" we asked her. Her response was very ambivalent. "I'm glad my family is still together," she said. "But I think my mother is just as unhappy in the marriage as she ever was." It is hard to assess the path not taken. However, we did hear many stories along these lines: "I was devastated when my parents broke up. But now it's hard for me to imagine how they stayed together for so many years. Though I'll always miss my family as it used to be, I can honestly say that my parents are better off apart."

## Helping Your Parents Get Help

One of the most important things you can do is encourage your parents to get good help. This can be an excellent way of expanding your parents' resources, without getting overly involved yourself. Most communities offer some form of support to divorcing individuals in the form of family service agencies, divorce mediation centers, support groups for the newly single. Every county in the country has its own Displaced Homemakers program, which offers support and guidance for separated, divorced, and widowed women. (For information, you may contact the National Displaced Homemakers Network, 1411 K St. NW, Suite 930, Washington, D.C. 20005, 202-628-6767.) Many communities have chapters of Women in Transition, a support group that is based on the excellent book of that title. How to locate this information? Look in the yellow pages under such headings as "Counselors," "Divorce Counseling," "Marriage, Family, Child & Individual Counselors," "Human Services Organizations," "Career & Vocational Counseling," "Social Service Organizations," or see if your library has an index of human resources in your area.

Some children find that their parents are reluctant at first to identify as a divorcé or a displaced homemaker. In this case, it is best not to push. Instead, you might encourage them to seek the support of a good friend or relative, especially if they know someone who has gone through a divorce. There are many excellent books to guide the newly divorced or divorcing, and a list is provided at the end of this chapter.

When should you encourage parents to seek professional counseling? When they seem depressed, disorganized, or disturbed for more than a few weeks, they may be amenable to the suggestion. When they are so paralyzed by anxiety or depression that they are unable to make certain urgent and important decisions or are making them in a rash and imprudent way, you may be more aggressive in pushing the idea. When they are engaging in behavior that is seriously detrimental to their health — excessive drinking, disturbed sleeping or eating patterns, reckless driving, or extremely promiscuous sexual behavior, you should press hard for treatment. Of course, any sign of suicidal tendencies should be treated with utmost seriousness.

## Basic Emotional Support

More important than anything is to give your assurance of continued love and support. A person whose marriage has failed after twenty or more years is often a person whose self-confidence has been shattered and who is haunted by feelings that it has all been a waste. As the tangible product of the marriage, you are vitally important; you are the living, breathing sign that *all was not for naught.* The bonds of marriage may have dissolved, but the parent-child bond has not. It is you who now offer the deepest sense of continuity, the link with the past and the promise of the future. In whatever way you can find — if you are not too racked by anger or hurt and can do so sincerely — express your love and concern.

It is often hard to remember that the parent who initiated the split also needs your love and support. Despite all the advantages of being the initiator, this person, too, may be in great pain, experiencing loneliness, guilt, fear of the uncertain future — and fear above all of losing contact with *you.* We spoke with one mother who, after years of unhappiness, had finally found the courage to leave her very domineering husband. Her children were distraught and angry, but one of them was able to empathize with her mother's pain. The mother told us:

> My daughter sent me a card. Inside it she had written, "I will always love and support you, no matter what you do." I can't tell you how much that meant to me. It was one of my first nights alone in a little motel room. I felt so frightened and alone. I put the card on my night table, and that's what got me through the night. I kept waking up, and then I'd turn the light on and read it again. . . .

Respect the mourning process, while encouraging a sense of openness toward the future. One divorce counselor we spoke with tells people, "It feels like your life is over now, but it's a *pause* — and a new life will emerge."[1] Help your parents to build bridges between their past and the future by reminding them of past strengths and accomplishments.

### *"Don't Just Do Something, Stand There —"*

A technique called *reflective listening* is one recommended by many therapists. Rather than feeling that you must interpret or give an answer to your parent's remarks, you listen attentively and rephrase what you hear. When your mother tells you for the eighth time, "How can I go on when my whole life has been demolished before my eyes?" you may respond by saying, "I understand that right now you feel devastated and have lost the structure your life has been based on." When your father says, "I can't manage without her; she took care of me," you can reply, "I know that right now you don't see how you can handle everyday living without her." As simple and contrived as these examples may seem, most people find it a tremendous comfort to feel they've been *heard*, that their pain has been acknowledged. As one counselor told us, "Because someone comes to you with their story doesn't necessarily mean that they're looking for you to fix it." Sometimes it's enough just to say, "That must be so hard."[2]

Some children complain that a parent is talking compulsively, going over and over the same ground. This is a fairly common response to extremely frightening, unusual, or disruptive occurrences. It's a way of grasping the reality and attempting to gain some sense of coherence and control over an otherwise overwhelming event.

Sometimes people do get stuck. Beyond a certain point, endless repetition may simply reinforce itself rather than free the mind to move on. If you find yourself growing acutely and increasingly uncomfortable with your parent's endless talk, then extricate yourself!

As an adult child, take responsibility for setting limits. As one counselor said, "Sometimes it's important to set the conditions for listening." This can mean setting the time frame. If your mother calls at a bad time and launches into her story, you can say, "How much time do you think you need? I'm really willing to listen, but right now I only have about five minutes." It's important to communicate to your parent that "This is not a good time" is not the same as "I don't want to hear."

Setting the conditions may also mean limiting the content of communication. Sometimes it's necessary to say, "Let's not talk about Dad anymore. Let's talk about something else." In such cases, you don't have to lecture on how "stuck in negativity" your parent is. Focus on your own feelings: "It just makes me too upset to hear you say those things about my father.''[3]

Expressing your love and concern and listening reflectively constitute basic emotional aid for divorcing parents. This aid is also practical, however, because people who feel depressed and abandoned find it hard to make decisions. And usually there are pressing practical matters to be resolved immediately.

## Practical Concerns

So many books exist to guide divorcing couples through the maze of practical decisions that it would be redundant to summarize their contents here. Instead, we have provided a list of titles at the end of this chapter.

There is an important connection between emotional and practical factors in the aftermath of divorce. On the one hand, dealing with the practical issues can help to sort out the emotional issues. However, the practical process will not proceed smoothly if there are deep unresolved emotional issues between the partners. Intense emotionality is normal for divorcing couples, but if it is so extreme over a long period of time as to seriously hamper the process of practical decisions, then you might want to suggest that your parents try some form of divorce counseling.

An added benefit of divorce counseling is that it lessens the burden on you. Despite your best intentions, you may *not* be the best person to sort out the emotional from the legal aspects of your parents' divorce. If your parents refuse to go together, it can still be very beneficial for one or both parents to go separately.

If the divorce has been a very *nonmutual* affair, then it is good to encourage the parent who did not want the divorce to take some initiative in the practical sphere. This will give your parent some sense of control and will often help to restore a bit of shattered self-esteem. It can be a difficult process, however. One woman told us:

When I encouraged my mother to go down and file for the divorce, she acted like I'd given her a length of rope to hang herself. Yet if I had made the first call to the lawyer myself, she would have treated *me* like the executioner. And so every step of the way, she just let Dad run the whole show.

This kind of ambivalence is why helping a parent can be so difficult and why it often feels like such a thankless task. It is also why you may not be the best person to help, for you yourself may be pulled by strong currents of ambivalence. If you feel confident in your ability to swim clear of such currents, then fix your sights on the far horizon. Your goal, despite any temporary resistance, is to plan for the future well-being of your parents and the family as a whole.

## Legal Affairs

Again, because there are so many excellent books on the legal aspect of divorce, our goal is to provide a basic orientation through this complicated and often daunting territory. Most of our remarks in this section are based on a book that we feel represents the most balanced, rigorous, and thoroughly documented study to date of what actually goes on in the process of negotiation: *The Process of Divorce,* by Kenneth Kressel (listed in the Bibliography and at the end of this chapter).

But before we go further, there is a basic question. *Should* you get involved in your parents' legal affairs?

Remember the touchstone questions listed earlier. Be aware that you may find yourself in the cross fire of intense and ambivalent feelings and that you risk incurring the long-term resentment of one or both parents. Rather than taking a stand on specific issues, it is wiser to help your parents with the basic background work: clarifying goals, gathering information, and seeking appropriate professional help.

In thinking about the goals of negotiation, keep a sense of perspective. Because the legal process often coincides with the intense initial phase of divorce, family members tend to get swept up in short-term needs. You may be furious at your mother for leaving your dad, but this does not cancel out the fact that she put him through graduate school, raised his children, kept his house for twenty years, and now deserves a measure of security. Intense hurt, anger, or the desire for revenge do not provide a good basis for reaching a satisfactory resolution.

What is a satisfactory resolution? The following criteria are excerpted from Kressel's book:

1. Resolution of all relevant issues.
2. Tolerable financial and emotional costs.
3. Agreements that are fair and equitable — relative to broadly prevailing norms and community expectations for comparable cases — and are perceived as such by the parties.
4. Agreements that protect the rights, interests, and welfare of affected third parties, especially children.
5. Satisfaction with the overall results.
6. The couples experience a sense of "ownership" of the agreement.
7. Parties comply with the terms of the agreement.
8. Spouses are better able (and certainly not less able) to cooperate.[4]

These outcomes are not better because they are "nicer" or "morally superior," though many people might judge them so. Their chief virtues are that they enable the process to proceed most smoothly and rapidly, they ensure a higher degree of satisfaction, and they entail less need for renegotiation, hence cutting down on financial costs and permitting earlier psychological closure. As one divorce counselor told us, "Divorcing partners each achieve a higher degree of security with middle-ground solutions."[5]

You may not feel that you can embrace these objectives. If you feel highly emotional, strongly motivated by anger, by the desire to punish or to protect one parent at the expense of another, then this is *not* the best way for you to help your parents. It is extremely difficult to sort out your parents' complex relationship, especially since you do not have all the facts. It is, on the other hand, extremely easy to sympathize with the abandoned parent, "the basket case." Sometimes there truly is a villain and a victim. However, many of our respondents told us that they had allowed their one-sided feelings to influence the legal process and later felt intense regret.

Another important point is that some degree of conflict between divorcing partners is to be expected during the negotiation process. Professionals in the field of divorce worry about those couples who seem to agree to everything. Kressel described what he called the autistic style of divorce, in which a couple seems phobically afraid of conflict.[6] The risk is that because genuine needs and desires will not be asserted, hidden resentments may fester and erupt at a later time. If you, as the child, cannot tolerate a measure of conflict between your parents, it may be best to keep your distance from the negotiating process.

If for these or other reasons you don't feel suited for helping your parents in the legal process, then you needn't feel as if you've failed them. Though they may not recognize it, you have done them a service by acknowledging your own limitations. There are many other ways to help your parents: always look for those most compatible with your feelings and in line with your actual abilities.

BASIC HOMEWORK

Divorce is a complex process, and the laws vary from state to state. Encourage your parents to familiarize themselves with the basic elements of the process and the specific variations in their state.[7] Many women, in particular, feel very intimidated by the mere thought of entering the legal system. A little information can go a long way toward boosting their confidence and making the experience more manageable. Helpful books exist, and a number of titles are listed at the end of this chapter.

Experts stress the importance of being prepared before the actual legal process begins. Not only should each parent have a good grasp of what the process will involve, but each should be able to provide an accurate picture of their economic status as a couple and a full account of what their individual needs will be. All documents and records pertaining to assets and liabilities should be gathered and organized. Each parent should draw up a realistic assessment of his or her expected cost of living, based on an analysis of the past two or three years' expenses. Being prepared saves time and money; it increases self-confidence and helps create an atmosphere of mutual respect among all parties involved in the legal process.

Impress upon your parents the need for full and honest disclosure. If one parent hides important information from the other, this will only result in an extended paper chase and ultimately in increased cost and aggravation for all.

### TYPES OF LEGAL HELP

*Lawyer*   The professional most often seen by divorcing couples is the lawyer. Kressel's advice is to choose a lawyer who promotes a cooperative atmosphere between the divorcing partners and who is sensitive to the emotional dynamics of divorce.[8]

It must be stressed, however, that while warmth and empathy are desirable qualities in a lawyer, a lawyer is not a psychological counselor. If your parent is using a significant portion of each session with the lawyer to process emotions, he or she should be encouraged to find another, more appropriate channel.

How do you find a lawyer? Encourage your parent to be *choosy*.[9] Most areas have a lawyers' referral service that is listed in the phone book. (Check the yellow pages under "Lawyers Referral Service.") This service will provide the names of attorneys who are experts on divorce law. Your parent can call the offices of three or four of these lawyers and make a brief appointment (about fifteen minutes), for which there should be no — or only a minimal — charge.

During the initial interviews, your parent should be forthright in asking questions. Is this lawyer an expert in local divorce laws? How accessible will he or she be? Is it possible to give an estimated time frame? What are the fees? And, of course, what is the basic approach to divorce: Does he or she favor a highly adversarial or a more cooperative approach?

Remember, it's not just that a cooperative stance is "nicer," but that it has been shown to result in a more effective, less expensive negotiation process and to produce greater mutual, long-term satisfaction. Of course, a good lawyer will encourage his or her client to be assertive in claiming a fair share. A lawyer who is "too nice" may result in a settlement that, over the long term, leads to resentment and renegotiation. For this same reason, your parents should be suspicious of any person or agency that advocates a quick, cheap divorce and that begins by getting both parties to waive a long list of potential requests.

Ultimately, to obtain the best possible solution, the divorcing partners must expect to take an active role. No expert can know their particular situation, its possibilities and its limitations, as intimately as they do. Clients who sit passively at their lawyer's feet may find themselves with a settlement that does not truly reflect their needs.

On the question of lawyers' fees: from the very first visit, a lawyer should be clear about all known and anticipated fees. Ideally, there should be some form of written memorandum describing the services the lawyer intends to perform and whatever fee information can be provided. Experts also advise divorcing people to keep a running log of all appointments, phone calls, and correspondence so that there are no unpleasant surprises at billing time and so any discrepancies can be checked.

For those who are unable to afford the services of a private lawyer, other legal services exist. There are legal clinics that attempt to cut costs by relying on paraprofessional help and standardized legal forms. If your parents' divorce promises to be a relatively simple affair, this might be an appropriate choice. It will certainly be economical in the short run, but ultimately the quality of service will depend on the quality of the lawyers and other staff involved. People are cautioned that, if they like the lawyer they meet at the initial interview, they should verify that he or she will actually be the one representing them.

For those who qualify, government-funded legal services are available. (Look under "Legal Services," "Legal Assistance," "Community Legal Services," or "Legal Aid" in the white pages of your phone book.) The main disadvantage of such services is that there is often a backlog of cases and hence a long waiting period. If your parent is in a crisis situation, that should be made clear during the initial phone call. Though the divorce itself may take a long time to go through, any pressing problems may be considered more promptly.

*Mediation*   Divorce mediation is a newer method of handling divorce that is rapidly gaining in popularity. Whether the services are offered through public or private auspices, the basic approach is the same. The method is based on a cooperative stance, with most if not all of the sessions involving face-to-face encounters between the divorcing partners, and with a mediator serving as a neutral facilitator. Though mediators tend to have a more psychological focus than most lawyers, the basic approach is a practical, task-oriented one. Mediators will often recommend psychological counseling as they feel it is needed.

Usually a divorcing couple is asked to refrain from seeking outside legal advice during the mediation process. Lawyers on staff or affiliated with the center may sometimes participate in the mediation. The written agreement produced by the mediation process is not in itself a legal document and must be reviewed by a lawyer before being submitted to the judge. (Each partner may want his or her own lawyer to review the agreement; other couples may wish to save money by agreeing on one lawyer who will serve as a neutral party.)

Advocates of divorce mediation contrast what they feel is its enlightened, cooperative stance with the outmoded, adversarial legal process that they believe fosters hostility and polarization. Another potential benefit is that the costs of a mediated divorce tend to be somewhat lower. If your parents are not interested in mediation, you and your siblings might consider making an appointment to speak with an experienced divorce mediator. Many adult children find themselves thrust into the position of being mediators, yet they lack any training or experience. A professional counselor can provide some helpful guidelines and, perhaps most important, can explain the hazards of attempting to mediate as a family member. Many professional divorce mediators have witnessed adult children attempting the role of mediator and can explain some of the pitfalls.

## Financial Matters

In approaching your parents' financial affairs, the same basic criteria exist as apply to the legal process as a whole. The goal is an equitable settlement, one that is reasonably satisfactory to both parties. Experts caution that some degree of dissatisfaction is generally inevitable: the aim is to minimize it. In the words of one expert in family law: "If *both* parties feel a little disappointed at the result, the settlement is probably a fair one."[10] Because of the intense feelings surrounding financial decisions, your best bet — unless there are major breakdowns in negotiation or serious inequities — is to do supportive backup work, rather than to involve yourself with specific decisions.

### DIVIDING THE ASSETS

Divorce law in forty-nine states requires that marital assets be divided. Forty-two states and the District of Columbia have *equitable-distribution laws* and seven have *community-property laws*. (Only Mississippi has neither.)

Whichever law is applicable to your parents' situation, the basic point of departure is the same. Marital assets must be identified and their value must be determined. Several of the books listed at the end of this chapter give specific instructions for this sometimes rather complicated process.

In the seven community-property states, distribution is usually a simple process of dividing by two. In equitable-distribution states, a complex set of criteria — such as length of marriage, number and age of children, health, education, and job prospects of each spouse — are factored into the final decision.[11]

*The House*   Before getting involved in any decisions about your parents' house, ask yourself if you can really be objective. Many adult children are very attached to the family house, and this may make it difficult, even impossible, for them to help with decisions that are truly in their parents' interest.

Once the legal decision has been made as to whether one parent will get the house or whether the house will be sold and the assets divided, both of your parents still need to decide just where and how they want to live. It is important for them not to do anything rash or impulsive. Many different needs must be factored into the equation, both practical and emotional. Some newly single people have a tremendous need for the security of the old house; others experience a sense of freedom and of fresh beginnings from moving out. Some find the calm of privacy helps them work through the transition; others are frightened to live alone and long for company.

If you can set aside your own needs on this score, you can help your parents to think through their options. Is your mother really up to the hassle and expense of moving? Maybe her desire for new surroundings would be satisfied by a bit of redecorating or by the fun of turning your father's former study into her own special room. People who've been living as a married couple for twenty and more years are often unaware of all the possibilities: renting a room to a friendly person, turning the house into a duplex and renting out half, group living, trailer parks, community apartment living, and so on.

One option that should be considered with utmost caution is that of inviting a parent to live in your household. One counselor we spoke with stressed the deleterious effects of such an arrangement:

> This creates a dependent situation for the parent, and this is reverse dependency, which is even harder psychologically. The worst situation of all is when a parent moves out of town to live with the child. A recently single person

needs some stability, continuity — the basic building blocks of their life — in place.[12]

Obviously, if resources are scant, options are more limited. The book *Women in Transition* has an excellent discussion of housing for the newly single, with special focus on those with low income. Though written for women, this section is applicable to men as well.[13]

*Possessions* According to professional mediators, it is best to have a couple agree on the method of division before they begin wrangling over specific possessions. Different methods exist, and the legal personnel who are helping your parents will no doubt be able to suggest different options. If one spouse is remaining in the house, he or she may keep most of the household objects, giving the other partner a "credit" for their estimated worth. Another method is to have the partners draw up a list of possessions and then check off which ones they especially want. Then, as one counselor told us, "Whenever there are two checks, they have to sit down and do some horse-trading."[14]

The emotions surrounding family possessions can be intense and unpredictable. We learned of one woman who was upset because her husband *didn't* want anything. It made her feel as though their whole past together meant nothing to him. As a family member, you are apt to have many strong attachments to family possessions and should probably not be involved in the actual process of dividing them at all.

COLLEGE COSTS

If you are a young adult who has not yet started or completed college, ask that your parents clarify their intentions on this score. If one or both parents promise support for your college education, this should be part of the formal settlement. One counselor we spoke with suggested that an equitable formula is to agree that parents will divide the difference between what the child can provide (through scholarships, other forms of financial aid, and working) and the cost of a four-year B.A. at a state college. Exactly how the parents divide this amount is a matter for negotiation.[15]

You yourself should look into just exactly what your needs will be: talk to the financial adviser at the schools you are considering; talk to other students; read the fine print on any relevant financial documents you may have received. The cost of college includes not only tuition but also room and board, books, travel, clothing, and other supplies. Needless to say, this is one area of your parents' settlement where you need make no pretense of being objective!

THE SPECIAL SITUATION OF WOMEN

If there is one parent who risks serious financial difficulty after divorce, it is most likely your mother. Women in general are at a significant financial disadvantage in our society. Opportunities for advancement in high-paying fields are limited for women. Traditional "women's work," in the helping and service professions, is notoriously underpaid. Even when women do the same work as men, they are paid less. According to recent statistics, a woman earns sixty cents for every dollar earned by a man.[16] Divorce almost always means a significant decline in the standard of living for women, while the same is not true for men.[17]

Older women face special difficulties. Many of them grew up with no expectation of working outside the home. These "displaced homemakers" often have little understanding about money matters, no formal job training or experience, and even less confidence in their ability to survive as single women.

If your mother fits this description, the first thing you may want to do is to help her become more informed about basic financial matters. Professionals who work with divorcing couples emphasize that women are often at a decided disadvantage during financial negotiations because they are so uninformed. One counselor told us, "Many of these women don't even know where their husband kept the checkbook."

Your mother should have a grasp of basic financial terms, and she should be primed on basic budget keeping. She should have a basic understanding of the financial transactions involved in divorce, and as clear a picture as possible as to what assets and liabilities she and your father have accumulated. But remember: the primary goal of informing your mother is to increase her confidence in her own ability to handle such matters. If you can't be informative without being condescending, then find someone else who can — or recommend one of the books from the list at the end of the chapter.

*Temporary Support*   Some women postpone filing for divorce, hoping their husbands will change their minds and come around. If you know that your father is adamant and that your mother's financial situation is precarious, urge her to begin the legal process quickly, so that she can get temporary support, or "maintenance," if needed. At a temporary hearing, a judge can rule that your mother must receive income to meet her basic needs and/or that your father must pay her legal expenses. It may also be important to secure her right to exclusive residence in the house and to make sure that any necessary insurance policies are maintained throughout this period.

*Health Insurance*   Of utmost importance is adequate health insurance coverage. Low-income women are eligible for Medicaid, but women in the middle brackets are often in the most precarious position. One divorce counselor we spoke with painted a very bleak picture of the many older divorcées she sees who are left financially strapped and without health insurance. Many of these women do not go to a doctor until it's a crisis situation — and then, often, it's too late.[18] The sad irony is that divorce itself increases the likelihood of serious illness.

Fortunately, there is a growing awareness of the dilemma. Depending on which state your mother lives in and the type of coverage that she and your father have had, she may be eligible for some form of conversion provision. Generally such coverage is not permanent, however, and so your mother's needs for long-term protection must be factored into the final settlement.

*Long-term Planning*   One divorce counselor told us, "When a woman can see that she is going to have long-term security, it is very empowering."[19] Planning for your mother's extended protection is a difficult process, but the practical and emotional rewards are significant.

Many financial counselors recommend to older divorcing women that any reasonable sum of money obtained from the division of assets (such as the sale of the house) should be invested to meet future needs.

Your mother may also be eligible for long-term support (sometimes called spousal maintenance) payments from your father. Just what these payments will be depends not only on what resources are available, but on your mother's ability to paint a realistic and convincing picture of her needs. For instance, your mother may want to ask for money to continue her education or advance her job training. If she has health problems, this may be a factor in the amount of support that she requires. You can help her in the process of defining her needs and goals, and there are many excellent books to guide you.

Many women do not have a good understanding of what their social security benefits will be. Currently, the former wife of a man who is getting retirement or disability benefits is entitled to a benefit on *his* record if she is at least sixty-two years old and had been married to him for at least ten years before the divorce. To call for information, your mother can look in the white pages under "Social Security Administration."

Your mother may also be reassured to know that, as of fairly recently, pension money accrued during the marriage may be considered a marital asset, hence entitling her to a portion.

In helping your mother plan for her future, remember that you are not out to punish your father but to see that your mother is assured of basic economic security, that she does not suffer a drastic drop in her standard of living, and that she is adequately compensated for all the years she worked as wife and mother. Even if your mother initiated the divorce, she should not face a life of economic insecurity. We heard several sad stories of mothers who felt guilty for leaving the marriage and so had asked for very little financial support. A few years later, with their emotions tempered, their fathers happily remarried, and their mothers destitute, the adult children regretted that they had not pushed for a more reasonable settlement.

*Vocational Counseling* Many women find they must get a job after their divorce. For older women who have never worked before or who have not worked since their children were born, the fear and anxiety can be tremendous. Their children, who grew up with a different set of images and expectations of the role of women, sometimes have trouble understanding the depth of this anxiety. Daughters sometimes feel threatened themselves by their mother's lack of self-confidence.

The challenge is to be understanding and empathetic, without buying into your mother's negative self-image. Encourage her to think about the many things she has done and can do. In raising a family and running the household, in hobbies and volunteer activities, many women have developed important and useful skills. They may think it doesn't count if they weren't paid for it, but in fact these past experiences can serve as a very useful bridge to a new career.

Many older women graduated from high school with language skills far superior to those of younger women graduating from high school and even junior college today. Such skills are at a premium in the current work world. As one professional counselor in the divorce field reported, "It's easy to teach someone word processing. What isn't easy is to make up for basic language skills if they weren't acquired earlier in life."[20]

Help your mother to be future oriented in her job search and to present herself as such. If she is not in immediately desperate straits, she should hold out for a job or job training that has some promise for the future, rather than accept the first low-wage job that comes along. Though she may need to start out at the low end of the pay scale, she can ask in the beginning, "Where might I expect to be five [ten, fifteen] years from now?" Of course, if health coverage is not adequately provided for in the divorce settlement, advise her to find a job with good health benefits.

Encourage her to get job counseling, which most communities offer. Many programs are specifically designed for women. Again, the Displaced Homemakers Network is an excellent source of support and information for women of all ages and backgrounds and exists in every county in the nation.

*Back to School*   Many older women feel hampered by their lack of education. For those women who did not finish high school, it can be a very important psychological milestone to complete their high school equivalency.

In recent years a significant number of older women have returned to college, and there are numerous programs to encourage and support their reentry. Besides offering enhanced career possibilities, college offers other benefits: a helpful sense of structure, a new sense of identity, a source of pride, and, most important, new friends — many of whom may be in a similar situation. Some older women are fearful that they will not be able to compete with the "young whippersnappers" around them. However, as one divorce counselor assures her clients, "Knowledge and judgment increase with age and experience, and the chief decline is in perceptual-motor speed, which is hardly a requisite for academic work unless one plans to be a professional dancer or athlete."[21]

You or your mother can do a survey of the colleges and universities in your area. The admissions office will be able to tell you if there are any special programs for the adult student. Call the financial aid office to find what forms of financial support may be specifically geared to the older woman.

## Violence Against Women

Sadly, violence against women is a daily reality in our society. It is not uncommon for women to be physically abused by their husbands or ex-husbands during the process of divorce or in its aftermath.

It is against the law to beat, threaten, rape, or sexually assault any woman. No man has the right to abuse his wife or ex-wife. If you have immediate fears for your mother's safety, the first priority is to get her to a safe place — a friend's or relative's house or a community shelter for battered women. Your mother should call the police during or immediately after an attack if she wants your father arrested, if she wants a report filed, or if she wants protection while moving to a safer place. A police report can be a very valuable record in case of future abuse; to this end, any evidence should be saved: clothing, photographs of injuries sustained, medical reports. If your mother is in fear of continued threats or physical injury, she may wish to request a court order of protection. This is a matter to discuss with her lawyer.[22]

Spouse abuse is a very serious emotional problem that affects the entire family. It is not just the abuser's problem. Typically, the abuser and the abused are locked into a deeply rooted pattern of interdependency. It is the rare child who emerges completely unscathed from such a background. If this has been a pattern in your family, it is highly advisable that you — as well as each of your parents — seek counseling.

## As Parents Age

The many cautions we've given about attempting to do too much for your parents take on a different meaning as your parents age and perhaps face serious physical limitations. This is a topic on which there has been a veritable explosion of information in recent years, and a number of helpful books are listed at the end of this chapter.

## Think Creatively

Many of those who feel their parents are doing exceptionally well in the aftermath of divorce feel that the key has been their parents' ability to think creatively rather than cling to the past or to rigid images of who they are and how their life should be.

Noelle's mother is a prime example. After the divorce, she initially felt stripped of her status and identity as "a professor's wife." When she moved to a new state with Noelle's young sister, her intention was to buy a small house for the two of them. She had a very clear image of the house that would be

appropriate: "A small, dark house for two lonely, cast-off girls."
But some deep impulse toward health gave her a different inspiration. Since after the settlement she had money from the sale of the family house, why not buy another big house and fill it with friends? That's what she did — and that house, far from being "a small, dark house" of loneliness and deprivation, became a center of warmth and welcome for friends and relatives from all over the world. Recently, she sold the house and fulfilled a long-held dream: "to move to southern France, live in a small apartment that's easy to take care of, do watercolors, and be visited by my family and friends."

Another mother we learned about, left by her husband after twenty-five years of marriage, took money from her settlement and had a tennis court built in her backyard. That way her home became a center of gravity for friends and family members.

Each of these decisions, of course, required a basic level of financial security. People who are struggling for economic survival may be skeptical of the very notion of creative solutions. But the basic principle is accessible to all. Divorce can be a passage to new experiences or to the rediscovery of certain buried treasures from the past. We heard many stories of parents who, since the divorce, had uncovered lost parts of themselves. One mother began to write again, a source of delight she hadn't experienced since her children were born. Another mother took up painting, transforming her husband's study into her studio. One father rediscovered his love of the out-of-doors.

Of course, a change that's healthy for your parents may make them seem, in your eyes, less familiar, less parentlike, less mature. The prime example here is when parents begin dating. But if it's healthy for them, if it makes them more energized, self-confident, less depressed — then it is your task to let go of *your* fixed images of Mom or Dad and give your blessing.

One divorce counselor made these statements when we asked her to tell us, in a nutshell, what she felt adult children should know about helping their parents: "Be supportive. Get information. Hold their hand when they go out for that first college application or job interview. But *don't* make decisions for them. The only decisions that count are those that people make for themselves."[23]

## Recommended Reading

De Angelis, Sidney. *You're Entitled! A Divorce Lawyer Talks to Women.* Chicago: Contemporary Books, 1989.

Friedman, James T. *The Divorce Handbook.* New York: Random House, 1984.

Kressel, Kenneth. *The Process of Divorce: How Professionals and Couples Negotiate Settlements.* New York: Basic Books, 1985.

Mowatt, Marian H. *Divorce Counseling: A Practical Guide.* Lexington, Mass.: D. C. Heath & Co., 1987.

Rogers, Mary. *Women, Divorce, and Money.* New York: McGraw Hill, 1981.

Silverstone, Barbara, and Helen Kandel Hyman. *You and Your Aging Parent.* New York: Pantheon, 1989.

Women in Transition, Inc. *Women in Transition: A Feminist Handbook on Separation and Divorce.* New York: Charles Scribner's Sons, 1975.

# 14

## A Message to Parents

A couple in their nineties has come before the judge to ask for a divorce. Incredulous, the judge asks them, "Why did you wait so long?"

"We were waiting for the children to die," is the response.

To any divorcing parent who has read these pages, this joke may not seem so funny. If there's one refrain throughout this book, it's "Divorce is hard for children — no matter how old they are." But it is not our intention to leave parents in despair. The majority of our respondents testified that once beyond the initial grief and upheaval, their parents' divorce has been an important catalyst for their own growth. Many acknowledged that their parents were happier in their new lives than they had ever been before. And many felt that the divorce had led them to more satisfying, more honest relationships with their parents as individuals.

There was, however, virtually no one for whom the transition was easy. Thus, the starting point for parents is to anticipate a difficult period of adjustment. One of the major obstacles for parents is the bilevel nature of the adult child's response. In fact, *adult child* says it all. Few parents are prepared for the depth and intensity of their children's reactions. For a variety of reasons, they tend to overestimate the adult side of their children.

Many parents have seen their children leading, in all external respects, a full and autonomous life. They are genuinely surprised to see the depth of their children's attachment to the family and its past.

When parents have waited until "it wouldn't be a problem for the children," the children's intense reactions may seem to make a mockery of their patience and forbearance. Many parents feel angry and shortchanged. "Waiting until the children are grown" not only provided a sense of timing but also of justification. "I stayed in an unhappy marriage until I was confident my children were grown and had their own lives," one mother told us. She felt that in doing so she had "earned" her divorce and was quite bitter when her children "didn't make it easy."

Sometimes lurking behind the anger and resentment is a sense of failure: "I must not have done my job as a parent if my adult children are so immature." When adult children react in unexpected ways, it threatens their parents' sense of accomplishment. Research shows that it is harder for parents to feel positive about their own life course when it seems that their adult children are not successfully launched.

Of course, many divorcing partners are struggling with their own ambivalence. And for the partner who initiated the divorce, there is the added burden of guilt. When children react with shock, grief, and rage, their parents' feelings of guilt and ambivalence are intensified. Here again, many parents feel a sense of unfairness: "I've taken care of you all these years. Now, in my hour of need, you're making things so much harder."

For all of these reasons, parents try to appeal to their children's rational, grown-up side. They communicate in a way that cuts off feelings: "You're an adult. You have your own life. You ought to be able to understand." Or they give lengthy explanations, bringing up the sins of the other parent, reviewing the failures and disappointments of the past. Both these approaches say, "Don't be upset. I don't want or can't bear to hear it."

At the most primal level of interaction, going back to the infant's first cry, parents don't like to see their children suffer. Parents of adult children try to squelch this instinctive response by denying that their adult children are suffering or have the right to suffer. But adult children must be allowed to mourn, to rage, to refuse to understand. Only by fully experiencing their feelings will they be able to understand, to accept, to move beyond.

Some degree of shock, rage, and grief was present in virtually all our respondents. For some children, however, the intensity was significantly moderated by the way their parents went about the divorce.

Of great significance here is how the divorce decision is reached. Judith Wallerstein's remarks in this regard apply equally to adult children. She wrote that children can more readily adjust to divorce when they understand it

> as a serious and carefully considered remedy for an important problem, when the divorce appears purposeful and rationally undertaken, and indeed succeeds in bringing relief and a happier outcome for one or both parents.
>
> Conversely, where the divorce is unplanned, undertaken impulsively, pursued in anger or guilt over fancied or real misdeeds, or where the divorce coincides with other unrelated family crises, the child's capacity to cope is severely burdened.[1]

Divorce is rarely a mutual decision. The less mutual it is, the more difficult it is for everyone in the family. When children feel that one parent is being cast off by the other, their own feelings of rage, injustice, and abandonment are especially intense. In such cases bitter alliances often form within the family, sometimes leading to long-term disturbances between family members.

Obviously, mutuality cannot be willed. When the disparity

between partners is very great, divorce counseling may be a significant help in depolarizing the situation. A skilled counselor can help the "abandoned" partner to feel less victimized by the process of divorce. At the same time, the parent initiating the divorce can help matters by acting in a responsible and humane manner. This means breaking the news to the other partner in a way that is direct and yet tactful. Adult children bitterly resent it when they feel that the news has been communicated in a sneaky, indirect, dishonest, humiliating, or unnecessarily brutal way. They especially resent it when they are left to break the news to the other parent.

Adult children are also very sensitive about how the news is first communicated to them. They want to be told in an honest, direct manner and in a way that allows for the full intensity of their response. They resent it when the news comes along with "We waited until it wouldn't be a problem for you." They feel manipulated when they're told in the midst of a formal gathering, in front of their small children, or moments before they have to dash to work or return to college.

Too often the news of divorce is accompanied by a flood of disturbing revelations. Parents should proceed slowly, not suddenly assuming a peer relationship. They need to be cautious about the nature and number of confidences they share. Before launching into intimate details, it's appropriate to ask, "Do you mind if I tell you something about our sexual lives?" or "Do you really think you're ready to hear this?" Most of our respondents eventually felt very positive about the new sense of equality that evolved in the parent-child relationship in the aftermath of divorce. It was hard for them when the change came too suddenly and when they were still reeling from the shock of the divorce.

It's especially important for each parent to be careful about making negative remarks concerning the other parent in their children's presence. There are some kinds of explanations that can help children to understand the divorce without undermining their feelings for the other parent. One young woman learned that her mother's first fiancé had been killed in an accident. Her mother told her, "When I met your father, I was

still grieving. He comforted me, and that's what drew us together. Later, as I grew stronger, our paths diverged." Implicit
in "our paths diverged" may be a number of negative feelings
about her ex-husband, but there is no need for the mother to
share these in detail with her daughter.

Parents and children face different tasks in the wake of divorce, and in some ways the children's task is more complex.
They have to let go *and* hold on at the same time. Once-married
partners may go their separate ways, but children — no matter
how old they are — will always be the children of their parents.

The same general principles apply when parents take up with
a new partner. Adult children appreciate being told in a direct
but tactful way. They don't want to meet on the street, nor do
they want a rhapsody on the glories of love. They need the
freedom to have negative reactions in the beginning and to
absorb the information little by little. Adult children will ask
for more information about the new person as they are ready to
hear it. They need to know that the details are available, without being swamped in the early stages. Even when the person
is someone they know, they need time to adjust to the situation
before meeting the new pair. The most helpful approach is for
parents to offer the opportunity to get together "when you are
ready" and to maintain one-to-one contact with their child
until that time comes.

Since it is tempting to displace anger and resentment onto
the "intruder," this slow and easy pace minimizes that tendency. The adult children can see that the parent-child relationship continues and that their reactions are respected.
Comments like "Jane would like to meet you when you feel
ready" or "George and I look forward to taking you out to
dinner sometime" help to convey that attitude.

Time, here, may be only a matter of weeks or months, or as
long as several years. The most important factor initially is the
adult child's need for continuity in the one-to-one relationship.
When the parent was committed to that and was able to avoid
pressuring for a new family unit, the period of acute discomfort
was shortened. The "child" in the adult child first needs reas-

surance: "I'm still your mom" and "I'll always be your dad." Then the adult side will emerge and accept the new relationships, the new ways of living and being a family.

Problems arise when parents are too anxious to have their children's validation of the new relationship. Most of our respondents reported that when their parents did not push, they naturally grew more accepting of the new relationship. If, over time, they saw that their parent was genuinely happier with the new partner, they were able to appreciate this fact. Often, it was what belatedly reconciled them to the divorce.

Especially resented among those we spoke with was the stepparent who tried to revise the family's past or to mediate between parent and child. Parents must take an active role in preventing such intrusions. Adult children can learn to accept and to appreciate a parent's new life, but they want to feel that their family's past and their relationship with their parent have been left intact.

By far the greatest gift that divorcing parents can give is a cooperative relationship between themselves. Conversely, a relationship that remains locked in negativity is the most damaging for all family relationships. As one woman wrote to us:

> My parents' continued hostility towards each other has wreaked such emotional havoc on my five siblings and myself that I could easily say that all other factors of their divorce are insignificant by comparison. Seventeen years after their separation they are still trying to manipulate their children's feelings for the other parent. This behavior has only diminished my opinion of both of my parents and has destroyed any respect I might have ever had for them. Sometimes I feel like I just maintain a relationship with them out of habit and for a sense of history.

The ideal is for parents to remain united as parents, no matter how their lives diverge. Most of our respondents were gradually able to accept that their parents had to go their separate ways. But they needed to feel that what was good about the past was validated by both parents. And there were significant times — holidays, crises, milestone events in their lives — when they deeply longed for their parents to be there together as parents.

When parents can successfully navigate the crisis of divorce, the rewards are great. They not only preserve their children's affection but gain their admiration. They communicate the important message:

> Life is unpredictable. People who once loved each other can grow apart. Things happen that plunge us into grief and confusion, but we can *come through*. Even at age forty-five . . . fifty-five . . . sixty-five . . . it is possible for people to start over, to find new sources of love, inspiration, adventure, and fulfillment. But we will not negate what we had. We can affirm what was best about our past, while moving on.

The parents of one young woman, Jennifer, provide an example of a divorce that was carefully and thoughtfully carried out. Ten years prior to the actual divorce, Jennifer's mother came to the decision that she wanted to leave the marriage, and she informed her husband of her decision. This was very hard for him, but she promised to stay until they were each prepared to lead separate lives and were confident that the children were mature enough. Meanwhile she began preparing herself; she went back to school and got a degree in a field that would enable her to support herself.

When the day finally came to announce the decision, both parents were present. They arranged for the whole family to meet together with a counselor, and each adult child had an opportunity to express his or her reactions before the others. After this initial meeting, their mother encouraged the children to continue counseling. During the settlement phase, she kept the adult children informed of the process and asked them repeatedly, "How do you feel about this?"

Now, eight years later, both parents are able to come together for important events in their children's lives. Jennifer is able to appreciate that both of her parents are much happier with their new partners.

Still, the transition was not without pain. Jennifer cried bitterly at the beginning, and there are still things that cause her pain. She feels her father's remarriage has drawn him further away from the rest of them. She misses coming together as a family, with both her siblings, and feels it would happen more often if her parents were still together.

And if there were no pain?

Psychologists say they worry most about the small children who make no protest when their parents say good-bye. Such blank response, they say, indicates a troubled bond, a lack of positive attachment, or a complete denial of reality. In an analogous way, when adult children grieve and rage at their parents' divorce, it's a sign of how deeply their family has mattered to them. Often, it's a sign that their parents gave them a past worth grieving over. In such cases, parents may need to come to the same realization as did the heroine of a recent novella:

> Even so, as I sit on my bed and pull off my stockings and rub my fifty-two-year-old toes, I think that I, too, have given my children the two cruelest gifts I had to give, which are these, the experience of perfect family happiness, and the certain knowledge that it could not last.[2]

The grief of adult children whose parents divorce is a cruel gift back to their parents. It's cruel because it brings more pain and confusion to parents at a difficult time. But it also says, "I care." Nothing treasured, nothing lost.

At bottom, this is all about letting go. Parents and adult children must release each other from the powerful grip of memories and expectations. For parents, this means allowing the full measure of their children's pain. For both, it means trusting in the insight, attributed to the poet Rainer Maria Rilke, that "one must live in oneself and think of the whole of life, of all its millions of possibilities, expanses and futures, in the face of which there is nothing past or lost."[3]

# 15

## The Mysterious Destination

### Noelle's Story: Part II

*Not long ago, my mother sold the house that she and my sister had moved to after the divorce. It was a beautiful house, with a French-slate roof and a view of the Hudson River, but it had seemed to us at first like a temporary crash pad or emergency shelter. Now, fourteen years later, it had long since come to be home for my brother, my sister, and me.*

*In the process of moving, my mother came across a box of letters that my father had written her over the years. She told me that they were very beautiful and affectionate letters, and I was surprised at how much it meant to me to know of the existence of that box.*

*I was surprised, as I've been surprised at other times — at the birth of my daughter, at innumerable Christmases, on many seemingly insignificant occasions when suddenly a memory stirs — at how much it still matters to me that there was once a true affection between my parents, and that it no longer exists.*

*And yet — so much has changed. . . .*

*For years after my parents' divorce I had a dream that my family was all together in a little car. That was the dream — no* plot, no action, no words — just that image: the five of us together in a little car, a quiet green landscape slipping past the windows, a sense of wholeness.

I no longer have that dream. I don't know when exactly it disappeared, but when I remember it now it seems like the vestige of an old self. It's not that the longing for wholeness has disappeared, but rather that the little car, that safe space that gathers my family together, *is* inside *me*.

This is so despite many tensions that still exist and many wounds that have never fully healed: my parents have no positive contact with each other; holidays and special events remain a recurrent source of anxiety; my father and I are still trying to heal a strained and distant relationship.

Yet at some very deep level, something has been restored, something has come to rest. How did it come about? I can't say exactly. It happened over time — a long time — but time itself is not the answer. It's been a complex process, a weave of many elements — part active and conscious; part passive and subterranean; part fortuitous, circumstantial, and linked to the lives of others.

For one thing, I have seen my parents make new lives for themselves. I have seen my father become more vital and energetic. I have seen my mother arrive at a level of confidence, adventurousness — at what I could only call selfhood — that, years earlier, would have seemed to her beyond the pale of possibility.

I have seen the sense of family shift and rearrange itself, as though the heart, like the brain, could learn a new circuitry. In the first few years there was always a sense of loss and disconnection at the core of family gatherings. Gradually, very gradually, that changed. We evolved new rituals; we gathered new friends into the family fold; we renewed some forgotten ties and grew closer to certain aunts, uncles, and cousins we'd never known so well before.

I have learned to sift through the past, performing a kind of archaeology, transforming what was once only breakage and painful reminder into an invaluable source of information. There are times when I feel almost grateful to the rupture for all it's enabled me to see, almost sorry for my friends whose families have stayed safely intact and unexamined.

*Here is a telling example. Not long ago I interviewed a woman who had experienced the "happy ending" that so many of us have wished for. Her parents had divorced and then, a few months later, moved back into the same house. Since then, they have lived as if nothing ever happened. She herself felt, and continues to feel, relieved of the profound embarrassment that their brief separation caused her. Yet she acknowledged, "Nothing is resolved between them." As she spoke, I had the image of a deep crack that had been smoothed over, a surface order restored — and a deep well of emotions left unexplored.*

*We all have our ways of working things through, and this woman had chosen to pour her energies into her own marriage, children, and vocation. But it made me feel grateful that so many of my family's demons had, in fact, leapt out of the cracks and introduced themselves. They have been difficult and sometimes frightening companions, but I recognize them now as indispensable guides.*

*Lastly, I have moved into the present — into my own experience of marriage and parenthood. In part it's been the sheer fact of marriage and having a child that has helped to free me from the past. Other passions, other claims, have forced my energy and attention in new directions. But to a large degree, the shift in perspective has been willed. As I saw myself repeating certain patterns, acting out of old, unresolved dark spaces and pockets of ignorance, I had as never before — in the shape of two beings who love me and need me and have a right to me — the motivation to say, "Enough. It is time to move on."*

*Sometimes it all seems to me like a kind of cosmic joke or test — like Beethoven going deaf. My primary attachment was to my family and, more specifically, to my father within the context of my family. Thus, the divorce shook me free of my prize possession, my self-definition, my primal sense of orientation. Now I see it as being freed of a certain idolatry. The task has been to embrace this freedom without bitterness.*

*Which of these changes came first? I can't say. Each has been indispensable to the process of healing, and they have all been deeply intertwined. Letting go of the past permits moving into the present. Moving into the present encourages letting go of the past.*

*There are moments when I feel a terrible regret or remorse; there are things I would have done so differently if I had understood what I understand today. Yet fundamentally, I don't believe the process can be short-circuited: the grief must be lived, the healing discovered in the grieving itself. If there is anything that can be short-circuited, it is the extra, unnecessary "stuff" — the false expectations, the rigid polarities, the unfounded hopelessness and blame — that so many of us experienced, because we went through it alone, without any support or recognition of the grief out of season.*

## The Range of Possibilities

For many of the people we interviewed, the divorce was five, ten, and fifteen years behind them. Their stories represent a tremendous range of outcomes, confirming the notion that just as there are different kinds of marriages, so there are different kinds of divorces.

Some reported severe, ongoing tensions among family members. Susan's story was fairly typical of this category. Five years after what she described as a protracted and nasty divorce, Susan's mother remains very embittered. Holidays and special events are a source of major tension. Because of this, Susan's father did not attend her graduation from college, and this was a serious disappointment to her. Though Susan is close to her mother, she is angry at her mother's attitude and said pessimistically, "She'll go to her grave having a problem with my dad."

Some have parents who have virtually no contact with each other. Unfortunately, this does not mean that they are emotionally free of each other. In fact, frequently it means the opposite: the level of intensity — of unresolved anger, guilt, attachment — remains so high that the partners cope by complete avoidance of each other. Though the family is spared overt hostilities, the situation is far from satisfactory. Laurel told us:

I can accept that my parents had to go their separate ways. What I find hard to forgive is that in all these years they haven't been able to work out a minimally pleasant relationship with one another. After all, they each spent most of their adult lives together, they had four children, and we all had a lot of happy times together. Yet they can't even communicate in the simplest way when there's a significant event in the life of one of us — like when my son was born. It creates such a gulf between the past and the present and it divides our family into this side and that. There are all these strange, artificial barriers. The way my father says "your mother" sends a chill up my spine. She's not just "my mother" — she was his wife for twenty-five years, and that doesn't just disappear.

It marked contrast to these examples, some of our respondents described a greater level of family harmony than had ever existed before. Roberta was twenty when her parents divorced thirteen years ago. She said:

We had a nice family . . . a nice life. I always had fun as a kid. We had extra things like vacations, a clubhouse on the river where we went every weekend. . . . But my parents always fought. The fighting was the most devastating, the worst thing. When I was a teenager, I would stay home . . . the referee. If I went out, I would worry all night long.

Though Roberta was very sad to hear that her parents were splitting up, the divorce itself was carried out in a friendly manner: "It was not a mean divorce. They were levelheaded. They split everything. It probably only took two months. Dad stayed in the house until he found a place to stay and we all helped him move. It wasn't a mean and vindictive divorce like their marriage was."

After the divorce, her father still came over every day and continued to do all the house and yard chores he had always done. "My parents are best of friends. They still talk several times a week. Us kids are the bond." Holidays for Roberta's family are often still the entire family group, including grandparents, aunts, and uncles. Even her mother's remarriage, three years after the divorce, did not disrupt the family ties. When Roberta's father had heart surgery, her mother took her turn at caring for him when he returned from the hospital. When her stepfather died recently, Roberta's father went to the funeral.

Roberta does find all this a little "weird," perhaps because it is so uncommon and people she talks to "can't believe it!" But for her, the worst trauma was her parents' fighting prior to the divorce. The postdivorce and remarriage transitions have gone far more smoothly than she ever imagined was possible. This family is an excellent example of how divorce can relieve unbearable conflict and how beneficial it is when parents can continue to offer support to each other and to be parents as a unit.

Certainly, the generalization holds that children — young or adult — are happier when their parents can remain on friendly terms, and we did find other examples of positive postdivorce relationships. It seems that for some long-married couples, the patterns of interconnection are strong enough to persist after divorce. Approximately 15 percent of those interviewed told us that their parents continue to have frequent contact with each other, that holidays go on much as before, that both parents maintain relationships with in-laws and family friends. It should be added that in most of these cases, the positive post-divorce relationship did not just happen of itself. Often it emerged from a protracted period of struggle. Just as a good marriage takes work, so — indeed all the more — does a minimum-damage divorce.

There is a shadow side to postdivorce harmony, as some of those we spoke with made clear. Several described the family gatherings with both parents present as a farce or a charade. One woman told us, "It's a sham; it just perpetuates the same denial as always." Emma said:

My parents were so civilized. They would go to events together, they would sit next to each other at the table. When my father's wife wasn't around, my parents *acted* like they were together. It made me angry. I remember once at some celebration my dad came over and asked me to dance and I said, "No. You don't even know how to dance." I think what made it hard is that I knew how much my mother still loved my dad. I would fantasize about Dad coming back to the house and my mother saying, "I'm very happy as I am, thank you."

In much the same vein another woman told us:

My father left my mother for her best friend, and she was devastated. She pieced her life back together, but she remains very emotionally tied to him. He's no longer with the first woman, but I know that he sees other women. Meanwhile he and my mother eat together several times a week, they go off on vacations together — with the result that nothing has really changed. I feel that she is still just as vulnerable to him, that it could all happen again. The actual divorce was devastating, but at least there seemed the possibility of some catharsis — and all that's been retracted, gone underground.

For these adult children who are highly aware of fundamental problems in their parents' relationship, mere continuity is not enough. They want to feel that something has been resolved and sometimes they experience the lack of resolution as a paralysis in their own life.

There were other adult children who told us that it was painful to realize that their parents still loved each other. Rosie said, "My parents never stopped loving each other. That's what made it so hard." It was heartbreaking for her when she visited her father in the old house and saw that he'd left her mother's clothes still hanging in the closet. Another young woman described one of the most painful moments associated with her father's death. She had just received the news and had come over to his apartment. His answering machine was on, and she could hear her mother's voice. Her mother had also received the news, and, through her sobs, she was repeating his name. For these daughters, it seems there was an especially heightened sense of loss and tragic waste. If the love was there, then why the heartache of divorce?

## Common Threads

Woven through these very disparate stories are some distinct, repeating threads.

Virtually all our respondents testified to a process that was long and ongoing. Just as most described the initial pain as far more intense than they would have imagined, so they were surprised at how long the repercussions lasted.

For some we spoke with, this was because the divorce came at a certain crucial time in their life and thus altered what would have been the natural process of maturation. Tess, whose parents divorced when she was twenty-three, told us, "I struggled so long with the various issues that their divorce brought up that I feel I am only now, in my midthirties, really going through the process of separation that was interrupted when they divorced." One of the problems, Tess felt, was that "I never got to accept my family for what it was. I was just at the age when you begin to see the reality — but then that reality was gone."

Rosie felt that the premature loss of her family made it harder for her to move forward in her own life. When her parents split up, her father remained in the family house. After his death three years ago, Rosie and her husband moved in. The house is in a bad neighborhood, and they would like to move out, but Rosie finds it very difficult:

When my mother left, she took only a few possessions, and my father left the house basically untouched. Everybody's stuff is in the attic — boxes and boxes of papers and pictures and belongings from both sides of the family, including some very old and some very precious things. I've started to go through things and sort them out, but it gets overwhelming. Sometimes I feel angry that I was left with all these things. But I'm very attached. We want to move, but I can't rush. I don't want to chop my arm off.

For Rosie, letting go of the house means a final coming-to-terms with the loss of her family.

Others felt that their parents' divorce had impelled them toward certain decisions with consequences they were still unraveling. One young woman had been living abroad for several years when her parents divorced. She flew home for a visit, found her family in a state of upheaval, and has lived in the same city ever since. A young man had given up a fellowship in order to take care of his younger siblings when his parents split up — some twenty years later, he still felt the repercussions of that choice. In some cases, it was not until our interview that any connection was made between the divorce and the change in life course. One young woman had dropped out of college to be near her parents at the time of their divorce. Yet she had begun the interview by saying, "Their divorce didn't have much of an impact on me at the time."

For others, certain ongoing, unresolved tensions perpetuate the pain of the divorce. As many as ten and fifteen years later, they still feel called upon to mediate between their parents. One woman whose parents divorced ten years ago told us, "I'm still the conduit for their relationship." Holidays remain a source of tension. In some cases, one parent has never fully recovered from the divorce, and this, for the children, represents a continuing anxiety.

A number of those we spoke with testified to a delayed reaction. Liza said that at the time of her parents' divorce, she felt too protective of her parents to reveal her own feelings. "I kept saying to myself, 'I'm grown up. I can handle this. I don't want to hurt their feelings.'" It wasn't until four years later, when she moved out of state, that the loss really hit her. "It made me realize that I didn't have a family anymore; I didn't have a home." Though her depression was such that she saw a therapist briefly during this time, "we never really talked about the divorce." The feelings had come up, but they weren't really dealt with explicitly. Instead, Liza felt that she did a lot of acting out through her relationships with men: "I would be in a relationship that wasn't good for me, and I just wouldn't be able to let go. I had such fear and insecurity." Now, thirteen years later, Liza has at last begun to face the divorce directly. In letters and in conversations, she's asked questions and expressed feelings to her parents that she never dared to before. She said, "Part of the process of getting ready for a more healthy relationship has been to finally begin talking to my parents about the divorce."

Finally, each significant change and each new stage of life means that the divorce is experienced in new ways. Liza told us, "When my dad moved to California several years after the divorce, I felt totally abandoned. In some ways it was worse than the divorce itself. It wouldn't have been so hard if my parents were still together and had moved far away, because then we'd still be a family."

When a parent remarries, when an adult child marries and has a child, and as that child grows, the divorce — however long ago it happened — takes on a new meaning and has a different impact. As Tess, who recently became a mother, described, "When I think of the long-range impact of my parents' divorce, the word that comes to mind is *juggling*. But what I'm juggling has changed. At first it was loyalties — now it's energy, pure and simple." One woman said, "I really miss being able to watch my parents grow old together." Others we met were worried about the repercussions of the divorce as their parents age and become more dependent.

A very positive aspect here is that as adult children go on maturing, they are able to come to a deeper, more balanced understanding of their parents and of their family's past. Anna explained, "There are things I can understand now in my thirties that I couldn't possibly have understood in my twenties." One man who had an extremely abusive father observed, "I always bought my mother's side of the story. I hated my father so much. Now, in my forties, I'm starting to understand some of what he went through. Some of the rage is turning to grief."

As they grow older, some actually find themselves in their parents' shoes. Diane told us, "What I learned going through my own divorce is that, for any given situation, there may be different, equally valid truths." Larry was twenty-one when his parents divorced; he had a very hard time accepting their new partners. Now at fifty-three, he himself is remarried, and his wife's son has not warmed up to him. This is painful for Larry, but he speaks with a hard-earned wisdom. "I have a plaque on the wall in my house. It shows big, spreading trees and all kinds of beautiful things that don't just happen overnight. And it has the words, 'All good things take time.'"

Though all our respondents agreed that the acute grief and disorientation of the first phase did not last more than a year or so, virtually all testified to a sense of loss that never disappeared completely and that occasionally resurfaced, often startling them in its intensity. One woman told us, "It seems that my parents' divorce was just the start of a snowball that is never ending. There are occurrences every day that always remind me of the split."

Those we interviewed were often shocked at the tears that came in response to our questions — so many years had passed, and they had thought themselves immune. Of all our questions, the biggest tearjerker was "What do you miss most about your family as it used to be?" Usually it was "the little things" that were remembered with the most emotion. When we asked Ron, he instantly responded, "Mom's cooking. She's become a vegetarian since the divorce and so it's always lasagna!" Then he said, "That's a real superficial answer, isn't it?" When we said, "No, maybe it isn't," he grew pensive. "What I miss is just the four of us together having a good time. And certain jokes we had — 'Mom broiling the buns' — that was one. What's hard is knowing we can't ever really get together again in the same way."

Diane missed being together and telling funny family stories — like the time her little brother "woke up in the middle of the night and peed in the laundry chute." As she put it, "There was no new information being conveyed in those stories, it was just a way of expressing 'We're a family.'"

Rosie told us:

A year after my mother left, I went over to our family house, where my dad was still living. I was doing something in the kitchen, and I reached into a drawer to get a dish towel. The towel I pulled out was one of those calendar towels. It said, "1975. God Bless Our Happy Home." I just broke down. In fact, it was the first time I really cried over the divorce.

The longing to have parents united, to have the family whole again, never completely disappears. One divorce counselor spoke of a middle-aged woman who said, as her mother's coffin was being lowered into the ground, "Well, I guess Mom and Dad are never going to get back together."

Even when they can readily acknowledge that their divorced parents are better off, even sometimes in the face of the most crushing evidence, the primal longing remains. Charles's story is a perfect example of this often deeply irrational longing. His parents had an openly conflictual marriage from as long as he could remember. Charles's father was an alcoholic and was often verbally and physically abusive. On countless occasions, Charles heard his older siblings urging his mother to leave. When his parents finally divorced in Charles's twenty-second year, he felt, above all, "numb. It hurt to have it openly acknowledged that my family was a failure, but I was cynical. I felt like I just couldn't feel anymore." When his parents remarried ten years later, much to his surprise, Charles felt a profound sense of relief. As he wrote to us, "I distinctly felt a subtle but strong integration (or at least, possibility) of a healing in myself with respect to relationships and commitment. As if — 'Oh, so I didn't come from so hopeless a place after all.'"

As we've seen, some children are pained by what seems to be a lingering, unresolved love between their parents. But the great majority of those we spoke with expressed the need to know that there was once a spark of love between their parents — or if not love, at least a glimmer of concern. Like Noelle and the box of letters, they clung to certain talismans. One woman saved a Post-it note on which her father had scrawled a message to her mother, "I wish you happiness in your new life." Though Marcelle's parents fought perpetually, she smiled when she described the strong magnetism that first drew them together: "I think it was like Tarzan and Jane. My father was this very handsome, rough boy from the country. My mother was this very refined, city girl." Marcelle was shocked and upset at first when, along with the news of divorce, she learned that she had been conceived accidentally. But in our interview, she laughed. "I can see a certain energy there. It appears I'm the result of an exploded condom." Children of any age need to feel that they are the "result" — not of mere fluke or indifference — but of some genuine passion or affection.

Yet when they were asked the question, "What would it be like if your parents had never divorced?" these same adult children had no trouble enumerating the positive aspects of the present situation.

As the years went by, most felt that they understood with greater clarity why their parents had needed to go their separate ways. Many felt that their parents had each found a way to a new and better life. They observed that their parents were involved in relationships that were much more affectionate and loving, or had found a new mate who was more compatible in life-style and values.

Many of our respondents felt that their mother had achieved a degree of confidence and autonomy undreamed of before. This, for a number of those we spoke with, was the most positive long-term outcome of their parents' divorce. Several daughters expressed how healing it was *for them* to see their mother emerge from years of self-doubt and dependency. As one woman told us, "When you're a daughter, your own self-image is so tied in with your mother's. So as my mother became stronger and more self-confident, so did I."

Another woman said, "I had a lot of anger towards my mother. I perceived her as being very wishy-washy, and I was always terrified that I would end up like her, with a husband that didn't really love or respect me. Ironically, the divorce has done more for her identity than anything — and this has helped me too."

Many adult children told us that they had achieved more honest family relationships. They felt that many habitual patterns of behavior, formerly performed unconsciously or suffered in silence, had been revealed, clarified, and acknowledged. Scary secrets had come out; rigid rules had been questioned; old complicities and unhealthy triangles had been dissolved. In their place, they felt a new openness. Many respondents expressed appreciation of a more equal, one-to-one relationship with each parent.

Several people explained to us how important friends had become in their life. Ron told us, "Since my parents' divorce, I've taken a lot more stock in friends." Kate said:

> My friends and I all help each other out, with child care and all kinds of things. My mother said to me, "Isn't it a shame you have to rely so much on friends?" and what I felt like saying to her was, "It's my family who's given me the biggest disappointment in my life. My friends have never let me down."

If their parents' divorce raises fears for their own intimate relationships, it also gives adult children a wealth of insights. Many told us how careful they had been before deciding to marry. They wanted to be sure it would last, especially since they understood the power of parents to hurt even their adult children through divorce. As a group, they expressed a tremendous commitment to "making it work." Though many expressed the need to be careful with their partners, they believed above all in being open. Most felt that the greatest mistake their parents had made was in letting things build up. They were adamant about the need to face problems as they arise. One woman told us, "Somewhere I came across a quote that really struck me. It was something like this, 'If couples could learn to divorce and remarry every day, there'd be no need for the Big Divorce.'"

When these adult children became parents themselves, some experienced the loss of divorce in new ways. Yet at the same time, many believed that by becoming parents the healing process was fully catalyzed.

Though our respondents expressed it in different ways, many felt that, through the medium of their parents' divorce, they had come themselves to a more authentic existence. "Carry on with your own life" is the advice most frequently, and often thoughtlessly, given — yet it is when their parents divorce that many adult children make the shocking discovery that they do not really *have* a separate life. They may be living thousands of miles away from their parents and have a marriage, family, and career but at the deepest level remain emotionally fused to their family of origin. This discovery represents perhaps the most critical passage for the adult child whose parents divorce.

It is a dangerous passage, because for some it involves a true crisis of identity — at a time when such crises are experienced as inappropriate, a sign of weakness and failure. And as we've seen, for adult children this sense of upheaval and disorientation often occurs in the context of major responsibilities. While these responsibilities can provide a beneficial, insulating structure for the adult child, they can also magnify the sense of pressure. How can I fall apart? How can I not know who I am? How can I have my most fundamental assumptions thrown into question when there is so much in my own life at stake — a career, a marriage, children?

Yet at the same time this passage represents the opportunity to experience a degree of growth and of liberation that is truly extraordinary. In the immediate aftermath of their parents' breakup, many adult children find themselves questioning their most deeply held values: "Why should I be devoted and self-sacrificing like my mother was? Look where it got her." "The divorce made it clear the white hats don't win." We heard many variations on the theme.

But after a while — and sometimes, it is a long while — many of these adult children recognize an element of bad faith in their laments. They have been more or less blindly, automatically, following a certain path because it is the one they've grown up with. Now there is the opportunity to question and to choose: "I will act this way, or I will not act this way, because it is meaningful to *me*, not because this is how my parents used to do it."

Significantly, many of those who are most shaken by their parents' divorce are "the good girls and boys" who have most wholly adopted their parents' values. Often, these are children who have passed through adolescence without serious rebellion. If, for them, the passage from blind devotion to true choice is most difficult and frightening, the outcome is often most inspiring. Diane told us:

> I spent much of my life acting independent in order to please people I was totally dependent on. I always appeared very competent and self-sufficient, but it was really all focused on pleasing my parents, and especially my father. This carried into other relationships. I really think I've used men like a strange kind of Rorschach test: "Tell me what you think, and then I'll know who I am." When the divorce happened, my father lost the power he'd always had over me. I saw him for what he was — a very fallible human being. It was incredibly painful, but it freed me to live my own life in a way I never had before.

In a culture that offers few clear and compelling models and even fewer meaningful rituals for the complex transition from youth to adulthood, parental divorce may function as a genuine rite of passage, an initiation into true maturity.

## The Meaning of Divorce

There is, in fact, a relatively new movement to see divorce as more normative, less pathological. Such a change in perspective promises much that is positive. Transitions are more bearable when they are perceived as meaningful, part of the natural scheme of things, grounded in common experience. They are more bearable when this perception is shared by the general community, in an openly acknowledged way, and when clear guidelines for making the difficult passage are available. If the sense of anomie is still one of the most painful aspects of divorce in our culture, it is felt with particular intensity by families experiencing late divorce. Grief is all the more difficult to bear and to heal when it is experienced as untimely and inappropriate. One of the chief motivations for writing this book has been to give adult children the comfort that comes from knowing, "I'm not alone. I'm not abnormal. Others have felt this way. Here are examples of how they have coped and how they have grown."

There has been an analogous movement in recent times to see childbirth as a normative event, safely within the healthy, natural scheme of things, and not a medical emergency. Yet childbirth is inherently painful — and so is divorce. Our culture's basic patterns of raising children induce profound and passionate attachments between parent and child, self and family — attachments that lie at the very core of each person's most fundamental sense of identity. Unless we are to radically alter the structure of marriage and family in our culture, it seems highly unlikely that children — of any age — will ever experience their parents' divorce as something other than a profoundly painful and disorienting event.

So let us give all the assurance we can that such cataclysms within the family are widely experienced and ultimately growth producing. Let us do all we can to provide positive models of behavior and to emphasize the possibility of a satisfactory resolution — but let us not gloss over the pain. For too many of the adult children we encountered, denial complicated and prolonged the process of healing.

In evolving a more balanced view of divorce, it is interesting to look at the definition we found in a dictionary. It is a definition composed of two parts:

*Divorce* — 1 (*n*): the sundering of things closely united.
2 (*v*): To turn aside to a new destination.

In the first of these, the tremendous pain of divorce reverberates. In the second, the possibility of healing shines through, the recognition that the tremendous pain of divorce can eventually open out into a path.

## Noelle: Reprise

*Not long ago, I attended a workshop for adult children of divorce. It was a small group, and the others present were adults who had been young children at the time of their parents' divorce. At one point the leader of the workshop asked the participants to sum up, in as few words as possible, what their parents' divorce had meant to them. When it was my turn, without hesitation I said, "A sense of* rupture, *at a very deep level, that never completely goes away. And a sense of* resiliency."

*When I said "resiliency," the image that came to mind was of flowers, pushing their way up through cracks in a hard cement sidewalk. And I can describe these flowers vividly, because I see them as a series of moments or glimpses, gathered from my own experience and from the many people who told me their stories.*

*I see my mother and me, leaning over the balcony of the apartment she has rented for the summer in Spain. It is eight years since the divorce, and this is the summer I will later think of as "the summer my mother rounded the corner" and finally emerged from the long, dark tunnel of fear and insecurity.*

*Below us, the tile roofs of the houses wind their way in wild, crooked patterns down the hillsides. The sky, after a long, hot day, grows suddenly intensely blue, the cliffs above us grow bright pink, and the air fills with night sounds: swallows, the chatter of old women knitting in doorways while the old men smoke, droves of young men laughing and drinking beer on the cathedral steps, young lovers going up and down the steep stone walks looking for a private piece of wall to lean against, and always the surprising sound of small children, still wide-awake at this late hour. . . .*

*As if out of nowhere — except that ever since the divorce it is always there, as an unspoken backdrop, the ground of our conversations — my mother turns to me and says, "My life is so much more interesting than it used to be."*

*So much reverberates in that bland word* interesting! *I could laugh out loud. I know what she means before she goes on to say more. That she would never have chosen to be thrust out of a marriage of twenty-five years. That she would never want to live*

*through the grief again, the terror of starting life over as an aban-*
*doned middle-aged woman. That she resisted every step of the*
*way. And that nonetheless here we stand, on this balcony in Spain*
*as on the prow of a ship heading out into the blue, and that our*
*being here, the beauty of this night, the freedom and exhilaration*
*it inspires, the sense of the vastness of life's possibilities, the mys-*
*tery of journeys and where they lead, the closeness between us —*
*that all this has come to us through the divorce, through the pain*
*and confusion that once seemed so hopeless, so impenetrable. I*
*think how far away we are from that first terrible winter.*

*And I see Anna, surrounded by tiger lilies, picking snow peas in*
*her garden. She holds her baby with one arm; his fists are full of*
*pea pods. She turns and says to me, "You know, my parents are*
friends *to me now in a way they never were before."*

*Or Karl, rocking back in his chair, absently ruffling the fur of his*
*cat, all his attention turned to his thoughts:*

> *I look back on all the years before the divorce, and I feel*
> *like I was just emotionally coasting. I had this "stable fam-*
> *ily" that acted as a kind of insulation for me. When it fell*
> *apart, it was like the roof caved in on some of my most basic*
> *assumptions about who I was, about relationships. It was*
> *incredibly painful. But now I can't imagine what I'd be like*
> *if it had never happened. It gives me the shivers to think I'd*
> *probably still be walking around with all that stuff locked up*
> *inside of me.*

*Or Vivian, sitting beside me on the porch steps and saying,*

> *There was a time when I couldn't imagine ever really*
> *coming through it. It felt that bleak. But I have. And what*
> *it's given me is an appreciation of fidelity that I never had*
> *before. I don't take any of it for granted anymore — the ties*
> *between people, the miracle of* staying with, *of seeing some-*
> *one through.*

\*       \*       \*

That light at the end of the tunnel. It's there — at least it's been there for most of the people who shared their stories with us. That moment when you suddenly find yourself, leaning over a balcony in Spain, picking snow peas in a garden, sitting on the porch steps — wherever it is, it's the mysterious destination you could not have imagined before. It's the moment you realize the miraculous adaptability of human beings, so far exceeding your expectations, the moment you know you've come through. You might trade it all back in a second to have your family as it used to be. But here you are: alive and well and knowing something's been given to you that wouldn't have come any other way.

# *Notes*

## Introduction

1. Data for this book were drawn from 107 people. Of these, 50 were personally interviewed in sessions lasting a minimum of one and a half hours. Some were interviewed on two or three different occasions, during a period of from one to five years. Six were close friends of the authors and communicated with them frequently over ten years.

In all, 91 people — including 34 of the interviewees — completed a printed questionnaire. The composition of this group was as follows (percentages are approximate):

*Sex*
Male: 26 respondents (28.6 percent)
Female: 65 respondents (71.4 percent)

*Age* (at time of divorce)
18–20: 27 respondents (29.7 percent)
21–30: 52 respondents (57.1 percent)
30 and over: 12 respondents (13.2 percent)

*Years Since Divorce* (at time of survey)
0–3 years: 19 respondents (20.9 percent)
3–10 years: 41 respondents (45.1 percent)
10 years and more: 31 respondents (34.1 percent)

## Chapter 2: Late Divorce

1. Wallerstein and Blakeslee, *Second Chances*, xii.
2. Kressel, *The Process of Divorce*, 33.

3. Vaughan's *Uncoupling* provides an excellent discussion of this process.

4. In the discussion that follows, we are indebted to an article by Hagestad and Smyer, "Dissolving Long-Term Relationships," 155–87.

5. The book *Divorced Families*, by Ahrons and Rodgers, is largely devoted to a discussion of divorce styles. See also Kressel, *The Process of Divorce*, 226–40.

6. Barbara Foley Wilson provided this breakdown of the figures:

> For men between the ages of fifty-five and fifty-nine, divorce rates increased 12 percent between 1980 and 1987.
> For men aged sixty to sixty-four, the rate of increase was 16 percent.
> For men sixty-five and older, it was 5 percent.
> For women aged fifty-five to fifty-nine, the 1987 divorce rate was 12 percent higher than the 1980 rate.
> For those sixty to sixty-four, the rate held steady.
> For those sixty-five and older, there was a 7 percent increase.

7. Barbara Foley Wilson, National Center for Health Statistics.

8. Kaufmann, "Reworking the Relationship," 14.

9. These descriptions correspond closely to the "devitalized" and "conflict-habituated" marriages described by Cuber and Harroff in *The Significant Americans*, 44–46.

10. Cain, "Plight of the Gray Divorcee," 90.

11. Hagestad and Smyer, "Dissolving Long-Term Relationships," 173.

12. Ibid., 167.

13. Wallerstein and Blakeslee, *Second Chances*, 49–53.

14. Wallerstein and Kelly, *Surviving the Breakup*, 23.

15. Ahrons and Rodgers, *Divorced Families*, 97.

16. Cain, "Plight of the Gray Divorcee," 91.

## Chapter 3: Toward a Deeper Understanding of the Family

1. In this discussion we are indebted primarily to the following sources: Bowen, *Family Therapy in Clinical Practice*; Kerr, "Chronic Anxiety and Defining a Self"; Laing, *The Politics of the Family and Other Essays*; Minunchin, *Families and Family Therapy*; and Nichols, *The Power of the Family*.

2. A substantial number of people told us that they had always felt they came from a happy family. Of our respondents, 75 percent described their families as close before the divorce, and of these 45 percent said "very" to "extremely" close.

## Chapter 4: What Any Child Feels When Parents Divorce

1. Cain, "Older Children and Divorce," 26. Cain reported that of her fifty college students, "all but three in the study recalled an immediate state of

shock followed by a lingering sense of disbelief. Even those who grew up amid a turbulent marriage were incredulous when a separation was announced."

2. Wallerstein and Blakeslee, *Second Chances*, 7.

3. Hennon and Burton, "Well-being of the Divorced Elderly," 15.

4. Kaufmann, "Reworking the Relationship," 13. This researcher found some interesting patterns of sex difference in the anger expressed by her group of thirty college students:

> In contrast with what I anticipated, I found far more anger expressed by the females than the males. I would suggest that here I may be tapping into the kind of high affective response to interpersonal relationships that has always been a part of women's lives, but now the affective response can include feelings of anger in addition to those feelings traditionally deemed "acceptable" for women, for example, anxiety, care, responsibility, and sadness.

In "Parental Divorce in Young Adulthood," 475, Cooney et al. also reported more anger among women than men.

Of our ninety-one respondents, both males and females registered nearly the same high levels of anger.

5. "Dear Abby," *Rochester Times Union*, Aug. 23, 1989.


## Chapter 5: The Unique Situation of the Adult Child of Divorce

1. Kaufmann, "Reworking the Relationship," 14.

2. Cooney et al., "Parental Divorce in Young Adulthood," 476.

3. See Wallerstein and Blakeslee, *Second Chances*, 154–60, and "If Parents Part: Young Adults Describe Their Own Anguish," *New York Times*, Nov. 11, 1985.


## Chapter 6: Coping with the Initial Phase

1. Cain, "Older Children and Divorce," 50.

2. The Pennsylvania researchers reported that "sixty-four percent of the [39] students initially worried about experiencing loyalty conflicts. A great deal of time and effort were expended in trying to balance the attention and time they gave each parent." Cooney et al., "Parental Divorce in Young Adulthood," 474.

Cain, "Older Children and Divorce," 54, found that while most of her subjects clearly considered one parent worthy of blame and the other of compassion, they struggled to behave with neutrality.

Kaufmann, "Reworking the Relationship," 11, reported that both sexes expressed far more loyalty to their mother, but that this did not save them from worries and guilt about their father.

3. Cooney et al., quoted in "Parents' Divorce Has Major Impact on College Students."

## Chapter 7: Adjusting to Parents as New People

1. Vaughan provides an excellent discussion of this process in her book *Uncoupling*.
2. Wallerstein and Blakeslee, *Second Chances*, 8.
3. Ibid.
4. Kaufmann, "Reworking the Relationship," 4–5.
5. Hagestad et al., "The Impact of Divorce in Middle Age," 251.

## Chapter 8: Adjusting to Parents' New Partners

1. Ahrons and Rodgers, *Divorced Families*, 20.
2. Ibid., 187.
3. Wallerstein and Kelly, *Surviving the Breakup*, 103.
4. Ahrons and Rodgers, *Divorced Families*, 190.
5. "When Families Divorce," PBS Television Soapbox Series, WGBY 74, Springfield, Mass., 1987.
6. Ahrons and Rodgers, *Divorced Families*, 162.
7. Wallerstein and Blakeslee, *Second Chances*, 251.

## Chapter 9: Serious Rifts and Long-term Estrangements

1. Wallerstein and Kelly, *Surviving the Breakup*, 102.
2. Cooney et al., "Parental Divorce in Young Adulthood," 474.
3. Kaufmann, "Reworking the Relationship," 3.
4. Howard, *Eppie*, 216–41.
5. Ibid., 234.
6. Ibid., 228.
7. Helpful books include Halpern, *An Adult Guide to Coming to Terms with Your Parents;* Lerner, *The Dance of Anger* and *The Dance of Intimacy;* and Travis, *Anger, the Misunderstood Emotion*.

## Chapter 10: Their Own Love Lives

1. Cain, "Older Children and Divorce," 54.
2. Ibid.
3. Kaufmann, "Reworking the Relationship," 15.

## Chapter 12: Holidays and Special Events

1. Ahrons and Rodgers, *Divorced Families*, 130.

2. Cooney et al., quoted in "Parents' Divorce Has Major Impact on College Students."

3. Visher and Visher, *Stepfamilies*, 179.

## Chapter 13: What to Do? Emotional and Practical Strategies

1. Peg Steffan, Displaced Homemakers Program, Rochester, N.Y.

2. Vicki Lewin, Divorce Mediation Center of Rochester, N.Y.

3. Ibid.

4. Kressel, *The Process of Divorce*, 26–27.

5. John Heister, Divorce Mediation Center of Rochester.

6. Kressel, *The Process of Divorce*, 229–31.

7. To learn about divorce law for a particular state, you might consider calling the county clerk for information or checking at a legal library. Under "Divorce," the subject volume of *Books in Print* lists titles of books on divorce law for virtually every state.

8. Kressel, *The Process of Divorce*, 168–71.

9. The book *Women in Transition*, 137, provides an excellent list of what to look for in a lawyer.

10. Friedman, *The Divorce Handbook*, 81.

11. De Angelis, *You're Entitled!*, 122–39.

12. Steffan.

13. *Women in Transition*, 327.

14. Heister.

15. Lewin.

16. Mowatt, *Divorce Counseling*, 46.

17. Lenore Weitzman, *The Divorce Revolution: The Unexpected Social and Economic Consequences for Women and Children in America*, quoted in Mowatt, *Divorce Counseling*, 46.

18. Steffan.

19. Ibid.

20. Ibid.

21. Mowatt, *Divorce Counseling*, 70.

22. Brooklyn Legal Services Corp., *Handbook for Beaten Women*, Brooklyn, N.Y.

23. Steffan.

## Chapter 14: A Message to Parents

1. Wallerstein and Kelly, *Surviving the Breakup*, 17.

2. Jane Smiley, *Ordinary Love* (New York: Alfred A. Knopf, 1990), 94.

3. Rainer Maria Rilke, quoted in *Fellowship in Prayer*, vol. 4, no. 3, June 1990.

# Bibliography

Books

Ahrons, Constance R., and Roy H. Rodgers. *Divorced Families, Meeting the Challenge of Divorce and Remarriage.* New York: W. W. Norton & Co., 1987.

Bowen, Murray. *Family Therapy in Clinical Practice.* New York: Jason Aronson, 1978.

Carter, Elizabeth, and Monica McGoldrick, eds. *The Changing Family Life Cycle: A Framework for Family Therapy.* New York: Gardner Press, 1988.

Cauhape, Elizabeth. *Fresh Starts: Men and Women After Divorce.* New York: Basic Books, 1983.

Cuber, John, and Peggy Harroff. *The Significant Americans: A Study of Sexual Behavior Among the Affluent.* New York: Appleton-Century, 1965.

De Angelis, Sidney. *You're Entitled! A Divorce Lawyer Talks to Women.* Chicago: Contemporary Books, 1989.

Friedman, James T. *The Divorce Handbook.* New York: Random House, 1984.

Halpern, Howard. *An Adult Guide to Coming to Terms with Your Parents.* New York: Simon & Schuster, 1976.

Howard, Margo. *Eppie: The Story of Ann Landers.* New York: Putnam, 1982.

Kressel, Kenneth. *The Process of Divorce: How Professionals and Couples Negotiate Settlements.* New York: Basic Books, 1985.

Laing, R. D. *The Politics of the Family and Other Essays.* New York: Random House, 1972.

Lerner, Harriet Goldhor. *The Dance of Anger: A Woman's Guide to Changing the Patterns of Intimate Relationships.* New York: Harper & Row, 1985.

―――. *The Dance of Intimacy: A Woman's Guide to Courageous Acts of Change in Key Relationships.* New York: Harper & Row, 1989.

Levinson, Daniel. *The Seasons of a Man's Life.* New York: Ballantine Books, 1978.

Minunchin, Salvador. *Families and Family Therapy.* Cambridge: Harvard University Press, 1981.

Mowatt, Marian H. *Divorce Counseling: A Practical Guide.* Lexington, Mass.: D. C. Heath & Co., 1987.

Nichols, Michael P. *The Power of the Family: Mastering the Hidden Dance of Family Relationships.* New York: Simon & Schuster, 1988.

Rogers, Mary. *Women, Divorce, and Money.* New York: McGraw Hill, 1981.

Sheehy, Gail. *Passages: Predictable Crises of Adult Life.* New York: Ballantine Books, 1978.

Silverstone, Barbara, and Helen Kandel Hyman. *You and Your Aging Parent.* New York: Pantheon, 1989.

Travis, Carol. *Anger, the Misunderstood Emotion.* New York: Simon & Schuster, 1982.

Vaughan, Diane. *Uncoupling: How and Why Relationships Come Apart.* New York: Random House, 1987.

Viorst, Judith. *Necessary Losses.* New York: Ballantine Books, 1986.

Visher, Emily B., and John S. Visher. *Stepfamilies: A Guide to Working with Stepparents and Stepchildren.* New York: Brunner/Mazel, 1979.

Wallerstein, Judith S., and Sandra Blakeslee. *Second Chances: Men, Women and Children a Decade After Divorce.* New York: Ticknor & Fields, 1989.

Wallerstein, Judith S., and Joan Berlin Kelly. *Surviving the Breakup: How Children and Parents Cope with Divorce.* New York: Basic Books, 1980.

Women in Transition. *Women in Transition: A Feminist Handbook on Separation and Divorce.* New York: Charles Scribner's Sons, 1975.

Articles from Magazines, Journals, and Anthologies

Bales, John. "Parents' Divorce Has Major Impact on College Students." *Observer Dispatch* (Utica, N.Y.), 1986.

Berardo, Donna H. "Divorce and Remarriage at Middle Age and Beyond." *Annals of the American Academy of Political Science,* 464 (Nov. 1982): 132–39.

Cain, Barbara. "Divorce Among Elderly Women: A Growing Social Phenomenon." *Social Casework* 69, no. 9 (Nov. 1988): 563–68.

———. "Plight of the Gray Divorcee." *New York Times Magazine,* Dec. 19, 1982, 90.

———. "The Price They Pay: Older Children and Divorce." *New York Times Magazine,* Feb. 18, 1990, 26–55.

Cooney, Teresa M. et al., "Parental Divorce in Young Adulthood: Some Preliminary Findings." *American Journal of Orthopsychiatry* 56, no. 3 (July 1986): 470–77.

Hagestad, Gunhild O., and Michael A. Smyer. "Dissolving Long-Term Relationships: Patterns of Divorcing in Middle Age." In *Personal Relationships*. Vol. 4. *Dissolving Personal Relationships*, edited by S. Duck. London: Academic Press, 1982, 155–87.

Hagestad, Gunhild O. et al. "The Impact of Divorce in Middle Age." In *Parenthood: A Psychodynamic Perspective*, edited by Rebecca Cohen et al. New York: Guilford Press, 1984, 247–62.

Hennon, Charles B., and John R. Burton. "Well-being of the Divorced Elderly and Their Dependency on Adult Children." Paper presented at the annual meeting of the National Council on Family Relations, Milwaukee, Wis., Oct. 13–17, 1981, 2–22.

Kaufmann, Katherine Stone. "Reworking the Relationship: College Students and Their Divorcing Parents." *Work in Progress* 34 (1988). Wellesley, Mass.: Stone Center for Developmental Services and Studies, Wellesley College, Wellesley, Mass.

Kerr, Michael. "Chronic Anxiety and Defining a Self." *Atlantic Monthly*, Sept. 1988, 35–58.

Smyer, Michael, and Brian F. Hofland. "Divorce and Family Support in Family Life." *Journal of Family Issues* 3 (Mar. 1982): 61–77.

Uhlenberg, Peter, and Mary Anne P. Myers. "Divorce and the Elderly." *Annals of the American Academy of Political Science* 464 (Nov. 1982): 276–82.

Wines, Leslie. "A New Kind of Stepmother." *Glamour Magazine*, Aug. 1983, 140–46.

## DATE DUE

| | | | |
|---|---|---|---|
| 11/26/03 | | | |
| 11/24/09 | | | |
| 4/8/10 | | | |
| 7/31/10 ILL | | | |
| 9/1/10 | | | |
| | | | |
| | | | |
| | | | |
| | | | |
| | | | |
| | | | |
| | | | |
| | | | |
| | | | |
| | | | |

Demco, Inc. 38-293